SHOOTING
COLUMBO

Books by David Koenig

Mouse Tales:
A Behind-the-Ears Look at Disneyland

Mouse Under Glass:
Secrets of Disney Animation & Theme Parks

More Mouse Tales:
A Closer Peek Backstage at Disneyland

Realityland:
True-Life Adventures at Walt Disney World

Danny Kaye:
King of Jesters

The People v. Disneyland:
How Lawsuits & Lawyers Transformed the Magic

The 55ers:
The Pioneers Who Settled Disneyland

Shooting Columbo:
The Lives & Deaths of TV's Rumpled Detective

SHOOTING
COLUMBO

THE LIVES AND DEATHS OF TV'S RUMPLED DETECTIVE

By David Koenig

BONAVENTURE PRESS

For my dearest friends—
Bill Jagielski, who loved Columbo *every bit as much as I do,*
and David Keefe, despite his inexplicable preference for The Rockford Files

Shooting Columbo: The Lives and Deaths of TV's Rumpled Detective

Published by
BONAVENTURE PRESS
Aliso Viejo, CA
USA
www.bonaventurepress.com

All rights reserved. No part of this book may be reproduced or transmitted in any form or by any means, electronic or mechanical, including scanning, photocopying, recording or by any information storage and retrieval system without written permission from the author, except for the inclusion of brief quotations in a review.

Cover art by Kevin Jakubowski
Edited by Hugh Allison

Copyright 2021 by David Koenig

Publisher's Cataloging in Publication Data
Koenig, David G., 1962-
     Shooting Columbo: The Lives and Deaths of TV's Rumpled Detective
         p. cm.
     Includes annotated references and index.

     1. Columbo (Television Program)   [1. Columbo (Television Program)
     2. Mystery and detective television programs.   3. Television programs] 1. Title.
     791.4572

Library of Congress Control Number: 2021938776

ISBN 978-1-937878-11-5 (Hardcover)

Printed in the USA
10 9 8 7 6 5 4 3 2 1

Contents

Preface   9

1. The Crime   11

2. The Masterminds   13

3. The Cop   20
Prescription: Murder

4. The Contract   26
Ransom for a Dead Man

5. Mutual Distrust   33
Death Lends a Hand   *Murder by the Book*
Dead Weight   *Lady in Waiting*
Suitable for Framing   *Blueprint for Murder*
Short Fuse

6. A Comfortable Fit   53
A Stitch in Crime   *Étude in Black*
The Greenhouse Jungle   *The Most Crucial Game*
Requiem for a Falling Star   *Double Shock*
Dagger of the Mind   *The Most Dangerous Match*

7. Music to Kill By   72

8. The Strike   76
Lovely But Lethal   *Any Old Port in a Storm*
Candidate for Crime   *Double Exposure*
Publish or Perish   *Mind Over Mayhem*
Swan Song   *A Friend in Deed*

9. The Scene of the Crime   95

10. Turbulence Ahead — 103
An Exercise in Fatality
By Dawn's Early Light
Troubled Waters
Negative Reaction
Playback
A Deadly State of Mind

11. The Peacekeeper — 120
A Case of Immunity
Now You See Him

12. Bon Voyage — 130
A Matter of Honor
Identity Crisis
Forgotten Lady
Last Salute to the Commodore

13. The Meltdown — 145
Fade In to Murder
Old Fashioned Murder

14. The Fixer — 155
The Bye-Bye Sky High I.Q. Murder Case
Make Me a Perfect Murder
How to Dial a Murder
Try and Catch Me
Murder Under Glass
The Conspirators

15. On Ice — 168

16. Second Life — 173
Murder, Smoke and Shadows
Sex and the Married Detective
Murder, a Self Portrait
Columbo Goes to the Guillotine
Grand Deceptions

17. Back to Basics — 185
Columbo Cries Wolf
Rest in Peace, Mrs. Columbo
Murder in Malibu
Agenda for Murder
Uneasy Lies the Crown

18. New Respect — 198
Caution: Murder Can Be Hazardous to Your Health
Columbo Goes to College
Columbo and the Murder of a Rock Star

19. Absolute Power — 206
Death Hits the Jackpot
A Bird in the Hand…
It's All in the Game
Strange Bedfellows
Ashes to Ashes
No Time to Die
Butterfly in Shades of Grey
Undercover
A Trace of Murder
Murder with Too Many Notes

20. Columbo's Last Case — 230
Columbo Likes the Nightlife

Notebook: Sources & Scribblings — 236

Index — 244

Acknowledgments

This book's cover and title page credit a single author, but it has truly been a group effort, a feat that could not have been accomplished without the assistance of others more talented, generous and better connected than me.

First and foremost, I am grateful for those who shared their memories and insight: Penny Adams, Jeffrey Bloom, Everett Chambers, Shera Danese, Richard "Dick" DeBenedictis, Charles "Charlie" Engel, Peter S. Fischer, Barry Glasser, Jeffrey Hatcher, Shirl Hendrix, Jack Horger, Dean Hargrove, Lucetta Kallis, Charles Kipps, Milt Kogan, Judy Lamppu, Alan J. Levi, Todd London, Jerrold L. "Jerry" Ludwig, Patricia (Ford) Mayo, Vincent McEveety Jr., Nancy A. Meyer, Jeffrey Reiner, Mark Bruce Rosin, Robert Seaman, David Simmons, and Katherine Wenglikowski.

Unfortunately, being forced to complete this project during a pandemic prevented me from meeting—and thanking in person—most of these kind souls. I hope to rectify that situation as soon as possible.

The health crisis also kept me from visiting a number of research facilities, which all went into lockdown mode for a year and counting. That meant I was unable to view several items that I had hoped to. But, miracle of miracles, most of the facilities that held vital materials employed at least one guardian angel who helped me complete my research. Chief among them were Hilary Swett, Javier Barrios, and their team at the Writers Guild Foundation (Theodore Flicker, Jackson Gillis, and Robert van Scoyk collections).

Equally exhaustive assistance was provided by Jane Parr at Boston University's Howard Gottlieb Research Center (Everett Chambers and Ken Kolb collections) and Lindsay Moen at the University of Iowa (Robert Metzler Collection).

I also was aided by Louise Hilton and Warren Sherk at the Academy of Motion Picture Arts and Sciences' Margaret Herrick Library (Millard Kaufman Papers),

Emily Wittenberg at the American Film Institute's Louis B. Mayer Library (Richard Levinson & William Link Collection), Heidi Marshall at Columbia College-Chicago (Robert Enrietto Collection), David Kloepfer and his team at Simon Fraser University (Daryl Duke Collection), and the staff of UCLA Library Special Collections (Douglas Benton, True Boardman, Lloyd Bochner, Susan Clark, Anthony & Nancy Lawrence, and Nick Smirnoff papers).

No one's contributions were more valuable nor more appreciated than those of Dene Kernohan. Dene had compiled a mountain of *Columbo* research of his own, including interviews with Jeffrey Hatcher, Charles Kipps, and Nancy Meyer, which he had hoped to one day use in a book of his own. Thank you, Dene.

Similarly, Gergely Hubai kindly allowed me to quote from his Dick DeBenedictis interview, which went into far greater depth than my own.

Jim and Melody Rondeau graciously supplied copies of rare scripts I could find nowhere else.

Charlie Christ, Randy Skretvedt, and Jordan Young provided additional research assistance.

Peter Meyer, Herbie J. Pilato, and Leslie Simmons put me in touch with wonderful interview subjects.

I thank Hugh Allison, the most precise editor I have ever encountered. Working alongside eagle-eyed Hugh is revelatory and maddening—and the project is always 100 times better because of it.

The incomparable cover illustration and design were created by supremely talented artist Kevin Jakubowski (www.kevinjakubowski.com).

My loving family—Laura, Zach and Rebecca Koenig—was bewilderingly supportive, as always. They gifted me with long hours of writing about, researching and watching *Columbo* (sometimes even joining me!). They even accompanied me on location tours. How lucky I am!

My other family members are also a blessing—Joe, Paul, Maryanne and especially my mom, Anne Koenig, who introduced me to the rumpled detective during the show's initial run on NBC.

And, most of all, I am indebted to my Lord and Savior Jesus Christ—for everything He has provided so far and has promised for tomorrow.

Preface

A great mystery, at its heart, is an intricate puzzle that stumps its audience despite providing all the pieces needed for solving it. My favorite mystery show is *Columbo*. Ironically, many people don't even consider *Columbo* a mystery, since the traditional solution—the murderer's identity—is usually revealed before the first commercial break.

To me, *Columbo* is better—the show gives its audience a head start. Hercule Poirot and Jessica Fletcher spend much of their time seemingly chasing red herrings, their thought processes often a secret to the viewer until the final reveal. At long last, the detective identifies and explains each clue. *Columbo*, on the other hand, is one long reveal. We are Sgt. Kramer with a cheat sheet, along for the ride yet still one step behind. We marvel at the ingenuity and—because of Peter Falk's engaging characterization—the *fun* of his reaching the solution. He's a magician performing expert sleight of hand in slow motion, with his sleeves rolled up.

I have always wondered about what went into the making of the show. Over the years there's been one great book about the series: *The Columbo Phile* by Mark Dawidziak, first published in 1989. Still, I've always held out hope for an even deeper, more comprehensive account. In fact, Dawidziak confided to me that he too hoped his book would not mark the end of "*Columbo* scholarship," but the beginning, one that inspired "carry-it-on research."

In 2006, Falk released his memoirs, *Just One More Thing*. I got a copy as soon as I could, anxious to learn additional secrets about his most famous character. To Falk's credit, the book is wonderful; it reads as if you're in the room with the author, hearing about his life in his own voice. Falk, though, was a storyteller, not a historian. He loved to share a good yarn, accuracy be damned. Whatever made for the most ripping tale, to Falk, that's what happened. The book contains more than a few verifiable exaggerations, like claiming *The Iceman Cometh* ran every night for seven hours, and outright fabrications, such as recounting how he first met John Cassavetes at a Lakers game—years after they'd already co-starred in a movie together.

Later, as I began comparing Falk interviews to scripts and studio records, I realized he regularly disregarded reality. It dawned on me that if I were to accurately chronicle the show's history, my trickiest puzzle would be separating fact from fiction among the words of Falk.

Fortunately, so many of the instigators and eyewitnesses to these adventures graciously shared their memories. Even more beneficially, I was granted access to the personal papers of more than a dozen other players in the story. These are firsthand reports, not shaded by bias nor dimmed by the passing of years. Chief among them were the business diaries of Bob Metzler, NBC's liaison to the series from 1975 to 1977. Metzler documented everything the production was up to, and I could trust the honesty of his assessments and veracity of his reporting of events and conversations. Metzler wasn't selling anything or trying to make himself look better. His notes were meant for his eyes only.

What I hope emerges from my account is a roller-coaster ride of what happens when the creation of two extremely protective geniuses is co-opted by—God forbid—an actor, one who was supremely creative, irresistibly winsome, uncontrollably volatile, and born to play the role. It's an adventure in which truth makes the best story of all.

– David Koenig
May 2021

1
The Crime

Every spring without fail, Peter Falk would begin his little cat-and-mouse game, toying with Universal Television, the producer of *Columbo*, and NBC, the TV network that aired the show. During press interviews, Falk would drop hints that the current season of his hit series was likely to be his last. The long hours and frantic production schedule were wearing on his health and his home life. There weren't enough good scripts. And he simply didn't have time for a regular gig due to movie commitments.

Behind the scenes, the executives at Universal rolled their eyes, tempted to call his bluff. NBC was a different story. The perennially third-place network desperately needed America's favorite detective on their fall schedule. Year after year, NBC made it clear to Universal that they had better come up with a way to produce another season of fresh episodes, even if the network had to cover part of the production cost. Inevitably, a deal got done, always with a hefty raise for Falk.

But the spring of 1978 was different. For the first time, NBC wasn't panicking at Falk playing hard to get. The actor received little contact from Universal regarding renewal of the series. Falk was bewildered. After seven seasons, sure, the show no longer lived in the Top 10 in the Nielsen ratings, but it typically did slide into the Top 20, reaching close to 20 million households per episode. *Columbo* was one of the few draws NBC had. How could it shun the rumpled detective?

For NBC, it was time to clear the decks. It had just hired away ABC's programming savant, Fred Silverman, who practically overnight had boosted ABC from worst to first, by green-lighting the likes of *Charlie's Angels, Laverne and Shirley,* and *Three's Company.* NBC needed to get younger and sexier. And that left little room on the schedule for a doddering middle-aged sleuth who ambled around in a threadbare raincoat, nagging suspects for two hours.

Columbo had become a national institution and inspired an endless stream of quirky TV detectives. Yet NBC didn't see offing the beloved character as sacrilege. The network figured that after seven years of contract ploys, walkouts, outrageous salary demands, heated tirades, and spiraling out-of-control budget overruns, Falk had it coming. It no longer made business sense to continue the series.

In its eyes, NBC wasn't burying the series. To them, it was Peter Falk who killed *Columbo*.

2
The Masterminds

Although opposites physically, tall wiry Richard Levinson and short stouter William Link were in most every other way the spitting image of each other. Born eight months apart, they grew up in the Philadelphia suburbs of the 1940s with near-identical middle-class childhoods, devouring comic books, collecting magic tricks, and hanging on every word of *Suspense, Inner Sanctum*, and other radio dramas. The boys first met in junior high, and became instant, inseparable friends and partners.

Bill Link recalled, "I was told to look out for a tall guy who loved mysteries and did magic, and he was told by his friends to look out for a short guy who loved mysteries and did magic. We literally met at lunchtime that first day of junior high school. And we became friends like that. We shared these interests; that was the main foundation for the friendship."

Both voracious readers, they loaned each other books as soon as they finished them. Most were mysteries, along the lines of *Ellery Queen*. Soon, the boys started writing together, staging neighborhood dramas and penning their high school's musicals. In 1952, the pair headed off to the Wharton School of Business at the University of Pennsylvania, presumably to prepare for careers in their fathers' trades—Levinson in auto parts and Link in textiles. Nonetheless, their writing partnership continued. They contributed to the college's literary and humor magazines, launched a new campus humor publication of their own called *Highball*, wrote weekly film reviews for the school paper, and supplied scripts and lyrics for five Penn musicals. While still in school, they sold their first short story to *Ellery Queen's Mystery Magazine*—even though it would take another four years before they'd sell another.

One week after graduating, Link was drafted into the Army. Suddenly without his writing partner and suspecting a draft notice of his own was inevitable, Levinson enlisted in a six-month reserve program. Two years later, Link was discharged and the team decided to give it a go as professional writers. They relocated to New York, where untold opportunities awaited to write for television. They arrived too late. While they were in the service, the majority of New York TV production had migrated to the West Coast and nearly all of the hour-long dramas were dead. The partners tried to eke out an existence as writers, selling just enough short stories to *Playboy, Alfred Hitchcock's Mystery Magazine*, and other publications to keep their dream alive. They finally sold their first TV script, and then a second, to *General Motors Presents* in Toronto. But since the programs aired only in Canada, no one they knew could see what they had done.

They submitted their next script, an Army drama called *Chain of Command*, to Hollywood, and it was accepted by the *Desilu Playhouse*. Encouraged, Levinson and Link packed their bags in the summer of 1959 and headed for California. With the medium's inexhaustible demand, the boys were soon hired as staff writers for Four Star Television, churning out scripts for *Johnny Ringo* and *Richard Diamond, Private Detective*, and other series for $1,000 a week.

In January 1960, the Writers Guild of America went on strike, a 146-day protest that prohibited Levinson and Link from contributing to filmed television shows. They could, however, write for live TV and when it was announced *The Chevy Mystery Show* would step in as a summer replacement for *The Dinah Shore Show*, they hatched the idea of expanding one of their short stories into an hour-long episode. They pitched their latest, published in the April 1960 issue of *Alfred Hitchcock's Mystery Magazine*, and the producer bit.

The story was an "inverted mystery," in which the reader is shown the crime and the culprit, and the story's detective must piece together the clues. The mystery wasn't a traditional whodunit—or even a howdunit—but rather a "how's-he-gonna-catch-him." Levinson and Link realized the more perfect the crime seemed to the audience, the more powerful and satisfying it would be to crack it before their eyes.

The central character was a brilliant psychiatrist who strangles his wife, then heads off to the airport with his mistress who has disguised herself as his wife. The couple stage a very public argument at the airport, and she storms off. He can now fly off on his own, establishing an ironclad alibi for when the wife's body is later discovered. Unfortunately for him, the detective assigned to the case, Lt. Fisher, is able to uncover a trail of loose ends, one annoying crumb after another, that all point to the doctor.

Levinson and Link had a novel idea for the investigator: they'd emulate the dogged, unpretentious cop, Petrovich, from Dostoevsky's Russian masterpiece *Crime and Punishment*. In the novel, Petrovich instinctively knows who the killer is, and continues to hound him, while feigning humility, until the suspect confesses.

The screenwriters had originally titled the short story "May I Come In," after the annoying detective's fateful arrival with the final batch of bad news for the villain. *Alfred Hitchcock's Mystery Magazine* renamed the story "Dear Corpus Delecti." For the one-hour live TV show, Levinson and Link renamed it again as *Enough Rope*. The show remained fairly faithful to the original story, although the authors did want to give the cop a more colorful name. In place of the nondescript "Fisher," "Columbo" popped into their heads. Decades later, it occurred to Link that they must have come across the name from their appreciation of the films and screenplays of Billy Wilder. The villain in *Some Like It Hot*? "Spats" Colombo.

Enough Rope aired live on July 31, 1960, starring Richard Carlson as the villainous Dr. Flemming and, as the detective, venerable character actor Bert Freed. Freed had made a career out of playing tough-guy cops, including a recurring role that same year as a police sergeant in John Cassavetes' TV series *Johnny Staccato*. Levinson and Link were thankful the show stuck closely to their script, but were disappointed by its poor direction and low production values.

They felt their work deserved better. Levinson and Link asked out of their contract with Four Star Television and returned to New York, hoping for success not in the grind of TV, but in the more respectable milieu of novels and Broadway dramas. Among their ideas was to expand *Enough Rope* into a full-length stage play. With the main plot points all in place, the challenge came in extending the intricate interplay between the killer and the cop. They had to sustain the tension between the detective, uncovering one clue after another, and the suspect, deftly deflecting. After typing up one exchange that ended with Columbo leaving the suspect's apartment, they realized the scene was too short. They could have Columbo also ask about what the man's wife was wearing, but then they'd have to retype an entire page of the script. Feeling lazy, they instead had the cop pop his head back in the doorway and ask, "Just one more thing...."

Producer Paul Gregory bought the rights and redubbed the play *Prescription: Murder*. He assembled an illustrious cast, eyeing an eventual Broadway run. Joseph Cotten (*The Third Man*) would star as Dr. Roy Flemming, Agnes Moorehead as his wife, Cotten's real-life wife Patricia Medina as his mistress, and Thomas Mitchell (*Gone with the Wind*, *It's a Wonderful Life*) as Lt. Columbo. Levinson and Link could not have dreamed of a more renowned cast—but quickly discovered the potential downside of working with A-listers. The boys found Cotten, Moorehead and Mitchell difficult to work with and intrinsically dismissive toward writers. Yet, even as 27-year-old neophytes, Levinson and Link attempted to stand their ground in protecting what they had written and changing only what they deemed necessary.

The stage play opened in San Francisco on January 15, 1962, with plans to reach Broadway by April. The troupe played primarily one- and two-night stands, each in a different city, as they worked their way eastward. Hyping the all-star cast, most performances sold out. Critics, on the whole, praised the actors but panned the "backwards mystery," pointing to the drama's slow pace and weak third act. Levinson and Link later claimed that they attempted to iron out flaws in the script, but were sidetracked by producer Gregory who didn't want to mess with a moneymaker and Mitchell, suffering from poor health, who refused to learn any new lines.

The cast, however, blamed Levinson and Link. They jokingly referred to the duo as "Leopold and Loeb," the infamous college students who in 1924 kidnapped and murdered a 14-year-old, to demonstrate that their intellectual superiority would allow them to get away with "the perfect crime." The actors said the writers were "very young and quite determined not to change a word of their script," nor would they allow any other writers to tamper without their approval.

In a letter to investors, Gregory revealed he was having problems with the writers, lamenting an "inability to secure sufficient quality rewrites to improve the major weakness in the script." So the producer made changes without them. Levinson and Link's attorney promptly sent Gregory a letter protesting his "presenting this unauthorized version of the play." Gregory responded that he had no choice, since the playwrights were not competent to provide acceptable rewrites and were unwilling to sign off on any changes made by others. In mid-February, Levinson and Link submitted several revisions, but they felt handcuffed by Cotten's proclivity toward overacting. They intentionally gave him only "spare dialogue" to prevent him from overdoing it. The writers attributed complaints of slow pacing to Cotten's being unable to "command excited interest."

Frustrated, Gregory decided the show would not be ready for Broadway until fall. Yet poor reviews and structural problems aside, the public continued to enjoy the show, especially Mitchell's performance as the wily detective. Dressed in a heavy overcoat, he meandered from one spot to another, dropping cigar ashes with every turn and playing up the Irish charm. Audiences adored him. After every performance, the crowds cheered and applauded wildly when Mitchell came out for his bow, then trailed off when Cotten, the purported star, walked up for his.

Prescription: Murder finally reached the Northeast in late February, for a one-

THE PROMOTERS of the initial run of *Prescription: Murder* continued advertising Thomas Mitchell as the detective months after he had left the cast and fully aware he would not be returning. This Doug Anderson cartoon ran in the *St. Louis Post-Dispatch* on March 25, 1962, caricaturing *(left to right)* Mitchell, Agnes Moorehead, Joseph Cotten, and Patricia Medina.

week booking in Philadelphia. Days into the engagement, Mitchell became too ill to go on. He was rushed to a hospital for surgery and then sent back home to California to "recuperate." In actuality, he was dying of cancer. His understudy, the competent-yet-uncharismatic Howard Wierum, took over as Columbo. For the remainder of the run, the producer and theaters continued to advertise the play as starring Thomas Mitchell. Audiences would not learn of the switch until hearing the precurtain announcement or spotting the change notice inserted into the playbill.

Without Mitchell, the play wasn't nearly as much fun. The reviews worsened. As the *Detroit Free Press* observed, "Thomas Mitchell was supposed to be the detective who solves the crime, but he was suffering from an illness possibly brought on by acute embarrassment."

As word of mouth spread, box office slipped. The show closed in Boston on May 26, after just 19 weeks. Levinson and Link considered themselves fortunate, since they would regain the rights and could prevent an unauthorized version making it to Broadway.

By now the writers realized their professional home lie in television—and in California. They returned to Hollywood and resumed series writing in earnest, only now freelance, on *Dr. Kildare, The Fugitive, The Man from U.N.C.L.E.*, and *The Alfred Hitchcock Hour*. They helped launch a short-lived spy show called *Jericho* and dreamed up their own detective series, *Mannix*, which would run for eight seasons on CBS.

Driven and ambitious, they worked tirelessly. Levinson would hammer away at the typewriter, smoking one cigarette after another and bellowing at a machine-gun pace. Link would pace back and forth, holding his own, albeit in quieter tones, and providing the zinger just when it was needed. They seemed to be wired to exactly the same wavelength, playing off of each other like a match of verbal ping pong, and often finishing each other's sentences. Both obsessed over every detail. They detested loose ends and gaps in logic. But, being so creative and headstrong, they frequently disagreed, heatedly arguing their point of view. Yet once the TV offers started pouring in, they realized just how unproductive their arguments were. They trusted each other's judgment, so they made a pact, one they would stick to for the entirety of their partnership: whenever they reached an impasse, they'd alternate whose suggestion they went with.

Their series output was prodigious, though frustrating when mishandled by a director or producer who tampered with their words or intent. They again aspired for better. But this time they would not forsake TV for the more respectable pastures of literature, Broadway or film. Instead they would bring the quality of those media to television. So it was with great interest that they saw what was happening at Universal Television.

Big-name movies were dominating the television ratings. So the three television networks began vying for films to broadcast. Rather than just peddle its backlist, Universal produced three movies made especially for television. NBC bought two of them. Both were big hits. Taking notice, CBS signed a deal with Warner Bros. to make movies for them, and ABC inked a deal with MGM. That left a big opportunity for Universal and its salesman extraordinaire, Hollywood agent-turned-studio-senior-VP Jennings Lang, in dealing with NBC. An enthusiastic, bearlike man with a million ideas, Lang proposed producing a massive package of made-for-TV movies just for NBC. Lang's idea was to call them "World Premieres"; they would each run two hours, offer the quality of theatrical films, and feature four to six name stars. But they would be filmed in as little as three weeks and budgeted from $700,000 to $1 million apiece.

NBC would be allowed to show each film twice, then all rights would revert to Universal. All films would also act as pilots, so if the ratings merited, NBC would get first crack at them as series. NBC ordered 15 World Premiere movies for the 1966-1967 TV season and ended up green-lighting two of them for series—*Ironside* with Raymond Burr as the wheelchair-bound investigator and *Fame Is the Name of the Game* with Anthony Franciosa as a crusading reporter. NBC wanted even more World Premieres for the next season, and the next.

Universal's sudden craving for content and the high production values of the World Premieres intrigued Levinson and Link. They had their agents submit *Prescription: Murder*. Universal thought it would work perfectly. Don Siegel (*Invasion of the Body Snatchers*) was signed to direct and produce. But soon after, Siegel left the project and was replaced with Richard Irving, a longtime Universal executive who directed and produced special projects on the side. Unlike the stereotypical studio bigwig, Irving genuinely wished to involve his writers and sought their input on creative decisions. He asked permission of Levinson and Link before changing the story's setting from New York to Los Angeles. He invited them to participate in the pre-production process and let them sit in on casting sessions. For the role of Lt. Columbo, the writers pushed for Lee J. Cobb (the hot-tempered juror in *12 Angry Men*). Cobb was unavailable. So Levinson and Link suggested Bing Crosby, remembering the crooner's serious work in *The Country Girl* (1954) and envisioning him laconically taking in a crime scene, with a pipe in place of a cigar. Crosby read the script and liked it, but declined. He was looking to lessen his workload and play more golf.

Irving had another idea. He'd just heard from the agent of Peter Falk, who had snagged the script off someone else's desk and loved it. "Peter Falk said he would *kill* to play that cop," Irving relayed.

Reactively, Levinson and Link resisted the idea. At 39, Falk was about half the age of Thomas Mitchell's Columbo. They also had become acquainted with Falk during their early days in New York, and were fond of him—*everybody* liked Peter. They just knew the actor could be a handful to deal with. Temperamental stage actors had already made *Prescription: Murder* hell for the writers. Certainly, there had to be better options than Peter Falk.

3
The Cop

Peter Falk didn't intend to be an actor; he just sort of stumbled into the profession. He was born in 1927 and grew up in Ossining, New York, where his father owned a clothing store and where—at age three—he had his right eye removed due to a cancerous tumor. His handicap, though, may have been a boon; being teased about his cockeyed glass eye taught him early on not to give a rip about what others said. He became an A student, a standout athlete in three sports, and a quick study at the local pool hall.

After high school, Falk enrolled at Hamilton College in Upstate New York but—bored—soon dropped out and joined the Merchant Marine as a cook. After two years, he returned to New York City, earning a political science degree from the New School for Social Research, followed by a master's degree in public administration from Syracuse University. For fun, he dabbled in acting, and kept at the hobby by appearing at a community theater in Hartford even after becoming an efficiency expert for the Connecticut Budget Bureau. Early on, Falk didn't think much of his thespian abilities. Acting was supposed to be art, performed by trained professionals. He considered what he did faking it. Falk was also notoriously indecisive. It would take 10 years of dating Syracuse classmate Alyce Mayo before they married. And, approaching 30, he still had no idea what he wanted to do with his life. He just knew it wasn't working as a numbers man for a government agency.

Falk, in fact, was amazingly gifted in almost everything he did, yet he was filled with self-doubt. He was equally distrustful of others, until they had proven their skill—and that they had his best interest at heart. As would become his habit in life, he was looking for direction from an expert, a genius, and he found one in Eva Le Gallienne. The renowned actress and drama coach saw him in a community theater performance of *Richard III* and wanted to know what he was doing in Hartford. "There is no theater here," she pronounced.

"I'm not an actor," Falk sheepishly explained.

"You should be," Le Gallienne replied.

Falk quit his job the next day. He moved to New York and began taking acting classes. On the strength of a letter of recommendation from Le Gallienne, he quickly landed a small role off-Broadway in Molière's *Don Juan*. Soon after, he was cast as the central bartender in Eugene O'Neill's *The Iceman Cometh*, starring the equally unknown Jason Robards.

In addition to providing tremendous exposure, the play taught Falk how to think on his feet. The drama ran nearly four hours long and took place on one set, a tavern with Falk behind the bar the entire time. The other actors, however, sat at tables, often with their heads down, waiting for their soliloquy. Occasionally, they would literally fall asleep waiting. Falk began carrying a broom around on stage. When he noticed an actor appear to be drifting off, he'd start sweeping in their direction and nudge them with the broom right before they were to deliver their next lines.

After two years off-Broadway, Falk was offered a movie contract by Columbia Pictures. The deal was contingent only on the personal okay of studio chief Harry Cohn. The meeting with Cohn did not go well, since he was bothered by Falk's "deficiency." Falk didn't know what he was referring to. Cohn spelled it out: "I'm concerned about your eye." For Falk, the glass eye wasn't a problem at all. He'd lived most of his life with it, and it gave him an unusual, memorable look. But Cohn wanted Falk to take a screen test to make sure that his eye didn't look odd on the big screen. Falk protested. The two argued, and Cohn abruptly cut him off: "Young man, for the same price I'll get an actor with two eyes."

Falk returned to off-Broadway, and started getting small roles in TV dramas and low-budget pictures. His biggest break came when he was cast as psychotic gangster Abe Reles in *Murder, Inc.* (1960), which earned him an Academy Award nomination and scores of offers to play similar mobsters.

Falk purposefully began looking for varied roles and, in 1961, found a pip playing a Greek truck driver who picks up a young pregnant hitchhiker in the TV drama *The Price of Tomatoes* on *The Dick Powell Theatre*. Unlike having him play a crazed villain, writer/first-time-producer Richard Alan Simmons cast Falk as a more sensitive, endearing character, just rough around the edges. The part garnered Falk his first Emmy and, for Simmons, the lifelong admiration of Falk.

Between a rash of other high-profile film and TV work, Falk agreed to work for Simmons on another *Dick Powell* drama a year later and to star for him

HEADLINING his first television series, *The Trials of O'Brien*, Peter Falk played an abrasive lawyer, drastically different from yet no less eccentric than Lt. Columbo.

in a weekly drama series in 1965. *The Trials of O'Brien* featured Falk as offbeat lawyer Danny O'Brien—fast-talking, moody, cocky, impatient and selectively charming. The pace of shooting was exhausting, with a new hour-long program completed every week for 22 weeks.

Critics loved the show. The public, not so much. On average, *The Trials of O'Brien* placed 97th out of 102 programs ranked by the Nielsen ratings. Falk blamed the poor showing on being scheduled on Saturday nights, when "you get an elderly crowd—the *Lawrence Welk* people—at home. The people from about 16 to 48 or 50 are going to enjoy our show the most, and Saturday night takes a lot of them out of town." CBS tried rescheduling the program for 10 p.m. on Fridays, but—facing off against the highly rated *Man from U.N.C.L.E.*—it fared no better. The series, to Falk's great relief, was not renewed.

It was back to guest shots on TV shows and supporting roles in movies—the goofy henchman Max in *The Great Race*, the police lieutenant in the Natalie Wood comedy *Penelope*, a schemer opposite Jack Lemmon and Elaine May in *Luv*.

Prescription: Murder

Not long after completing *Luv*, Falk stumbled onto the pilot script for *Prescription: Murder*. The part of the detective intrigued him, and he had his agent contact Universal.

"I ran across the script someplace—I probably picked it up on somebody's desk—and I fell in love with the character," Falk recalled. "I really wanted to play that part, and I went after it. They said I was too young and was not right. There aren't that many parts that I really want."

Dick Levinson and Bill Link had their concerns, but their resistance crumbled as time went on and they were unable to suggest someone better. Falk got the part.

Universal's Wardrobe Department costumed him like a typical TV detective—drab suitcoat and trousers, pressed white shirt, black tie. But Falk had his own thoughts about the character's overcoat referred to in the script. He misread it as "raincoat," and remembered a tan trench coat he had picked up a couple of years earlier, when a sudden rainstorm caused him to duck into a shop on 57th Street in Manhattan. Falk went home and fished the wrinkled garment out of his closet.

Levinson and Link's adaptation of their stage play was fairly straightforward. Some scenes only alluded to on stage, such as the argument between Dr. Flemming and his disguised mistress on the airplane, could actually be shown on-screen.

Their biggest switch was the ending. Columbo, convinced that Flemming is guilty but lacking incontrovertible proof, must find a way to get the murderer to incriminate himself. In the play, Columbo stages a fake suicide of Flemming's mistress, Susan, prompting the killer to become remorseful; Susan was his true love and he is so crushed by her death that he implores Columbo to take him to police headquarters so he can confess. Levinson and Link had penned the hokey ending to create sympathy for their star. But they now realized that the real star was the detective. They no longer felt any compunction to make the murderer remorseful or decent. Instead, for the TV version, they had Flemming, upon witnessing the fake suicide, brag about how he never cared about Susan and that she was just a plaything to accomplish his plot. He even suggests that if Susan had not killed herself, she may have met with an untimely, uh, accident. Only, Columbo has had Susan hiding nearby and, hearing the truth, she readily agrees to testify against the doctor.

Prescription: Murder first aired on NBC on February 20, 1968. Levinson and Link both tuned in at home, intent on picking apart anything that didn't translate as well to the screen as they had hoped. Their criticisms were quickly forgotten, as they found themselves mesmerized by Falk's performance. His

COLUMBO, looking a tad less scruffy than he would in later appearances, confronts Dr. Flemming, played by Gene Barry, in *Prescription: Murder*. *[Credit: NBCUniversal]*

engaging presence. His long, awkward pauses. His fidgeting with the cigar. His wandering gaze. And that glass eye, that wonderful glass eye, wasn't a distraction at all; it gave the character an endearing, almost quizzical squint. Levinson and Link couldn't take their eyes off of him.

Neither, in fact, could 25 million other TV viewers. More than 40 percent of all television sets were tuned to NBC. For the week, the show ranked fourth among all programs, and NBC immediately gave the go-ahead to give Columbo his own weekly series. There was only one problem. Falk, anxious to continue his rising movie career and with *The Trials of O'Brien* seared in his memory, declined. He had no interest in doing another weekly TV series.

Prescription: Murder

Filmed: June – July 1967
Stars: Gene Barry, Peter Falk, Katherine Justice, William Windom, Nina Foch
Director: Richard Irving
Producer: Richard Irving
Teleplay: Richard Levinson & William Link
Original Play: Richard Levinson & William Link
Original Air Date: Feb. 20, 1968
Nielsen Ranking: #4 (24.2 points, 41.1 share)

4
The Contract

*P*restriction: Murder didn't just earn Peter Falk an offer from NBC; it also earned Dick Levinson and Bill Link an invitation to become contract writers for Universal. They would receive a guaranteed salary, the opportunity to work on an unlimited number of projects, and the possibility to gain perpetual royalties on any new properties they helped to create.

Initially, the writers declined, knowing that Universal had a reputation as a "sausage factory," cranking out an endless stream of cookie-cutter films and TV shows. They feared they would be shuttled from one project to the next, performing emergency rewrites and unable to create anything of their own.

Universal's head of TV production, however, usually got his way. Tall, rangy, forceful and combative, Sid Sheinberg kept after the boys. He made it clear that with those he truly believed in, he got out of their way and backed them to the hilt. Not long after, Sheinberg would make a similar promise to a 20-year-old student filmmaker out of Cal State Long Beach, a kid named Steven Spielberg. Eventually, Levinson and Link reconsidered. The proposed deal included a 12-month option, so if they were unhappy after the first year, they could walk away.

Besides, Universal was the biggest game in town and had a standing deal with NBC for more than a dozen World Premieres a year. Indeed, Universal executives, anxious to keep the wunderkinds happy and replicate the success of *Prescription: Murder*, quickly assigned them to write a wholly original movie of the week, *Istanbul Express*, a detective yarn starring Gene Barry and produced and directed by Dick Irving.

Levinson and Link then were asked to write for *The Name of the Game,* a new series being spun off from a World Premiere. Levinson and Link would write two episodes, and produce the first, alongside executive producer Dick Irving and first-time associate producer Dean Hargrove. Levinson and Link found no joy in the non-writing duties of producing, such as setting the budget, hiring the cast and crew, and signing off on the sets, costumes and editing. But they did covet the power it gave them. They now officially had final say to ensure their vision made it to the screen and prevent meddlers from messing it up. "Our best work was us—not one word changed by anybody else," Link said.

As he explained, "We became producers because we had to protect what we had written. We sometimes saw what directors did when they came to our material, and we didn't like it. So we created an insurance policy by becoming producers of our own things. We simply had to do that."

Falk, meanwhile, had pursued a movie career, hoping for a starring role in something of significance. Instead, he was forced to settle for supporting parts in largely forgettable pictures. On one, *Machine Gun McCain* (1969), he found himself co-starring with John Cassavetes, the actor and avant-garde director.

Tall, handsome and supremely creative, Cassavetes oozed confidence. Falk was instantly captivated. He just could not understand why someone so gifted would waste his time acting in such a conventional picture. Cassavetes explained that it was the price of artistic freedom. His own films were made with his own money, the way he wanted, and with the people he wanted, with no studio interference. That meant he had to pick up run-of-the-mill acting jobs to finance his visions.

Falk was hooked. He agreed to appear in his next film, *Husbands*, sharing billing with Cassavetes and the actor who would complete their carousing lifelong threesome, Ben Gazzara. Falk was ill-prepared for Cassavetes' unconventional filmmaking style—the script was minimal; much of it was still percolating in Cassavetes' head. Cassavetes relied on his actors to improvise, to be real. His sets were less formal, less structured. He believed in actors learning their lines just before delivering them, and adding, subtracting, making the words their own. Unlike other directors who would call, "Action," Cassavetes would just start the cameras rolling and let the actors ease naturally into the scene, occasionally catching something unexpected and magical.

At first, Falk chafed against the lack of structure. He had little idea what was next. He hated it, and told Cassavetes he would never work for him again. But day by day, the excitement, variety, spontaneity and unpredictability won him over, and he could not wait to work with Cassavetes again. Falk also began incorporating this new freedom into his acting in other projects, determined to create his own art.

JOHN CASSAVETES *(left)* became mentor, friend, carousing partner, and co-worker to Falk and Ben Gazzara, here in *Husbands* (1970).

During the ensuing years, NBC continued pleading with Universal for a weekly *Columbo* series. Falk wanted no part of it. Cassavetes and Elaine May both encouraged him to avoid such one-dimensional roles. At the same time, Universal was perfecting a new kind of series—nicknamed "the wheel"—designed for shows in which the material was too heady or too difficult to produce on a weekly basis or featuring stars who would not commit to a weekly show. In 1968, they rolled out *The Name of the Game*. The three stars—Gene Barry as the high-powered publisher, Anthony Franciosa as an investigative reporter, and Robert Stack as the crusading editor—rotated as the lead from week to week. With a budget of $400,000 per 90-minute show, it was hip and cool, if not highly rated. The following year, NBC-Universal premiered a similar wheel, *The Bold Ones*, and in 1970 they launched *Four-In-One*, which began with six straight weeks of *McCloud*, followed by similar mini-runs of *San Francisco International Airport*, *Night Gallery*, and *The Psychiatrist*.

Universal wondered if making *Columbo* part of a wheel would convince Falk to sign on the dotted line, since he would just have to make six episodes a year, leaving him with 10 months to work on movies and other projects.

After years of rejections, Universal and NBC had low expectations. Little did they know that Falk had recently been swindled out of about $100,000 by his business manager and was looking for a way to make a lot of money quickly, both for financial security and—like Cassavetes—to help fund pet movie projects. Stunningly, Falk said yes. He was amenable to making a half-dozen 90-minute *Columbos* that would alternate with *McCloud* and a third program to be named later.

Ransom for a Dead Man

Before proceeding with the series, NBC requested a two-hour pilot. Levinson and Link were incredulous. Wasn't *Prescription: Murder* a pilot? Didn't its strong ratings prove the audience wanted more of Columbo? In all likelihood, NBC didn't want a second pilot to prove there was an audience for *Columbo*, but rather to whet the public's appetite for the fall season. After all, NBC had been begging Falk to commit to a series for two-and-a-half years. The third spoke in the wheel, Rock Hudson's *McMillan & Wife*, was also asked to shoot a two-hour "pilot," which would air on the Friday following the first regular *Columbo*, even after several other *McMillan & Wifes* were already in the can. These weren't tests. A second *Columbo* pilot gave NBC an extra installment of the show they had been dying for, and a two-hour one at that.

Universal's first choice to both write and produce the second *Columbo* pilot was Levinson and Link. They, however, were knee-deep in developing *The Psychiatrist*—and had already been interrupted to help launch *McCloud*. They agreed to supply a story idea for a *Columbo* pilot, but nothing more. To write the full script, they suggested Dean Hargrove, who had worked for them on *The Name of the Game*. Yet Hargrove had quickly progressed from associate producer to primary producer of that series' Gene Barry episodes. Hargrove also learned that while the new offer was technically a pilot, the main character had already been established, so he would just be a writer. There would be no royalties once the series started. Hargrove declined.

Universal then approached Stanford Whitmore, co-creator of *McCloud*. He turned down the *Columbo* pilot for the same reasons. Sheinberg went back to Hargrove to sweeten the pot. "Listen," Sheinberg said, "we'll find a way to express what you would have gotten in other ways. But we're not going to call it a royalty because that would get us into all sorts of conflicts." Translated, if Hargrove wrote the picture, he'd receive a nice bonus, producer credit on the pilot, and would head the first season if it became a series.

Hargrove relented. He started with Levinson and Link's two-page treatment, *Ransom for a Dead Man*, in which high-powered attorney Leslie Williams murders her husband, disposes of the body, and manufactures a ransom note, to intimate that he has been kidnapped. She pretends to throw the $300,000 ransom money out of her plane at a drop point, but secretly she holds on to it. She later uses that cash to try to bribe a suspicious stepdaughter to leave the country—only to learn the teen was in cahoots with Columbo, hoping to flush out the traceable bills.

Hargrove began by studying *Prescription: Murder*, to get to know the character and identify any plot points that could become part of the show's formula—namely Columbo arrives to investigate a crime, is continually bothered by a series of small, almost insignificant inconsistencies, zeroes in on a suspect, and begins pestering him until he finally, inadvertently gives himself away. The idea was to get the murderer to hang himself due to his one personal flaw. For *Prescription: Murder's* Dr. Flemming that was arrogance; for Leslie Williams, it would be greed and lack of conscience—she assumed the stepdaughter could be bought off.

Hargrove's script played up aspects highlighted in the first pilot—Columbo's forgetfulness, his intense politeness, his fascination with objects in the homes he enters, his frequently referring to his wife and telling brief anecdotes about other relatives, the catchphrase "one more thing," the ever-present cigar, and the oft-absent pencil.

To accentuate Columbo's nonintimidating nature, the writer had him underestimated not just by the villain, but also by the other professional investigators. Instead of first appearing 33 minutes into the show, as in *Prescription: Murder*, Columbo arrives 12.5 minutes in, long before anyone has any inkling that a murder has been committed. Columbo spends his first scenes poking around the periphery, listening in on the FBI agents' conversations, and getting in their way. When he asks the villain where the bathroom is, she speaks to him slowly and emphatically, as if he's an uncomprehending child.

Hargrove was also able to introduce several new elements—Columbo's love of chili, his simultaneous fascination and bewilderment with new technology (which ultimately leads to a clue), more action, and more humor. Most memorably, Hargrove had Williams take a fearful Columbo up in her private plane and hand him the controls, to great comic effect. The scene inside the cockpit was not to be shot until the final day of filming, on Stage 42. That gave Hargrove extra time to continually revise the scene, adding one of the best laughs just before shooting began. After Williams, having rattled her interrogator, takes back the controls and levels the plane, she says she's ready to answer any questions. But Columbo needs a moment to compose himself. Hargrove lengthened the beat, inserting an additional shot of the plane flying calmly. Williams asks again if he's ready to talk, and an ashen Columbo replies, "Not yet."

Hargrove also liked the raincoat and suggested that Falk make his entire wardrobe monochromatic. Falk knew that if he was to create a recurring character, he needed a more unique look—and it wouldn't hurt for the wardrobe to also be comfortable. He brought in a pair of old, high-topped brown shoes from home, and a muddy dark-green tie with tiny white dots. He selected a baggier, easier fitting raincoat—one he'd use for the next 20 years. The studio Wardrobe Department had a blue-and-white suit that fit well. "I made them dye the suit brown," Falk said. "Everything I wear, including my shirts, must be some shade of brown. I became crazy about the color in 1965 when I visited Italy. Everything is brown there, including the buildings. The Italians really understand that color best."

Falk, in fact, took the opportunity to make Columbo's whole look more disheveled. He left his hair a little shaggier, and wore shirts that were more yellowed and slightly wrinkled.

He broadened his performance, as well. He slowed down his delivery, lengthened pauses, avoided eye contact, got increasingly distracted, and used more animated gesturing.

Initially, some expressions bordered on mugging. Since the script had Columbo appear before the murder is discovered, the detective spends the first half of the picture not interrogating the villain, but studying her from a distance, staring at and pondering her behavior. In later episodes, Falk would display Columbo's reactions as he questioned his subject; in *Ransom for a Dead Man*, his takes are isolated and more drawn out, almost as if he's performing *Columbo for Dummies*.

Falk also, for the first time, would work to get one of his and Cassavetes' actor buddies into an episode. He suggested Timothy Carey as the counterman at Barney's Beanery. Throughout the series, Falk used his pull to get work for many of his cronies.

To play ice-cold murderer Leslie Williams, Hargrove pushed for Lee Grant. "The studio wanted Hope Lange (*The Ghost & Mrs. Muir*)," Hargrove recalled. "But I knew Lee from having done *Name of the Game* with her and was a great admirer of hers and her career in totality, so I held out for her. As a matter of fact, I had to go through a lot of physical hoops to get her into it because she was doing another show somewhere. We had to limo her back and forth, and wrap the schedule (around hers) to get her. As I had hoped, she was perfect in the show and a perfect foil for Peter Falk."

Dick Irving both executive produced and directed, integrating a host of effects—dramatic freeze-frames, unique camera angles, zooms, split-second flashbacks, tense editing by Ed Abroms, and a haunting score by Billy Goldenberg.

As expected, *Ransom for a Dead Man* premiered to strong ratings. Within days of the airing, NBC gave Universal the green-light to proceed with the series. The network wanted six 90-minute *Columbos*. Falk was willing, with one proviso. He had also agreed to star on Broadway alongside Lee Grant in Neil Simon's *The Prisoner of Second Avenue* in the fall. He needed to have all six episodes finished before the first one aired.

Ransom for a Dead Man

Working Title: *World Premiere: Columbo*
Filmed: Nov. 27 – Dec. 23, 1970
Stars: Peter Falk, Lee Grant, John Fink, Harold Gould
Director: Richard Irving
Executive Producer: Richard Irving
Producer: Dean Hargrove
Teleplay: Dean Hargrove
Story: Richard Levinson & William Link
Air Date: March 1, 1971

5
Mutual Distrust

Sid Sheinberg may have bribed Dean Hargrove to write *Ransom for a Dead Man* by dangling a producership in front of him. Yet his first choice to shepherd Season 1 of *Columbo* had always been Levinson and Link. The duo knew the character better than anyone, had more experience with mysteries, and was fast becoming the studio's golden boys. Universal was convinced that the success of *Columbo* would determine the fate of the wheel.

"So," Hargrove recounted, "the studio asked me if I would step aside for a year and let (Levinson and Link) set the show and determine what the mechanics would be, and then take over the show. I thought this was actually a good idea, because Dick and Bill really knew the mystery format. I had only done the one *Columbo* movie. So it was a chance for me to watch how they worked and how the show functioned. I stepped aside to do a show called *McCloud* with Dennis Weaver, which was not my happiest time."

Persuading Levinson and Link was more difficult. Sheinberg called them to a meeting in his office on the fifteenth floor of Universal's charcoal glass headquarters, known menacingly as The Black Tower. Sheinberg said he wanted them to produce six 90-minute episodes in five months. They would determine the format, originate the scripts, set the casts, crews and budgets, and oversee filming and all phases of post-production. Levinson and Link thought there was no way it could be done. Sheinberg said he agreed—that that's what everyone *else* in the world thought. Sheinberg did not. He believed *they* could do it, and he would not take no for an answer. After a marathon meeting, Levinson and Link staggered out of Sheinberg's office, having just agreed to the impossible—and not quite sure why.

The pair moved to a larger suite of offices and began assembling their top assistants. Robert F. O'Neill became their first hire. Steady and reliable, O'Neill had served as associate producer on *Dr. Kildare*, *Jericho* and *Mission: Impossible*, and was just coming off of *The Name of the Game*. As story editor they chose 26-year-old Steven Bochco, a decade before he would become a household name as the creator of *Hill Street Blues*. At that point, the only credits he had were writing one episode of *The Name of the Game* and doctoring three others. The team needed someone like Bochco who could write and rewrite well and fast.

The producers then began to set the "Rules of *Columbo*," using *Prescription: Murder* as the template. Every episode was to be structured as an inverted mystery and styled after the adventures of Ellery Queen and Agatha Christie, English drawing-room mysteries, rather than a cop show. They would take place in a sanitized, almost fantasy Los Angeles, devoid of shootouts, car chases, drug busts, or prostitutes. In their place would be stately mansions inhabited by proper, haughty professionals to provide a sharp contrast to the motley detective. The murderers' supreme self-confidence would convince them that the unassuming investigator is no match for their intellect.

The killer should also be highly unlikable. Levinson explained, "In *Ransom for a Dead Man*, most people wanted Lee Grant to get away with the murder and frankly so did we. That's because she played a sympathetic character. In the series, our murderers won't be sympathetic, so you'll want Columbo to win."

Each adventure would begin with a perfect murder, ingeniously planned and expertly covered up. Ironclad alibi intact, the murderer—and the audience—would be convinced the plan was foolproof. Columbo, though, will arrive and quickly spot a small, seemingly inconsequential inconsistency that makes him suspect the murderer. He will then uncover a string of clues, one by one, that reinforce his case, until he unveils one "gotcha" clue, the "pop" as Peter Falk would call it, which truly incriminates the guilty party, frequently initiated by some trickery on the part of Columbo.

The show was to be distinctly nonviolent. Columbo would not carry a gun or throw a punch. Any mayhem—like, say, the requisite murder—was to be portrayed artistically or, better yet, unseen.

Our hero might talk incessantly about his wife or nephew, but we'd never see them, or his home or police headquarters; he'd just drift in and out of the stories, vaguely, magically. The true mystery of the show was to be Columbo himself.

To stir freelance writers' imaginations and familiarize them with the format, the producers invited 60-some scribes to a screening of *Ransom for a Dead Man*. The writers in attendance quickly recognized how difficult it would be to sustain the drama with two characters just talking to each other for 90 minutes. When

WILLIAM LINK and Richard Levinson, behind typewriter, at work in the early 1970s.

the picture ended, only two freelancers showed any interest in contributing.

The brunt of the writing would fall on Bochco. "I was just a kid in a tiny cubbyhole across from Bill and Dick," he said. "They would summon: 'Okay, we have an idea for this episode.' And I'd deliver them a first draft, and they'd give me notes very quickly, and then I'd write a second draft, and they'd take my script and rewrite it. They taught me."

In the meantime, Falk was growing increasingly wary about returning to series TV. He had already insisted on being able to name his own line producer on three of the six episodes, to ensure his input was heard. He did not know Levinson and

Link well, just that they had little experience as producers. Falk considered them secretive and disinclined to keeping him in the loop. Indeed, they were highly protective of their work and scrambling to get it finished under ridiculously short deadlines. Falk started making frequent visits to their office to check in on their progress and to discuss each story and character. The producers, used to making rapid-fire decisions and moving on to the next crisis, found themselves dragged into arguments over the finer points of their show with the star, who preferred to ponder and waver. Falk didn't like being rushed or ignored. The producers grew defensive. This was their domain. Every day, shouting matches erupted that rattled the halls of Universal.

"One of the things that complicated that first year tremendously was that (Levinson and Link) were endlessly at war with Peter Falk," Bochco related. "I love Peter Falk, but he and Bill and Dick went at it every day. And they just had these terrible blowouts. I could hear (it) from across the hall. But when it was done, Peter would poke his head in my office: 'Hiya, kid, how's it going? How ya doing? I loved your script....' It was Jekyll and Hyde."

After about four weeks, Falk demanded that someone he trusted be placed on the production staff, to be mindful of his interests. Soon after, Falk miraculously began acquiring copies of treatments and first drafts of scripts. The work was rough and not ready to be reviewed, so Falk naturally was dissatisfied. The producers tried explaining that the scripts would be hugely improved—and privately vowed, from then on, to lock all of their drafts in a cabinet before leaving for the night. The battles intensified, threatening to throw the show off schedule.

In desperation, Levinson and Link went to The Black Tower for help. Falk was suspended, barred from the lot, until the producers had need for him.

Once they finally had their first scripts completed, Levinson and Link proudly shipped copies to NBC. The network had "conceptual concerns." Peter Falk is the lead—yet his character doesn't show up for 20 minutes. Why do we never see his wife? Better yet, Columbo should be single, so he's free for romantic interludes. Where are the other regular characters, particularly a young, handsome partner? Worst of all, the scripts are really talky—where's the fast pace? The danger?

Upon receiving NBC's notes, Levinson and Link threatened to quit. Not only were they fundamentally opposed to the changes and thought they would ruin the show, they argued on practical grounds: if the show was going to meet its air dates, it had to be completed before Falk left for New York, which meant there was no more time for rewrites. The episodes had to be filmed as written or they literally could not be finished. NBC backed off.

Death Lends a Hand

Levinson and Link originally thought to name their first episode after *Prescription: Murder's* earlier title, *Enough Rope*, but at the last moment switched to *Death Lends a Hand*—a sly reference to how the murder would be committed: private investigator Brimmer (Robert Culp) angrily backhands an uncooperative person he's trailing and she falls, striking her head on a coffee table.

The episode would show, for the first time, Columbo driving, so Levinson and Link decided to pick out three nondescript vehicles and would let Falk make the final decision. The day before filming began, Link took the actor to Universal's massive, multilevel prop car lot to show him their recommendations. "Nah," Falk said. "Those are no good." He began walking down the rows, past hundreds and hundreds of vehicles of every shape and size. In a back corner, he spotted a stubby gray nose jutting out from behind a larger sedan. The nose belonged to an unkempt 1959 Peugeot 403 Cabriolet. Falk knew it was the right one. Link was incredulous. "Peter," he asked, "why would a down-to-earth, blue-collar L.A. homicide cop be driving an exotic thing like that?" "It'll be fine," Falk replied, and since the decision was minor and time was short, Link let him have his way.

Columbo was originally supposed to be introduced being pulled over by a highway patrolman who discovers the Lieutenant has an expired driver's license. Falk protested. Columbo might be sloppy, but he would never drive around without valid ID. After another round of arguments, Levinson and Link proposed a compromise. The motorcycle cop would discover Columbo's license "expires next week."

Even after filming began, Falk remained a thorn in Levinson and Link's sides. Each episode was allotted 10 days to shoot; Falk considered the schedule merely a suggestion. He usually did not start memorizing the script until he arrived on the set that morning, insisting the scene would play fresher. He then required numerous takes until he nailed it and, considering his indecisiveness, that number could rise into the dozens. In each take, he tried out different words, phrasing and reactions. In fact, Falk changed around almost every line he was given to make it sound more like "the real" Columbo.

Typically, Levinson and Link were hyper-protective of every syllable of their scripts. But they quickly realized that with Falk no one knew the sound of Columbo better than he did, because he had poured so much of himself into the character. Levinson soon advised Bochco to "under-write" for him. "Peter Falk IS Columbo," Levinson instructed. "You don't have to write all of that stuff, because that's Peter. You don't have to write Peter, because Peter's Peter. If you write that stuff and then Peter does that, on top of being Peter, it's over the top."

Falk would also bring shooting to a standstill to discuss plot and character with the director, as the rest of the cast and crew stood idle. Filming would go deep into the evening, with the crew collecting overtime.

Prescription: Murder had taken 18 days to shoot—two over schedule—enraging studio head Lew Wasserman. There was not time for even this mild luxury when producing a series of six 90-minute pictures that needed to be shot one right after the other. Asked to pick up the pace, Falk would explode into angry diatribes about the Universal assembly line, ranting like one of the mobsters he played earlier in his career. The executives would sheepishly slink back to their offices.

The actor regularly visited the cutting room to check on each episode's progress and offer his input. The producers advised the editors to close their doors or, when they saw Falk coming, shut down for the day. When Falk expressed interest in watching the dailies, they began scheduling them at times when Falk was away from the lot shooting on location.

Levinson and Link were able to hire an accomplished Academy Award-winning cinematographer, Russell Metty, as director of photography for the first five episodes. His skills and credentials were impeccable—*Touch of Evil* for Orson Welles, *Spartacus* for Stanley Kubrick, *Bringing Up Baby* for Howard Hawks—but at 64, the crusty old "D.P." had seen it all and thought he knew it all. He insisted on lighting the show darkly, in shadows. The producers tried explaining to him that it wasn't that type of mystery. They wanted the show lit more like a Technicolor musical. Metty refused. In desperation, Levinson and Link bought him a box of fine Havana cigars and treated him to lunch at the best restaurant on the Universal lot. Metty softened, and agreed to brighten the scenes.

Murder by the Book

As Levinson and Link scurried to think up new plots, they would pull other writers out of the Universal hallways to bounce ideas off of. One, screenwriter/soon-to-become-cult-filmmaker Larry Cohen, had a devilish suggestion: what if the murderer and victim were a mystery writing team, a la Levinson and Link? The basic conceit—the author with all the talent is killed after telling his partner he wants to strike out on his own—was then handed off to Bochco to expand into a full script.

For *Murder by the Book*, Bochco named his writing team the equally alliterative Ferris and Franklin. Soon everyone around the studio began chattering about which real-life partner was the talented one and which was the coattail rider. The joke became "Did Link kill Levinson, or did Levinson kill Link?"

Other subtle touches gave nods to Levinson and Link. Franklin presents as a gift one of his Mrs. Melville novels called *Prescription: Murder*. Another of their titles (*Mrs. Melville in London*) and the last line Ferris types from their next novel ("The wet umbrella gave you away") point to a Season 2 episode, *Dagger of the Mind*.

About three weeks before each episode was to begin filming, the producers selected its director. The director received a temporary cubbyhole where he consulted on casting, crew, story and locations, and mapped out his camera shots for each scene, sometimes using storyboards. The director then conferred with Wardrobe, set designers, prop men, and the camera team to make sure everything fit within his vision, and of course directed the action once filming began.

Levinson and Link wanted a professional quality for the series, as if each entry was a motion picture unto itself. So they sought the best, most accomplished directors available. Sid Sheinberg encouraged them to mix in someone younger, someone who was willing to take chances and do something unconventional. Sheinberg suggested Steven Spielberg, the talented 24-year-old he and Wasserman were grooming. Spielberg had completed a *Name of the Game* for Dean Hargrove, and two shows each of *Night Gallery* and *The Psychiatrist*. Levinson and Link viewed a rough cut of a *Psychiatrist* and were sold. They just had to convince Falk, who held the right to refuse their choice of director. Falk did not want any surprises. They showed Falk *The Psychiatrist* and he too was impressed.

Falk was even more dazzled once production began. Spielberg planned meticulously and employed techniques the other veterans on the set had never heard of before. His very first shot began with an overhead on Franklin's car driving toward his partner's office, then pulled back to reveal the camera was actually filming from inside Ferris' upper-floor glass office, where Ferris types madly away. Falk remembered, "For the first time in any television show that I had ever done, we did a scene and I had no idea where the camera was. I'm not sure, but I think it was across the street in a second-story window."

Spielberg still had to work with the crusty old director of photography, Russ Metty, who had little respect for the "hotshot" director or his unorthodox techniques. Metty would complain to the producers, "He's a kid! Does he get a milk and cookie break? Is the diaper truck going to interfere with my generator?"

Metty was particularly upset about shooting inside the Sunset Boulevard office behind an entire wall of glass. "Where the hell do you expect me to put my lights?" Levinson and Link backed Spielberg: "He's the director. Do what he says."

Unlike most other *Columbo* directors, who were off to the next project once they filmed their final frame, Spielberg remained involved through all aspects of post-production, from scoring and sound mixing to editing. For the scene where Franklin bludgeons a female witness, Spielberg suggested closing in on her scream, but removing her shriek from the dialogue track, leaving only the soft background music. Link loved the idea. Levinson hated it, considering it too abstract. But Levinson was outnumbered, so he let it go.

When the producers saw the director's first cut of the picture, they didn't want to change a single frame. It was perfect. Spielberg was irked. He thought there were several seconds of footage that could be trimmed. The producers gave him their blessing to cut a little more.

They also were relieved to see that their choice of murderer, Jack Cassidy, played every bit as effectively as Robert Culp in *Death Lends a Hand*, only suave instead of seething. Culp and Cassidy's arrogance perfectly complemented Columbo's humility. Both Culp and Cassidy would be asked back twice more to play *Columbo* killers.

In fact, Levinson and Link were so delighted with the completed episode that they recommended *Murder by the Book* be bumped ahead of *Death Lends a Hand* and scheduled as the series opener.

Dead Weight

For the next three shows of the season, Levinson and Link were to step aside and hand the reins to Falk's handpicked choice for interim producer, Everett Chambers. Falk had known the equally feisty Chambers since the early 1950s when they both attended the New School for Social Research in New York. Chambers worked briefly as an actor, then director, before becoming a producer on John Cassavetes' series *Johnny Staccato*. Through 1971, Chambers was executive producing the new series *Monty Nash* starring Harry Guardino, but agreed to oversee three *Columbos* as a favor to Falk.

"Levinson and Link were not crazy about me coming on," Chambers said. "They wanted to have total control of the show and over Peter. And they got their nose out of joint, because Peter then catered to me rather than to them. He never expressed any of that when he wanted something; he would come to me to try to get it."

Chambers, like Falk, could be a brawler. He related, "Unfortunately or fortunately in my career, I was known as *not* a company man, particularly at Universal, where they always thought of me as the non-company man."

Chambers also was happy to work in small parts for Falk's acting buddies. Falk, like Cassavetes, was intensely loyal to his cronies and, now that he had his own series, was always looking for opportunities to support his friends. Plus, he simply enjoyed being around his pals. Chambers brought back Timothy Carey as chili vendor Bert and cast gruff Val Avery as a boathand in *Dead Weight*, and Fred

Draper as a cab driver in the next episode. Soon enough, Falk would find parts for buddies John Finnegan, Vito Scotti, and Bruce Kirby, who all would be called back over and over again, comprising a virtual *Columbo* Repertory Company.

But no one was better cared for than Mike Lally, a 70-something-year-old, lifelong extra from New York. He had started in the early days of sound movies—though sound wasn't really a prerequisite. Lally rarely if ever spoke on-screen before *Columbo*; he usually helped fill out crowds in the backgrounds of hundreds of movies and TV shows. Occasionally, his rough yet faintly sympathetic face got him cast as a dialogue-less bartender, guard or cop.

He stood about Falk's size, so Falk insisted he become one of his two stand-ins on every episode of *Columbo*. The old-timer became his confidante and his advance man, making sure his boss had everything he needed in his trailer. On filming days when the studio sent a driver out to pick up Falk, they'd be instructed to pick up Lally on the way.

The first script Chambers was given was the show's first freelance script, *Dead Weight* written by John T. Dugan, just as he was coming off as story editor of *Adam-12*. To play proud villain General Hollister, Chambers initially tried to get Robert Ryan or Lloyd Bridges, but both were unavailable. Instead, he cast against type with Eddie Albert, who had just wrapped his sixth and final season of *Green Acres*. Suzanne Pleshette would play the witness whom the General romances so she will question that she really saw a uniformed man commit murder in the General's bayfront home.

Despite the intriguing setup, Dugan's script was a notch below the previous entries, and Falk wanted the series to be better. In fact, he thought *he* could do better. Levinson and Link challenged him to write his own script. Falk tried, through the summer, but got stuck in Act II. He packed away his drafts for another day and instead requested to direct an episode. Universal and NBC had Sunday nights riding on *Columbo* and the wheel. The studio had no interest in experimenting with a first-time director who was known for being slow and methodical.

The Tower turned him down flat. They said they were concerned that if Falk concentrated too much on directing, his acting would suffer. Undeterred, Falk pushed harder. Universal proposed a compromise: Falk could direct... an episode of *Night Gallery*. Spielberg got his start on *Night Gallery*, they explained. Falk didn't want to direct *Night Gallery*. He was only interested in *Columbo*.

The production was supposed to take 10 days, but gradually started falling behind. Finally, Falk turned to Chambers: "Everett, how do I get to direct?"

"You get sick," Chambers answered. "If you're in the middle of a series and you get sick, you've got the power."

On day 11, the crew began filming the final scene on the Memorial Hall set on Stage 22. Falk arrived an hour late for his makeup, rehearsed briefly, and then started shooting the scene with Suzanne Pleshette. One script page in, Falk abruptly stopped, said he was unable to work, and returned to his dressing room. About a half-hour later, Falk returned to the set, but after 15 minutes attempting to get set up, he walked off again, stating that he felt sick. Universal sent its studio doctor to examine him. The doctor couldn't find anything wrong with him, so he prescribed over-the-counter medication and declared Falk fit to return to work.

After an hour, the assistant director went to call him down to the set, but Falk said he needed to rest for another hour or two. The delay set off the director, Jack Smight, a true old-schooler who started in TV in 1949 and worked steadily on series like *Route 66* and *The Alfred Hitchcock Hour* before moving onto big-budget action movies like Paul Newman's *Harper*. Furious, Smight called The Tower.

Seconds later, Dick Irving phoned Chambers to find out what the hell was going on. "I don't know," Chambers bluffed. "He's not well. I'll go talk to him."

On his way to Falk's dressing room, Chambers ran into Cassavetes and had him come along. When they arrived, Falk continued moaning, "I just feel terrible!" So the three of them hopped into Cassavetes' car and drove to Cassavetes' doctor, who decreed, "You have high blood pressure. You've got to take it easy. I'll give you a prescription and send you home." Armed with a doctor's note, Falk figured he had even more power.

Smight filmed as much as he could without Falk and then shut down at 4:20 in the afternoon. Universal promptly suspended Falk for a second time. The next morning, Levinson and Link outfitted Falk's other stand-in, Richard Lance, in the familiar raincoat. Lance had similarly shaggy hair to Falk, and was about the same short stature—so they referred to him as "the Midget." For the rest of the picture, including most of the final scene and Columbo's conversation on the General's doorstep, Smight filmed the other actors over the stand-in's shoulder, or filmed the double in longshot, with plans to later loop in Falk's dialogue.

When NBC heard of the suspension, the network made clear that Universal had better get the matter resolved. *Columbo* was the most anticipated new show of the fall. Reluctantly, Universal promised Falk that he could direct a future *Columbo*. The actor returned to the set, anxious to finish the episode. He had hoped to reshoot the scenes he missed. "No," Smight informed him, "I've finished the picture." The director was so angry, he refused to shoot Falk's close-ups, leaving the work to Chambers.

By standing up to Falk, Smight "was my hero," said Suzanne Pleshette, who was terrified that the delays would make her late for her next assignment. Although the actors had been friends since their teens, "I didn't talk to Peter for a year. I thought he behaved really, really badly."

Eddie Albert was less charitable. When he saw Falk back on the lot, he said, "I always wanted to meet you. I always wanted to work with you. You're a real asshole."

The show finished two days late and nearly 10 percent over its $400,000 budget. It also forced the producers of *Adam-12* to scramble for a new set when *Columbo* was late to vacate Stage 22.

Dead Weight did provide fans with an answer to one long-standing mystery, even if it was the wrong answer. One of Levinson and Link's "Rules of *Columbo*" was that, just as the audience would never see Columbo's wife, Columbo was never to divulge his first name. Link noted, "No, he never had a first name. And I have to be honest with you, Dick and I didn't know what his first name was, either. We considered it. We had a pact with Peter, though, way back at the beginning, that we would never tell the audience his first name—we wanted to keep them intrigued."

Yet *Dead Weight* called for a scene in which Columbo must flash his badge and police ID. So a Universal propman designed an ID card with Columbo's picture and a quick signature: "Frank Columbo," never thinking that viewers would be able to decipher his scrawl on their state-of-the-art 19-inch Zeniths.

The wallet, badge and ID remained part of Columbo's standard wardrobe for seven seasons. Even Bill Link had no idea that Columbo was carrying around fake ID, until fans were able to freeze-frame home videos on their high-definition TVs.

Lady in Waiting

Immediately after shooting wrapped on *Dead Weight*, Chambers consolidated his attention on the next episode, *Lady in Waiting*. The Bochco script concerned a woman who wants to take over the family business, so she shoots her domineering brother, claiming she mistook him for an intruder. Though Chambers may have held the title of producer, Levinson and Link were determined to re-exert their control over the show. As Chambers recounted, "The director, Norman Lloyd, and I went out (scouting) for locations. I came back and (Levinson and Link) had cast the leading lady without any consultation with me, which is really not done. And then a couple of days later they went in and redressed one of the sets, so I really got pissed off. It was a power move on their part."

Through production, Falk kept asking which episode he would be directing. Levinson and Link deferred to The Black Tower. The Tower kept putting him off. Each day, Falk arrived at the set a little later. For each scene, he took a little bit longer to study his lines. Each time the cameras were ready to roll, he seemed to be in the middle of a phone call. A production assistant began tracking the delays—17 minutes, six minutes, 21 minutes, five minutes—as the rest of the cast and crew stood around, unable to proceed.

Halfway through production, Falk heard that veteran director Hy Averback had been assigned to helm the fifth show. There was only one more episode left in the season. It was time to make another dramatic move.

On the sixth day of shooting, Falk had a mid-afternoon call time to film the boardroom scene in a seminar room inside the Universal production office. He arrived on time, studied his lines, and waited on the sidelines for his cue to enter the scene. When it was time, he refused. Falk said he was leaving for the day "on the advice of my attorney." He left the set and five minutes later was in his car driving off the lot. The company shot as much of the sequence as they were able to without Falk, before shutting down an hour early. The stunt cost the production a half-day.

The next morning, with no Falk, the crew quickly reshuffled their schedule to shoot any scenes they could without him. For a scene in which Leslie Nielsen, playing the boyfriend/lawyer, converses with Columbo after a trial, they called back in Lance, the diminutive double. Unsure of just how much Lance would be needed, they converted him from a member of the Screen Extras Guild to the Screen Actors Guild.

For a third time, Universal placed Falk on suspension. No matter, Falk's lawyer Bert Fields informed the studio. Peter would not be returning until he, as promised, was given his directing assignment. Universal was ready to dig in its heels; NBC was not. The network had viewed rough cuts of *Death Lends a Hand* and *Murder by the Book*. They knew they had a hit. They issued Universal an ultimatum: get Falk back on set. The executives in The Tower felt humiliated. Actors never stood up to the studio and won, yet they had no choice but to give Falk his way. To save face, Universal struck a deal. The anticipated schedule had the sixth show being completed by the end of August—two full weeks before Falk needed to catch a plane for New York. Universal would let Falk direct show number six, if he agreed to appear in a seventh *Columbo* right after. If Peter Falk the director made a mess of things, they'd have a backup episode to fulfill their contract to NBC. More likely, Falk would do fine and they'd have an extra episode to sell to NBC.

Falk returned to the set, jubilant. He asked Levinson and Link how things went without him. "We had problems while you were gone," Levinson confessed. "We had to close down."

Falk asked why.

"The Midget wants to direct."

Suitable for Framing

During filming of *Lady in Waiting*, Chambers had begun casting the next episode, *Suitable for Framing*. He liked Gene Barry, Robert Wagner, or especially Patrick O'Neal to play villainous art collector Dale Kingston. Yet after Levinson and Link started to usurp his power, the producer knew he could not go on. Chambers recalled, "I met Peter after work, and I said, 'Peter, this is not working out for me. I don't like that. I think it's unprofessional, and I'd like you to release me.' He said okay, so I left after two episodes."

Levinson and Link stepped in to produce *Suitable for Framing* and selected as the murderer *The Wild Wild West*'s Ross Martin, a choice whom Chambers had been against. Levinson and Link actually wanted to use Chambers' top choice, Patrick O'Neal, as the murderer in the following episode.

The script for *Suitable for Framing* came from Jackson Gillis, one of the two freelancers who stuck around after the private screening of *Ransom for a Dead Man*. Whereas the screening had scared off most of the other writers, the 55-year-old Gillis was tantalized. Mystery was his game. He had started penning radio dramas, like *Suspense* and *The Whistler*, three decades earlier and then freelanced literally hundreds of TV scripts, including *The Adventures of Spin and Marty* and *The Hardy Boys* for *The Mickey Mouse Club*, 13 episodes of *Adventures of Superman*, and 31 *Perry Masons*. He also spent one season as story consultant for *Perry Mason* and the next four as associate producer.

Highly skilled in plotting, Gillis introduced to the series the "Act II Switcheroo," a *Perry Mason* mainstay, in which about halfway through the show the audience is surprised to see that the motive, intended victim, or even murderer is not what or who they thought it was. The trick was doubly effective in *Columbo*, because after the first 20 minutes, viewers assumed they knew everything about the crime. In *Suitable for Framing*, we are shocked to learn that Dale Kingston would not be inheriting his slain uncle's art collection—and he knew it. His true scheme was to frame the actual heir, the uncle's ex-wife, so the art would ultimately pass on to him. Gillis incorporated a second-act switch in most of his future *Columbos*.

Yet Gillis' greatest strength was dreaming up ingenious clues, and years earlier he had thought up a humdinger that he was just waiting to work into the right project: what if the murderer was identified not by his own fingerprints, but the fingerprints of the detective? In *Suitable for Framing*, Gillis had Columbo thrust his hand inside Kingston's attaché, which he suspects contains artwork stolen from the murder victim. Later, when the pilfered paintings surface, Kingston's prints are nowhere to be found, but they do bear Columbo's. Bill Link considered it the best clue the show ever had.

Just as encouraging, Gillis' first draft was near perfect. Levinson and Link left every scene intact, aside from polishing the dialogue, changing a Bohemian artist's name from Clem Franklin to Sam Franklin, and having the discarded murder weapon discovered by a gardener instead of by two neighbor kids playing football. The script's only flaw was it ran about four minutes short. One fix was lengthening the scene in which Columbo questions the artist at his studio, as a nude model poses in the background. In the original script, the model's only function was to pose as "Columbo does his best to keep his eyes away." Instead, Columbo's embarrassment dominates the scene, as he becomes flustered and intensely uncomfortable, particularly when the naked woman tries to interact with him.

Also added late was a scene in which Columbo visits the gossipy landlady of Kingston's murdered accomplice/girlfriend. For more than three minutes, the landlady, played by Mary Wickes, gives the detective the Columbo treatment, rambling and veering off on tangents, as *he* tries to figure out how to cut the conversation short.

The humorous additions were completely extraneous to the plot, but proved to be highlights in one of the show's best-ever episodes.

Blueprint for Murder

Levinson and Link had long since realized that Universal would fold in their standoff with Falk. So they had Bochco already preparing a devilishly difficult script for Falk to direct as payback. During production of *Suitable for Framing*, they presented Falk with the script he was to helm—one intentionally fashioned to test even the most accomplished of directors. At close to a half-million dollars, it was also the biggest budgeted of all the Season 1 *Columbos*. In *Blueprint for Murder*, commercial architect Elliot Markham kills his uncooperative investor and plans to bury the body in a massive concrete pylon. But he cleverly waits until *after* he's egged Columbo into unearthing one pylon, so he can be sure the detective, chastened by his superiors, won't be allowed to go to the trouble and expense of digging up another one.

The producers had already chosen the site: the Century City Plaza skyscraper and parking structure being built on Santa Monica Boulevard. A massive hole had already been excavated, where construction was underway every day, all day long, with heavy equipment constantly echoing through the haze of dust. Of the 10 filming days, six of them would be out on location.

To his credit, Falk prepared diligently. He pored over the script and sought advice from Cassavetes, Spielberg and other directors. But the assignment magnified one of Falk's weaknesses—he was inherently indecisive and now everyone was waiting on him for instructions. After his first production meeting,

Falk lamented, "Nobody clued me I was to arrive with all the answers. Here cameramen and art directors and lighting men sit around waiting for me to make decisions. If I'd known, I'da faked something!"

He spent his days off at the excavation site lining up his shots. "I go out there with these guys trailing me to find places to shoot," he said. "I finally decide on one site and a construction worker taps me on the shoulder and says, 'If you're gonna shoot there, buddy, you better be fast; tomorrow that won't be there.'"

The constantly changing scenery did, however, help Falk make quicker decisions. If in viewing the dailies, he was unsure about one take, he might not have the option of reshooting, because by the time he returned to the site the next morning, his "set" might be gone.

As production wore on, Falk caught a cold and lost his voice. Levinson and Link would visit the excavation site to look down from the rim of the hole and smile at his misery. Falk would shake his fist at them and soldier on. He refused to complain. "This was feasible," he reasoned. "For one thing, this is the one they asked me to do. For another, the script is the script that was ready."

Once he finally finished, Falk was in no hurry to direct again—especially another *Columbo*. "Now that I've done it, I agree that it's tough," Falk admitted at the time. "I don't think the acting suffered at all but I do think the directing suffers. My acting performance was looser and better. I was so concerned about the camera angles that I didn't have time to work myself up into being tense about the acting. Uptightness never helps."

Indeed, Falk's performance seems especially calm and natural. One shortcoming was that Falk the director's treatment of the clues comes across as a touch heavy-handed—his camera zooms in on and lingers on evidence a little too long. For a key clue about the killer switching the victim's radio from country to classical, Falk chose cartoonishly corny music, and played it ridiculously loudly and left it blaring—for the audience to hear—even after the killer had left the car and was walking through a house.

Other scenes are particularly effective, including two borrowed from earlier episodes. In one tense sequence, the killer gets a flat tire while driving to dispose of the corpse in his trunk. A highway patrolman pulls him over and offers to help him get his spare. Bochco had originally written the scene—virtually word for word—for *Murder by the Book*, but it was cut.

The dramatic final reveal was clearly inspired by the ending to *Death Lends a Hand*, in which Columbo—having planted a seed—induces the killer to try to cover up his crime late at night. Columbo is then waiting for him, suddenly flipping on the lights and catching him in the act. (The same stunt would be repeated again and again, including in *Requiem for a Falling Star, Swan Song,* and *Double Exposure*.)

After the episode aired, Falk was asked if he thought the way Columbo tricked the criminal was legal. "Oh, don't ask me about entrapment," Falk said. "I don't know whether I can get a conviction out of any of them. This is not a hard-hitting documentary crime show, it's a conceit."

Whether *Columbo* was renewed or not, Levinson and Link knew that *Blueprint for Murder* would be the final episode aired of those they produced. So they wanted to leave their hero a better man. In the show, they had a doctor advise the detective to quit smoking. Just as they abhorred showing violence, neither did they want to promote lighting up, despite the fact that Levinson was a three-packs-a-day chain smoker. In the final scene, after solving the case, Columbo pulls out a cigar and begins to light up, then hesitates. He instead tosses it to the ground and snuffs it into the dirt. Falk played along for the purpose of the script, but would resume smoking in the next season; the cigar was just too good a prop.

Short Fuse

Right after completing filming on *Blueprint for Murder*, Falk jumped into the extra picture, *Short Fuse*. He was staring at a 10-day schedule, with no margin for error if he was going make his flight to New York on September 15. Levinson and Link gave Jackson Gillis the story idea: ne'er-do-well Roger Stanford bumps off his uncle so he can take over the family chemical company, by hiding a bomb in his cigar box. As a thank you for his superb editing, Levinson and Link allowed Ed Abroms to try his hand at directing. Gillis hurried to turn in his script, but with only two weeks to polish it before the cameras started rolling, they were left with a more plodding adventure than usual.

Gillis, the master of the pop, did devise another memorable climax. He needed Stanford, played by Roddy McDowall, to admit that he had planted the bomb in a cigar box. So Gillis had to have Columbo discover the box intact and then trap Stanford in a confined space where he thinks the unexploded bomb is about to go off. The Palm Springs Aerial Tramway had recently been used for an episode of *Mission: Impossible* and the Walter Matthau movie *Kotch*. Gillis suggested the finale be staged aboard a tramcar slowly descending from the 8,500-foot-high mountain. During the off-season, the Palm Springs tram was closed to the public every Tuesday and Wednesday, giving the crew two days to complete their work.

As originally scripted, the episode was to end with Columbo looking down at the fine cigars strewn upon the tramcar floor, bemoaning, "It's such a shame. These are such beautiful cigars...."

At the last moment, the writers tweaked the finale. They had Columbo pick up several of the spilled cigars and slip them into his inside coat pocket. When it's pointed out that they're supposed to be evidence, he laments having to return them.

Although it was his first directing assignment, Abroms became one of the few *Columbo* directors to shoot an episode on schedule. As an elite film cutter, he knew exactly when he had gotten what he needed on film and did not feel the need for a third—or thirteenth—take. He also had a trick for getting the action moving, giving Falk fewer opportunities to dwell on each line and request additional takes: he shot a number of scenes from great distances and had Falk and McDowall record their dialogue later. It didn't hurt that Falk knew he had a hard deadline to make his Broadway rehearsals and was also preoccupied with checking in on post-production of *Blueprint for Murder*.

On Wednesday September 15, 1971, the morning after wrapping *Short Fuse*, Falk caught his plane to New York. That evening at 8:30 p.m., *The NBC Mystery Movie* premiered with *Murder by the Book*, facing off against the formidable *Medical Center* on CBS and a string of sitcoms on ABC. *Columbo* outdrew them all, as it would all season. Since *McMillan & Wife* and *McCloud's* ratings proved not as strong, *Medical Center* would rank No. 13 for the full season and the *NBC Mystery Movie* No. 14, buoyed by big numbers for every *Columbo* episode, as well as NBC's decision to rerun each one twice more through the spring and summer.

Critics roundly hailed *Columbo* as the best new show of the season. The audience grew week by week. Comedians began working Columbo impressions into their sets. Columbomania was exploding.

The reaction was arguably too much for Falk. After each performance of *The Prisoner of Second Avenue*, he'd meet with reporters and well-wishers, who expressed little interest in his stage performance. "When people come backstage, they don't talk about the play. It's *Columbo, Columbo, Columbo*," Falk moaned. "I'm going nuts."

Levinson and Link didn't get to enjoy the praise, either. As soon as they finished post-production on their last *Columbo*, they were off to work on their next TV movie. They did, however, watch *Columbo* when it aired, tracked the reviews, and personally answered much of the fan mail that came their way. Of particular interest were the complaints. A Mrs. George Gross of Hawthorne, New Jersey, wrote in to complain about all the drinking in *Dead Weight*. "Mainly because of Peter Falk, *Columbo* had been our favorite program—until last night, with Eddie Albert," she wrote. "The second line in the program: 'Can we get you a *drink*?' and from then on that was the theme—one drink after another. Disgusting to non-drinkers and must be disturbing to former alcoholics who are trying to go straight."

Another viewer, A. Gritanza, submitted a critique after each episode, offering

PETER FALK grasps the Emmy he won at the Television Academy's 24th annual awards for the best performance by an actor in a leading role in a dramatic series on May 6, 1972. Julie Andrews accepted the best actress prize for *Elizabeth R's* Glenda Jackson. During his career, Falk would be nominated for 15 Emmys, taking home five.

pointers on how to make the clues clearer. *Death Lends a Hand*, Gritanza wrote, was "very good except Robert Culp was overdone and not really a challenge to our hero." In addition, the viewer thought they were made to wait much too long for Columbo's entrance.

Mrs. Ernestine Smith of La Jolla, California, thought the gotcha clue in *Lady in Waiting* was too obvious: "With reference to tonight's show: Ouch! With writers like Steven Bochco, you're going to lose all of Peter Falk's fans. What idiot couldn't tell right away the significance of the boyfriend driving up just as the shots are heard and *before* the alarm!"

Fortunately, tens of millions of other viewers were more forgiving, as was the Television Academy. That spring, *Columbo* was nominated for 10 Emmy Awards, taking home four. The show lost to *Masterpiece Theatre's Elizabeth R* on PBS for Outstanding Drama Series and Outstanding New Series, Billy Goldenberg lost for his *Lady in Waiting* score, and Ed Abroms lost for directing *Short Fuse*. Falk won as Best Actor in a Dramatic Series, Abroms won for editing *Death Lends a Hand*, and Lloyd Ahern won for photographing *Blueprint for Murder*.

In the writing category, *Columbo* was assured a win, since the show garnered all three nominations. The only question was whether it would be Levinson and Link for *Death Lends a Hand*, Bochco for *Murder by the Book*, or Gillis for *Suitable for Framing*. Levinson and Link were convinced Bochco would win, since they considered his script the strongest.

"Dick Levinson schmucked me," Bochco recalled. "He kept saying, 'Oh, you're gonna win this, yours is the best one, there's no question,' and actually I think it was the best one. It just happened to have my name on it; Bill and Dick of course had their thumbprints all over every word of it. So I went out and bought a tuxedo with blue denim with blue velvet lapels. And of course they won, as they should have, because it was their show, they created it. No one was gonna give a little pisher like me an Emmy. And I was devastated—that SOB, he conned me into thinking I was going to win."

Season 1 – 1971-1972

Murder by the Book
Filmed: May 29 – June 14, 1971
Stars: Peter Falk, Jack Cassidy, Martin Milner, Rosemary Forsyth, Barbara Colby
Director: Steven Spielberg
Producers: Richard Levinson & William Link
Teleplay: Steven Bochco
Air Date: Sept. 15, 1971
Nielsen Ranking: #8 (26.5 points)

Death Lends a Hand
Working Title: *Enough Rope*
Filmed: May 1971
Guest Stars: Robert Culp, Ray Milland, Patricia Crowley
Director: Bernard Kowalski
Producers: Richard Levinson & William Link
Teleplay: Richard Levinson & William Link
Air Date: Oct. 6, 1971
Ranking: #5

Dead Weight
Working Title: *Seed of Doubt*
Filmed: June 16 – July 1, 1971
Guest Stars: Eddie Albert, Suzanne Pleshette
Director: Jack Smight
Executive Producers: Richard Levinson & William Link
Producer: Everett Chambers
Teleplay: John T. Dugan
Air Date: Oct. 27, 1971
Ranking: #6

Suitable for Framing
Working Title: *The Crimson Frame*
Filmed: July – Aug. 1971
Guest Stars: Ross Martin, Don Ameche, Kim Hunter, Mary Wickes, Vic Tayback
Director: Hy Averback
Producers: Richard Levinson & William Link
Teleplay: Jackson Gillis
Air Date: Nov. 17, 1971
Ranking: #19

Lady in Waiting
Filmed: July 6 – 19, 1971
Guest Stars: Susan Clark, Jessie Royce Landis, Richard Anderson, Leslie Nielsen
Director: Norman Lloyd
Executive Producers: Richard Levinson & William Link
Producer: Everett Chambers
Teleplay: Steven Bochco
Story: Barney Slater
Air Date: Dec. 15, 1971
Ranking: #17

Short Fuse
Working Title: *Formula for Death*
Filming Completed: Sept. 14, 1971
Guest Stars: Roddy McDowall, Anne Francis
Director: Edward M. Abroms
Producers: Richard Levinson & William Link
Teleplay: Jackson Gillis
Story: Lester Pine & Tina Pine, Jackson Gillis
Air Date: Jan. 19, 1972
Ranking: #5

Blueprint for Murder
Filmed: Aug. 16 – 27, 1971
Guest Stars: Patrick O'Neal, Janis Paige, Forrest Tucker
Director: Peter Falk
Producers: Richard Levinson & William Link
Teleplay: Steven Bochco
Story: William Kelley
Air Date: Feb. 9, 1972
Ranking: #7

6
A Comfortable Fit

Hoping to capitalize on the success of the *NBC Mystery Movie*, Universal pitched the network on a second wheel comprised of Richard Widmark in *Madigan*, George Peppard as *Banacek*, and James Farentino in *Cool Million*. NBC slotted the new shows on Wednesdays, and promoted *Columbo*, *McCloud* and *McMillan & Wife* to the even greener pastures of Sunday nights, to take over *Bonanza's* longtime slot. Peter Falk did complain that he thought NBC was overusing *Columbo*, running each episode three times. So, to cut down on reruns and ideally to strike lightning again, Universal gave the Sunday wheel a fourth spoke—*Hec Ramsey*, featuring Richard Boone as a gunfighter turned forensic detective in the Old West.

Still, Falk gave the impression he was in no hurry to return to Los Angeles. During the final weeks of *The Prisoner of Second Avenue*, he started making rumblings about quitting *Columbo* and possibly continuing the play. He had no intention of staying in New York; he merely wanted greater leverage in his contract negotiations with Universal. Unsurprisingly, Falk left the play when his commitment ended on June 3, 1972. He returned to California, to discover that it was Levinson and Link who would be exiting *Columbo*. Unbeknownst to Falk, the producers never had any intention of continuing past the first year. In fact, eight months earlier, as soon as they wrapped the last episode of Season 1, they had already started moving on to new projects, leaving little opportunity to savor their success.

Falk was genuinely disappointed. Levinson and Link were stunned. Had he forgotten the shouting matches and the subterfuge? Why did he suddenly want them to stick around? "Because now I trust you," he said.

IN SEASON 2 the show ran as smoothly as it ever would under the guidance of producer Dean Hargrove *(left)* and executive story consultant Jackson Gillis *(right)*. *[Credits: Dean Hargrove, Candida Gillis]*

Temperamentally, however, their replacement was a better fit with Falk. A large yet rather quiet man, equally bright and easygoing, Dean Hargrove had the advantage of knowing who the real boss on the show was. Hargrove strove to get along with his star, rarely had conflicts, and infrequently received notes on his scripts. Falk had seen the good work Hargrove produced on *Ransom for a Dead Man*, and how he was able to juggle numerous projects simultaneously and smoothly. While producing *McCloud*, Hargrove also wrote and produced a pilot for the wheel that wasn't picked up—*Cutter*, about a black private eye in Chicago. And within weeks of taking over *Columbo*, Hargrove agreed to simultaneously co-executive produce *Madigan* as part of the new *Wednesday Night Mystery* series.

Before they reteamed in person, though, Falk called to tell Hargrove, "Don't take this personally, but I can't talk to you."

As Hargrove remembered, "I said, 'O… kay….' I found out that his lawyer, Bert Fields, had called the studio and said, 'Peter can no longer work under these conditions,' which was another way of saying he wanted more money. Of course, one of the things the studio did immediately was to offer him a larger percentage of the show—something they could always do with Telly Savalas, who would always be happy if he got another 10 percent of the net, which is basically useless.

You're never going to see that money. Peter would always say, 'I don't want the back end. I want the money now.'"

Falk was contracted to make $40,000 an episode. He wanted a per-show raise, while reducing the number of episodes to six. "I'd rather not do more shows unless we can keep a high degree of quality," he argued. Universal wanted eight shows, and for Falk to sign a seven-year contract. They ultimately agreed to a higher salary for one year, totaling eight episodes. Falk's contract also contained a "back-to-back" provision, stipulating that by the time one episode was finished, the next should be ready to film, making it easier for him to work between movie commitments.

"Peter was always a gentleman," Hargrove noted. "He didn't cause anyone any real problems. But he knew he was riding the lightning and things were going his way, so he could kind of do what he wanted to do. I wouldn't say he abused it, but he knew the power that he had and he took his time to make himself feel comfortable. And it was difficult for him to feel comfortable because he was never that comfortable himself with the work. He was always uncertain with the work, even though he got tremendous accolades for doing it."

A Stitch in Crime

Levinson and Link had been working through the spring of 1972 to give Hargrove a fast takeoff. They left him with three complete scripts, plus treatments or, at minimum, story ideas for the other five episodes. Universal also agreed to continue paying Levinson and Link to read the first drafts of all future *Columbo* scripts and to send Hargrove and Dick Irving their detailed comments, typically two- to four-page memos.

What also helped was that once *Columbo* premiered, the familiarity and big ratings prompted more freelancers to begin pitching ideas to the show. Three pitches were deemed solid enough to expand into outlines and ultimately full scripts, with the strongest—Shirl Hendryx's *A Stitch in Crime*—to be filmed first. Hendryx's ingenious script introduced a twist—a slow-motion, ticking-clock murder, designed to play out the length of the episode: ambitious surgeon Dr. Barry Mayfield performs a heart operation on his kindly mentor, Dr. Hiedeman, using special suture, which in days will dissolve and kill him. But when a nurse gets suspicious, Mayfield follows her to her car in the parking structure and whacks her with a tire iron. Columbo must not only solve the nurse's murder, but do it in time to save Hiedeman.

Hendryx recalled, "I had the idea earlier when I was having an operation on my shoulder, and I remember the doctor had a conversation with his nurse about the kinds of sutures. I asked about the difference between permanent and dissolving suture. I have an evil mind and thought somebody could get in trouble with this. It got in my mind and several months later it dawned on me that that could fit into a *Columbo*. I called a couple of surgeons, referred by the Writers Guild. The first one said, 'This could never happen. By the time the suture dissolves, the flesh will have taken over. And the one type of suture is thicker than the other.' I was about to give up, but called the head of surgery at a hospital in San Bernardino. She said, 'Of course that could happen. That's a wonderful idea!'"

Although the writer admits he can't recall if it was his idea or someone else's at a story meeting, Hendryx's script also introduced what would become a new quirk for the title character. As originally scripted, Columbo arrives at the parking structure early in the morning, bleary-eyed and hungry. He parks near a catering truck and asks how much for an apple. Told 25 cents—even for a small one—he instead buys two hard-boiled eggs. He proceeds to crack one on the hood of the victim's car and the other on the murder weapon, while dribbling shells about the crime scene.

In the final script, there's no catering truck or talk of apples. Columbo magically fishes one egg out of his pocket and the scene ends with the black humor of him cracking it on the tire iron. Columbo suddenly appearing with hard-boiled eggs would become a recurring schtick throughout the series.

In early drafts, Hendryx plotted for the nurse's amorous roommate, Marsha, having been spurned by Dr. Mayfield, to make a play for Columbo. After she invites him in, she was to say coyly, "Come now, Lieutenant. This wouldn't just be your way of making acquaintances with members of the opposite sex, would it?"

"No," he responds firmly.

She puts a friendly hand on his knee, and asks, "You're certain that I can't get you something?"

"No, I'm definitely on duty, Miss."

She begins wiping his brow. "You are beginning to perspire—isn't there something I can do?"

Columbo, visibly uncomfortable, starts talking about his wife, so Marsha will back off and allow him to question her.

In its place, Hendryx wrote a new lead-in to the scene, in which Marsha invites him in to offer a home remedy for his sneezing. The cure works but, in an unused bit, after Marsha says good-bye, *she* sneezes.

Falk too displayed a characteristic of Columbo not alluded to in the script, and to be shown only rarely in future episodes: rage. During the final confrontation in Mayfield's office, Columbo informs the doctor that he believes the nurse was upset after Hiedeman's operation because she suspected the use of dissolving suture—which would be murder. Mayfield begins laughing, feigning disbelief: "You don't really believe all the foolish things you say, do you?" Columbo was to respond resolutely: "I believe you killed Sharon Martin—and you're trying to kill Dr. Hiedeman." Before parting, he encourages Mayfield to take good care of Hiedeman, because if he died they would have to perform an autopsy. Falk filmed the dialogue exactly as written, but with the added dimension of sudden rage. Columbo cuts off Mayfield's chortling dismissiveness by slamming a coffee cup onto the desk and snarling his next line like a mobster. He delivers his parting words not as a suggestion, but as a cold threat. Columbo had previously dropped his clueless servility when he threatened to hound the murderer's accomplice in *Prescription: Murder*, but that was clearly an act to get the young lady to crack. This time, Falk made it feel as if Columbo was so repulsed by Mayfield, he simply could not hold back his anger.

Hendryx worked on revisions with Levinson, Link, Hargrove and *Columbo's* new executive story consultant, Jackson Gillis. The assignment was a return to the office for Gillis who, apart from five years on the *Perry Mason* staff, had spent the bulk of his 20-year career developing his own material, from the solitude of his own home. That said, Gillis wasn't a story editor like Steven Bochco; he would read the scripts and offer direction, but he wasn't rewriting them.

Bochco, like Levinson and Link, had had enough of the grind. Over the next year, he would contribute several more scripts on the side to *Columbo*, while trying to break into producing. He would start as associate producer of the *Banacek* pilot, and then write and produce a TV movie for Lee Grant. Bochco would then spend three years as story editor on *McMillan & Wife*, before developing a string of his own series, including *The Invisible Man*, *Richie Brockelman, Private Eye*, *Hill Street Blues*, *Hooperman*, *Cop Rock*, *L.A. Law*, *Doogie Howser, M.D.*, and *NYPD Blue*.

Étude in Black

Before leaving, Bochco had written the Season 2 premiere, based on an idea by Levinson and Link. They had been asked by Falk to come up with a starring vehicle for his buddy, John Cassavetes, who had aggressively avoided TV work for the last four years. To get Cassavetes to appear, Falk had promised to co-star in his next movie, *A Woman Under the Influence*, with Cassavetes' wife, Gena Rowlands, and pay half of the $250,000 cost to produce the film. In *Étude in Black*, Cassavetes would play a conceited orchestra conductor who kills his mistress.

Hargrove found Cassavetes just as insufferable as his *Étude in Black* character. Cassavetes thumbed his nose at television and television professionals. Hargrove considered Cassavetes a troublemaker and an egomaniac. The friction between the two was immediate.

To more quickly identify a usable take, the crew attached a videotape camera to the master film camera, providing them with instant replays of the scenes they just shot. Falk loved the new toy. "I think it's wonderful," he said. "So do I," Cassavetes added flatly, before stressing that he would never use the gimmick on one of *his* films.

During post-production, Cassavetes dropped in on the scoring session, to hear Dick DeBenedictis' thrilling score played by a full 30-piece orchestra comprised of the top sidemen in Hollywood. The episode's director, Nicholas Colasanto (who 10 years later would find fame playing Coach on *Cheers*) enthused, "Hey, John, really, really good, eh?" Cassavetes shrugged, "Yeah, for what it is."

For Season 2, NBC was insistent on one change: the show needed a second continuing character, ideally a younger cop or a family member Columbo could confide in. Levinson and Link relented. Sort of. For *Étude in Black*, they instructed Bochco to give Columbo a dog.

Initially, the idea was for him to have a puppy. Colasanto disagreed, "No, he should have a dog that looks like him." So they found an oversized, aging, lethargic basset hound. Though he was a dog lover, Falk did not want a sidekick; Columbo had enough quirks, he certainly didn't need a pet. But Colasanto asked him to at least give the pooch a look. Falk walked onto the doctor's room set for his first day of shooting, took one look at the inert blob of wrinkles, and melted. The mutt was perfect.

Throughout the episode, everywhere Columbo went, he solicited suggestions for a name for his new pet. In Bochco's original ending, he was supposed to decide on one. "You know, I think I got the name," Columbo says, after the murderer is led away.

"What name?" asks his colleague.

"For my dog. I think I'll call him Maestro. It has real style."

In the end, it was decided to give the dog no name. Eventually, Columbo just started calling him "Dog."

The Greenhouse Jungle

To write the next script, Gillis pulled out of retirement Jonathan Latimer. The scribe had started as a Chicago crime reporter covering Al Capone, before becoming a mystery novelist and screenwriter in the 1930s, and Gillis' most productive staff writer during his time associate-producing *Perry Mason*. Latimer concocted *The Greenhouse Jungle*, the tale of orchid fancier Jarvis Goodland who, disgusted by his weakling nephew Tony and Tony's cheating wife Cathy, helps the young man fake his kidnapping. Tony agrees, intending to use the ransom money to buy off his wife's boyfriend, musclebound Ken. Instead, Goodland kills Tony, keeps the cash, and tries to pin the murder on Cathy.

Although most *Columbo* villains try to sweet-talk the detective before his persistence begins to annoy them, Latimer had both Jarvis (played by a constantly bellowing Ray Milland) and Cathy furious with Columbo from the second they meet him. Cathy was supposed to begin warming to him about two-thirds of the way in, after Columbo follows her to a planned boat trip with Ken. Following a brief interrogation, Columbo was to agree to leave them alone. But as he steps back over the railing toward the dock, he remembers just one more thing—some mysterious lover of Cathy's told Tony he would stop seeing her for $50,000. Confused, Cathy stares at her boytoy. Just then, Columbo loses his footing and starts to fall off the boat. Cathy reaches out and grabs his arm, stopping his fall. Columbo thanks her. But instead of letting go of him, Cathy turns back to glare at her boyfriend: "Goodbye, Ken." Ken glowers at Columbo, slams down his grease-rag, jumps off the boat, and huffs off without looking back. Columbo meekly apologizes, but Cathy stops him: "Don't blame yourself. I'm not surprised. You've just never… made a mess of your life because the only man you ever really loved was… was just too weak to—" Her voice breaks. She runs down into the boat's cabin. Cathy's grabbing Columbo's arm was intended to foreshadow the episode's final moment, when, after clearing her name, Columbo offers his hand to the anguished woman and volunteers to drive her home.

Ultimately, it was decided to end the boat confrontation with Cathy looking suspiciously at Ken, and delete Columbo's fall and Ken's exit. Cathy continues her mistreatment of Columbo until the last moment, when she finally recognizes how hard he has been working to clear her name. The delayed realization made her acceptance of his arm at the end all the more sweet.

To satisfy NBC's longing for a memorable assistant for Columbo to play off of, Latimer for the first time created an aide who was both prominent in the story and had a personality. Falk insisted on using his acting pal from New York, Bob Dishy, to play go-getter Sgt. Wilson. Though Dishy proved a perfect foil, the producers were in no hurry to ask him back. What made his Wilson character so enjoyable—how his officious nature and by-the-book policework contrasted with Columbo's and allowed the murderer to lead him to the wrong conclusions—could have led the series to become repetitive.

The most memorable scene of *The Greenhouse Jungle* had Columbo and Wilson making their way down a hill to inspect the wreckage of Tony's sportscar. "Here, I'll show you the quick way down," Wilson announces, as Columbo lags behind. As scripted, "the descent looks unnervingly steep. That Wilson is skipping and sliding down it like a gazelle does not help Columbo at all. Now, worse, Wilson has halted partway down to look back up—waiting for Columbo. Columbo steels himself for the end. Columbo comes down like a beginning skier shoved by an enemy onto an advanced slope. He not only reaches Wilson, he passes him. Albeit unintentionally. As he goes by Wilson in full, uncontrollable slide, he says, 'Little steep.' At the floor of the canyon, Columbo abruptly arrives in foreground. Though still alive, he is absolutely rigid—eyes a little glazed. 'The quickest way down, all right,' he says."

Falk asked to do the stunt himself. He started out slowly, apprehensively, then began to stagger, lurching forward, faster and faster, his arms flailing wildly, until he hit the bottom at full speed and flipped into a ditch. Falk didn't have time to deliver his lines until, after a beat, he was on his back on the canyon floor. He then had to repeat the stunt so it could be filmed from different angles.

The Most Crucial Game

Freelancer John T. Dugan (*Dead Weight*) submitted a spec script for the next episode. In *The Most Crucial Game*, Paul Hanlon, the general manager of a pro football team, clubs to death the team's owner with a block of ice as he climbs out of his swimming pool.

The crime's setting inspired Falk's most memorable ad-lib. While examining the pool, Columbo was to get his shoes wet. Later, as Columbo is somberly speaking with the victim's attorney, Falk leaned in close to the gentleman and unexpectedly whispered, "Sir, you don't mind if I ask you a personal question, do you? What'd you pay for those shoes?" Flustered, the lawyer answered, "I think about $60." Columbo, his eyes widening, explained that he stepped into water and ruined his, and wondered, "You don't know where I could get a pair that looks like that for around 16 or 17?" The "What'd you pay for those shoes?" line was such a hit that for the rest of his life, strangers would come up to Falk on the street and ask him how much he paid for his shoes—or his tie, pants, whatever he was wearing.

To play the hot-headed Hanlon, Hargrove immediately thought of Robert Culp, even though Culp had already played a murderer during the first season. "No one raised an eyebrow because Culp was the perfect example of what a *Columbo* villain should be—wealthy, slick, arrogant, smart and there weren't a lot of guys around who did what he did," Hargrove explained. "Culp was as unpleasant in life as he was on-screen, but he was just the perfect *Columbo* villain."

FALK HOOPS it up with Lakers Jim McMillian *(left)* and LeRoy Ellis during a break in filming *The Most Crucial Game*. [Credit: Los Angeles Times Photographic Archive, Special Collections, Charles E. Young Research Library, UCLA]

During pre-production, Universal was contacted by a press agent for the National Basketball Association, which was looking to generate publicity for the league by having some of its players guest-star on various TV programs. Hargrove thought the athletes fit well with the episode's sports setting and Falk was a huge fan of the Knicks and the Lakers. So Hargrove signed six Lakers to appear—Happy Hairston, LeRoy Ellis, Flynn Robinson, Pat Riley, Keith Erickson, and Jim McMillian. For most of them, it was their acting debut—even though all they had to do was scrimmage three-on-three while Columbo and Hanlon spoke on the sidelines. Yet one of the players, Happy Hairston, who had a cameo the year before in *Brian's Song*, caught the eye of director Jeremy Kagan. Impressed by Hairston's good looks and presence, Kagan noted that Happy had true acting potential. When Hairston retired from basketball three years later, he did become an actor, appearing in a string of TV shows and the movies *The Concorde… Airport '79* and *The Paper*.

Requiem for a Falling Star

For his first script of the season, Jackson Gillis basically took Anne Baxter's titular character from *All About Eve* (1950) and imagined her 20 years later, no longer a scheming starlet but now a fading movie idol, even more melodramatic than Margo Channing, the part played by co-star Bette Davis. Gillis wrote the part specifically for Baxter and named her character Nora Chandler, "Chandler" reminiscent of Channing and "Nora" a name Baxter had used multiple times before, including in one of her better-known film noirs, *The Blue Gardenia*.

In *Requiem for a Falling Star*, Nora Chandler discovers her longtime assistant Jean intends to marry a gossip columnist. Chandler lies in wait at the writer's house and kills Jean when she arrives driving her fiancé's car, leaving everyone to think he was the intended victim. But again Gillis pulled an Act II Switcheroo. Chandler actually wanted *Jean* dead to ensure she wouldn't blab about her murderous past.

Gillis tried to build in as many authentic ties to Hollywood as possible. Costume designer Edith Head, a close friend of Baxter's, agreed to appear as herself, in a scene shot in her office, where she picks out a new tie for Columbo. *Dragnet's* Jack Webb, who at the time was executive producing *Adam-12, Emergency!* and the *Hec Ramsey* pilot, also consented to a brief cameo. As the Lieutenant follows a studio executive to the entrance of The Black Tower, just as the exec walks in, Webb was to walk out, pleasantly nodding at the detective. Columbo would gulp and stare in awe, as we cut to commercial. At the last minute, Webb pulled out.

Also going unused was one of Columbo's distractions. As he and Chandler walk across the lot, Columbo was to stop in his tracks and look down at a little sign. He whispers, "Hey—is that really where Lucille Ball parks her car?"

Other stars did make uncredited, split-second appearances—but so fleetingly Universal didn't think it would need their permission. Eight-by-tens of Clark Gable, W.C. Fields, Humphrey Bogart, and a dozen other celebrities were hung on the walls of the gossip columnist's office. Fittingly, Nora Chandler's walls were covered with pictures of herself.

Requiem for a Falling Star was the first of five *Columbos* to be based at a movie studio—a setting Universal loved, since most of the episode could be filmed around the lot.

NBC was delighted with the series' progress. Among what were anticipated to be the season's strongest shows, the network decided to hold *A Stitch in Crime* for February sweeps, and schedule *Étude in Black* as the season opener on September 17, *Columbo's* first time on a Sunday night. CBS would counter with *Mannix* and *Barnaby Jones*; more intimidatingly, ABC would program a new movie every Sunday at 9:00, starting with the James Bond film *Goldfinger*. To hold on to more of *Columbo's* audience, NBC asked Universal if there was any way to extend *Étude in Black* from 90 minutes to two hours, as was being planned for a special "Columbo goes to London" episode for November sweeps week.

Dick Irving had a clever way of selling the idea to Falk: a two-hour show would better honor his friend Cassavetes and make his part even bigger.

Falk liked the idea, and approached Hargrove: "You know, I don't think there's enough of John in the show. We ought to do more for him." Hargrove was incredulous. The show was completed and set to air in two weeks. No matter. The studio—and Falk—insisted he find a way to pull together 24 more minutes of footage.

Hargrove recalled, "Now Link and Levinson were brought in, and we're all trying to scramble and say where can we find material, because these things are fairly tightly plotted. It's not like you can do a show where you have a Thanksgiving dinner and everybody comes home. So we were all struggling, even to the point where we were saying, 'Well, we can pick up a minute doing that. We can see him driving to the murder scene and back. We'll pick up another 25 seconds.' We were desperate trying to find stuff."

Over Labor Day weekend, Hargrove quickly wrote two additional scenes, one to draw out Columbo's arrival at the murder scene by having him review the victim's photo album (with a colleague who then vanishes for the rest of the scene), and the other consisting of Columbo questioning the victim's young neighbor at her ballet lesson.

Hargrove figured he could add another minute or two by stretching out the murderer's traveling between the Hollywood Bowl, the garage, and the victim's apartment, and adding several more traveling shots, known as "run-bys." It fell on Hargrove to convince Cassavetes to go along.

"It was my job to call John and explain to him what was going on," Hargrove recounted. "I said, 'We're doing some additional material…,' and he said, 'Well, I'd like to see it. I want to make sure it's good for me.' I said, 'Of course, we will get you the material. It's almost finished.' We sent it over to him. And he called me and said, 'I don't know, and there's this thing in here where I drive to the murder scene and I drive back. Well, I'm not going to do that.' And I asked, 'Well, why not?' And he said, 'I am not a run-by actor.' Now you can't get too deep into what that means, all I know is he was being unpleasant. He was kind of throwing his weight around and just expressing the lesser part of his nature."

Consequently, Hargrove had no desire to write any more material for Cassavetes. Falk said not to worry; he'd take care of it. Falk noted that *Étude in Black* was missing one thing that was a highlight of previous episodes: the classic one-on-one confrontation between Columbo and his prime suspect, at the suspect's home. Falk figured that, with his and Cassavetes' improvisational skills, they really didn't need a script. The scene starts with a long, drawn-out shot of Columbo pulling up and parking in front of Maestro Alex Benedict's house. A "houseboy" (Pat Morita) answers the door, mistakes him for a musician, and eventually hops up the stairs to beckon Benedict. After a spell, Benedict descends the stairway only for Columbo to begin asking him a series of random questions that serve no purpose—how much did your house cost? How much do you pay in taxes? How much do you make? And finally, can I have your autograph? During the bizarre interrogation, the Maestro continually demands to know what's the point—the same question the audience would also be wondering. (They might also be curious how Cassavetes' short hair in this scene magically grew back in the next.)

The editor scrambled to cut the scene into the episode, and scheduled a screening time for Falk, Hargrove and Cassavetes to view it. Falk, knowing Cassavetes and Hargrove didn't get along, contacted the producer beforehand to say, "I don't want to be there with you two in the same room."

"That's okay," Hargrove said. "I'll watch it later."

The episode was so last minute in being patched together that Universal could not get it in time to NBC affiliates in Canada, where the *NBC Mystery Movie* ran two days earlier, on Friday nights. Canada had to settle for the 90-minute version. In the ratings, the U.S. premiere was beaten badly by *Goldfinger* (No. 2 in the ratings vs. *Columbo's* No. 14). NBC, however, was pleased, since its competition would only get softer and the extra half-hour significantly outperformed what it would have gotten from the show it replaced, *Night Gallery*.

Double Shock

In the meantime, Levinson, Link and Gillis hatched an idea to change up the formula. In *Double Shock*, we think we see celebrity chef Dexter Paris kill his grandfather, only to realize our chief suspect has an identical twin. The viewer is not sure which brother is the killer, until Columbo demonstrates that the brothers were in cahoots.

Originally, Gillis' script had Dexter interrupting his grandfather's bath to bring him a wedding present: a portable TV set. The old man remarks that he hates television—just before Dexter plugs the appliance in and drops it in the tub. Gillis later turned the grandfather into the twins' uncle, and—to tie into Dexter's profession—changed the deadly appliance into an electric hand mixer.

The first draft had Columbo confronting Dexter at the opening of a local Gourmet Shoppe, where the chef is promoting his new line of signature cookware. Instead, the event was changed to the filming of a live cooking show, so that Columbo could volunteer to assist him. The script gave minimal instructions, but Falk ad-libbed the scene to perfection, beginning as reluctant and embarrassed, bumbling along until he winds up tickled with glee. The demonstration didn't get the detective any further along in his investigation, but did provide Falk with a tour de force for making the character supremely endearing to audiences.

Mission: Impossible's first master of disguise, Martin Landau, was an inspired choice to play the murderous brothers. Director Robert Butler recalled, "I had worked for Disney, so I knew the execution of twins, I knew how to do that and make it believable for the time. It's a little cornball now, but then it was good. Marty did a wonderful job of playing two distinct characters. One was carefree and joie de vivre and the other was kind of serious, and as soon as Marty walked on from Wardrobe, the attitude, the air, you knew which twin you were looking at. He did a masterful job."

Butler quickly discovered, though, that he was working at Peter Falk's pace: "Since Peter wanted to get everything as right as it could be, we just took forever. I kept looking over my shoulder, there was no one there. He had control of that show. Peter had been an accountant as a young guy... he did some arithmetic and decided he could do anything he wanted to (on *Columbo*) and they were still going to make mountains of money, (so I should) not believe all the horror stories. He wasn't dictatorial; he just said, 'Let's try this.' 'Peter, you got it.' He was just a very good guy to work *with*—I started to say work *for*, and I guess that's the truth. He had the power."

Hargrove confirmed that during Season 2, shooting started to regularly creep past schedule, as Falk grew even pickier about the work. "Peter never prepared," Hargrove said. "He came in with a script, he sort of learned it as he was rehearsing, and, of course, as great as he was, he was a very insecure performer. I noticed that after the director would say, 'Cut,' before he would say, 'Print,' Peter would raise his hand to the lens with one finger up to say, 'Give me another.' In my interpretation as I watched this over time, he really didn't trust anybody about the value of what he'd done, and not even himself that much. So the process took longer and the schedules on the show started getting longer and longer, and what happens many times and certainly happened here was that when things would go over or long like that, everybody would just point at Peter and say he was the problem. Well, sometimes that was true and sometimes it wasn't. But that was the handy excuse when things were going on, and the shows kept getting longer and longer."

Dagger of the Mind

To the press, NBC claimed that it was so elated with the success of the extended *Étude in Black*, it immediately ordered another two-hour show, this one to be set in London. Yet that had been the plan from the beginning. When Levinson and Link were coming up with ideas for Season 1, they thought of sending Columbo to the land of Sherlock Holmes and Agatha Christie, to come to the aid of Scotland Yard. NBC agreed to pay extra to shoot the episode partially overseas, if it received the extra half-hour.

Levinson and Link's idea, fleshed out by Jackson Gillis, was to pattern the story after *Macbeth*—with the murderers husband-and-wife Shakespearean actors, arrogant Nicholas Frame and ambitious Lillian Stanhope. Instead of a king whose kingdom they covet, their victim became theater impresario Sir Roger Haversham, who discovers that Lilly wooed him only so he would back their production of *Macbeth*.

Universal flew six of the actors and a portion of the crew to London for a short week of filming. U.K.-based professionals, including a new director of photography, were hired for the international portion.

That said, only about a fourth of the scenes would be filmed in London, mostly exteriors that featured iconic buildings or sights, like the Tower of London. Just two interiors were shot overseas: a hippie fortuneteller's pad and Detective Chief Superintendent Durk's gentlemen's club. All other interiors would be filmed on the Universal lot or at the Greystone Mansion in Beverly Hills, which was used as Haversham's country estate.

To further consolidate costs, shortly before flying out the *Columbo* crew, Hargrove sent a skeleton *Madigan* team to London to use some of the same contacts and second-unit footage.

Falk didn't like the idea—he thought it too gimmicky—but seemed to enjoy his visit. While in costume, the actor was complimented by one local attendant. "You're wise, sir, to have brought your raincoat." Falk smiled, "You'd better believe it."

Unexpectedly, the *Columbo* team returned from London with more footage than even the longer running time allowed. NBC wanted to show as much of London as possible, including a two-minute sequence Falk had ad-libbed scrambling through the crowds near Buckingham Palace, trying to take pictures of the changing of the guard.

That meant something had to go. The biggest cut was the original three-minute opening scene, inspired by the passage of *Macbeth* in which three witches foretell Macbeth's doom. *Dagger of the Mind* was to open with Nick Frame consulting wacky spiritualist Angus. Attired in "a wild mixture of mod, the occult, and careless home laundry," Angus stood behind a steaming concoction in a huge iron pot, as he incants, "Double, double toil and trouble, fire burn and cauldron bubble…." Making his way through "the star-decked mobiles and other mystical clutter," Nick interrupts Angus and demands he foretell the fate of his play. Angus is more interested in his bubbling pot of cioppino.

"Just the reading," Nick insists. "Success or failure?"

Angus has tired of Nick asking him the same question before every new show, particularly considering the actor's "distinguished record of failures."

"Angus, I've got to know. I'm late already for the final run-through."

Angus sighs and sits down behind a table covered with tarot cards, all face down. Yet he is having trouble deciphering the "astral voices," until Nick puts money on the table. After more bickering, Angus suddenly jumps up, flipping over the table, and roars with laughter. "Success is your answer," Angus proclaims. "After all these years, it's going to be success!"

Jubilant, Nick exits. Angus stoops down to pick up a fallen tarot card. As he turns it over, his chuckling stops. It is a card of death, a hanged man dangling from a gallows. (Later, when Haversham's butler is found hanging from his rafters, the camera was to linger on his shadow, framed to look exactly like the hanged man on the tarot card.)

Deleting the fortunetelling scene necessitated a few other tweaks. When Nick first arrives at the theater, Lilly whispers, "Angus! What did he say?" The line had to be edited out, cutting straight to Nick's ecstatic response: "How would you like to do *A Doll's House* in New York?" Later, when the couple is tying a bicycle to the back of their car, two lines had to be cut. Nick, suddenly uncertain, wonders, "If only there were time to consult Angus again… the witches on the heath!" And Lilly snaps, "Angus is a fool!" To cover up the unnatural break in the two-shot, the editor inserted a close-up of Nick tying a knot.

A final snip near the end was more likely a censor's cut. At the wax museum, Columbo flicks a bead into a goblet to demonstrate to Durk how a pearl from Lilly's broken necklace ended up in Haversham's umbrella. Tourists were then supposed to be shown streaming in to view the exhibits, among them buxom script girl Miss Dudley. Without thinking, Columbo flicks another bead in the direction of the goblet; it lands in Miss Dudley's cleavage.

The Most Dangerous Match

Through July and August of 1972, the biggest sensation on television was the World Chess Championship between eccentric American genius Bobby

Fischer and the reigning World Chess Champion, Russian Boris Spassky. Billed as "The Match of the Century," the series of games marked the first time a chess competition was ever broadcast in the United States in primetime, with reporters from around the world breathlessly covering the drama. Interest in chess rose to an all-time high.

Levinson and Link had always viewed a Columbo investigation as a chess match, so with Jackson Gillis they devised the story of high-strung American chess champion Emmett Clayton, paranoid that he will lose his title, murdering his Russian competitor, Tomlin Dudek, by pushing him into a mechanical grinder.

The Most Dangerous Match opens with a memorable, artsy nightmare sequence to show Clayton's dread of the coming competition. Lost and frightened, Clayton runs through a haze past large white statues. The camera pulls back to show he's on a giant marble chessboard and the statues are giant chess pieces. The king begins sliding toward him. He accidentally knocks over a knight. He sees the king has Dudek's face. Now all the pieces are closing in on him. Dudek falls. The king gets closer. Clayton tries to roll out of the way—right off his hotel-room bed, as he awakens in a cold sweat.

Gillis had originally given even greater detail to the nightmare. The pieces were to emit an eerie screeching as they slid across the marble. All the pieces would be revealed to have the face of Dudek. Thunderous applause would erupt when Clayton tipped over the knight, and all of the Dudek figures would bow to the mounting applause.

Laurence Harvey (*The Manchurian Candidate*) played Clayton as a tortured eccentric, desperate to hide his pain. Unknown to his colleagues on the set, Harvey was suffering from stomach cancer that would take his life at age 45—just eight months after the episode aired.

By the end of the season, the last of Levinson and Link's story ideas had been exhausted. Hargrove and Gillis needed help. Falk pushed to hire Larry Cohen, the writer/director who years before had cast Falk in an early TV role that led to *Murder, Inc*. According to Cohen, Falk "demanded" Cohen be hired as payback for insufficiently compensating him for inspiring *Murder by the Book*. While mapping out the first season, Levinson and Link had asked Cohen for writing help, and he suggested the idea of a best-selling author getting bumped off when he tries to break up with his coattail-riding writing partner.

"I gave (the idea) to Levinson and Link as a gift, and they turned around and gave it to Steven Bochco, who got an Emmy nomination on a picture directed by Spielberg," Cohen said. "He never said thank you, but he's been collecting the residuals on my story for 30 years now. I got no thanks at all. And Levinson and Link never really thanked me much either. Universal sent me a color television as a gift. I hated that television set. I thought I was such a bigshot, I could give away a story. But I learned and regretted."

Cohen was leaving for a year's sabbatical in England, so he didn't want to write full scripts or even treatments. He did agree to jot down a series of two-page story ideas as a "murder consultant."

Cohen explained, "I made a deal not to write any scripts, but just supply a dozen murders and modus operandi. For $100,000! And I did it all in two weeks in London, walking around Hyde Park and dictating into a tape recorder. Now that's a deal."

After modest ratings for the season premiere, *Columbo* rebounded, finishing between No. 2 and No. 6 for the remainder of the season and heartily outdrawing the numbers for Season 1. CBS's *All in the Family* on Saturday nights was the only program that consistently outdrew it. *Columbo* did not fare as well at the Emmys, striking out in four categories—it lost to *The Waltons* as Best Drama Series, Falk lost to Richard Thomas (John-Boy) as Best Actor, director Ed Abroms (*The Most Dangerous Match*) lost to *Kung Fu*, and writer Bochco (*Étude in Black*) lost to *The Waltons*.

Columbo may have slipped in the eyes of critics, but the show had actually improved through the second season, as Falk perfected the character's mannerisms, expressions and speech patterns. Most of them were his own. Little by little, he drew upon more of his own endearing hesitancy, curiosity, contemplativeness and disorganization. The line began to blur between where Peter Falk stopped and Lt. Columbo began. He was confident the show could remain a hit, so long as the writers maintained the quality and kept the formula fresh.

Season 2 – 1972-1973

Étude in Black
Working Title: *Étude for Murder*
Filmed: Late June – July, early Sept. 1972
Stars: Peter Falk, John Cassavetes, Blythe Danner, Myrna Loy
Director: Nicholas Colasanto
Producer: Dean Hargrove
Teleplay: Steven Bochco
Story: Richard Levinson & William Link
Air Date: Sept. 17, 1972
Nielsen Ranking: #14

The Greenhouse Jungle
Filmed: July 1972
Guest Stars: Ray Milland, Bob Dishy, Sandra Smith
Director: Boris Sagal
Producer: Dean Hargrove
Teleplay: Jonathan Latimer
Air Date: Oct. 15, 1972
Ranking: #2

The Most Crucial Game
Working Title: *Sudden Death Payoff*
Filmed: August 1972
Guest Stars: Robert Culp, Dean Jagger, James Gregory, Valerie Harper, Dean Stockwell
Director: Jeremy Kagan
Producer: Dean Hargrove
Teleplay: John T. Dugan
Air Date: Nov. 5, 1972
Ranking: #4

Dagger of the Mind
Working Title: *Out, Damned Spot!*
Filmed: October 1972
Guest Stars: Richard Basehart, Honor Blackman, Wilfrid Hyde-White
Director: Richard Quine
Producer: Dean Hargrove
Teleplay: Jackson Gillis
Story: Richard Levinson & William Link
Air Date: Nov. 26, 1972
Ranking: #3 (29.0 points)

Requiem for a Falling Star
Working Title: *Murder by Starlight*
Filmed: August 1972
Guest Stars: Anne Baxter, Pippa Scott, Kevin McCarthy, Mel Ferrer
Director: Richard Quine
Producer: Dean Hargrove
Teleplay: Jackson Gillis
Air Date: Jan. 21, 1973
Ranking: #6 (28.5 points)

A Stitch in Crime
Working Titles: *A Special Kind of Death, The Specialist*
Filmed: June 1972
Guest Stars: Leonard Nimoy, Anne Francis
Director: Hy Averback
Producer: Dean Hargrove
Teleplay: Shirl Hendryx
Air Date: Feb. 11, 1973
Ranking: #2 (32.4 points, 46 share)

The Most Dangerous Match
Working Title: *Fool's Mate*
Filmed: Oct. – Nov. 1972
Guest Stars: Laurence Harvey, Lloyd Bochner, Jack Kruschen
Director: Edward M. Abroms
Producer: Dean Hargrove
Teleplay: Jackson Gillis
Story: Jackson Gillis, Richard Levinson & William Link
Air Date: March 4, 1973
Ranking: #5 (26.3 points)

Double Shock
Working Titles: *Recipe for Dying, Murder Times Two*
Filmed: September 1972
Guest Stars: Martin Landau, Jeannette Nolan, Julie Newmar
Director: Robert Butler
Producer: Dean Hargrove
Teleplay: Steven Bochco
Story: Jackson Gillis, Richard Levinson & William Link
Air Date: March 25, 1973
Ranking: #2

7
Music to Kill By

Music played an integral role in establishing the mood of every *Columbo* episode. From the beginning, Levinson and Link wanted each adventure to have its own distinct look, feel and sound. They feared the inverted mystery format and Columbo's character could grow formulaic, so unique, top-notch production values could help make each installment stand on its own.

The producer was responsible for selecting the composer. Universal's Music Department did not hold a group of composers under contract, but always had ready recommendations of who could write a certain kind of music for any kind of show.

The producer needed to have his composer selected by the time the episode was filmed and edited. Decisions on the score were left to the composer, although the producers and sometimes the director might offer suggestions. In place of music, Spielberg opened *Murder by the Book* with the rhythmic sounds of a typewriter. He then had Billy Goldenberg craft a score that mimicked the typing of keys. He even closed the show with Goldenberg's haunting theme played in concert with the sounds of a typewriter.

Columbo's producers were almost always pleased with what the composer dreamed up—except on *The Greenhouse Jungle*. For the score, Dean Hargrove turned to avant-garde Swiss-American Paul Glass, who regularly composed for *Night Gallery*. Glass decided that because Ray Milland's character collected flowers and was such a disagreeable person, he would write a concerto for heckelphone—a low, unconventional-sounding oboe.

On hearing the score, Hargrove was mortified. "He came in with a totally atonal score," the producer recalled. "You know, it doesn't have to be dance music, but it does have to be a good dramatic score. His score, in that sense, didn't make sense."

Hargrove scrapped all of Glass' music and brought in Oliver Nelson, who crafted a completely new score in about a week.

The producer also decided *where* music was needed. Once the film was cut, he or, more commonly, his associate producer and post-production supervisor would meet with the composer for a "spotting session." The producers would point out where music was intended to start and stop, as a music editor noted the point on each reel where the music was to be inserted. The composer, working from his own copy of the film, typically had seven to 10 days to write the score, which was then recorded by a full orchestra.

In the early years, the composer would also conduct the studio orchestra as it recorded his score. In time, the shows transitioned to "click tracks"—a metronomic pulse that was provided to each musician so they could play their parts on their own, to the specified tempo and in sync with the picture.

Each track was labeled and then added to the appropriate frames of the film, along with dubbed dialogue and sound effects. Tracks were then mixed to proper sound levels to create a master print, ready for broadcast.

When Hargrove took over for Season 2, he brought along Dick DeBenedictis, a protégé of Goldenberg's who had gotten his start crafting specialty material for Carol Burnett. Goldenberg suggested Hargrove use DeBenedictis for *McCloud*. DeBenedictis would end up writing the music for 23 *Columbos*, as well as dozens of other Hargrove productions over the next 25 years.

Initially, DeBenedictis tried to write in the style of Goldenberg, giving each show its own "villain theme" or "caper theme," of which variations would be used throughout the episode. Villain themes typically were used when the killer had an illustrative identity, such as heavy brass for a military man. A caper theme represented how a crime was committed, such as a stabbing or striking with a blunt object.

Other music cues might accompany the police at work, another lead character, or other facets of the story. "In film, you're writing to support the drama," DeBenedictis said. "You're trying to match the emotions evoked by the show."

DeBenedictis' first *Columbo* assignment was *Étude in Black*. The score, he recalled, "was very tricky because a part of the picture itself had John Cassavettes at the Hollywood Bowl for various orchestral settings, so we were doing legitimate symphonic music. I had to help select that music, but then I had to be careful in the score because I was doing a legitimate score as well—that is, it wasn't a rhythmic section score. It wasn't Hawaiian. It wasn't a rock-and-roll or any kind of jazz score. It was a legitimate score written more along the lines of classical music terms, but I had to be careful not to interfere with the music that was being used in the body of the show to explore (Cassavetes') character. That was tricky. So I kind of came up with thematic material that would allow me to avoid conflicts with the classical music that was going on, and I chose classical music that was of a particular era so that it would not clash with my stuff, which was a little bit more modern."

Besides turning out fine work, DeBenedictis had another trick for being asked to work on future episodes. He shared, "What I would do is while I was scoring one episode or one show, I would score the theme for another show and play it for the producer and say, 'How do you like this?' I'd kind of sneak it in at the end of the session. And generally they liked what I came up with."

A minimum of music was picked up from one episode to the next. DeBenedictis said, "It would depend, first of all, on time and, second of all, on the union contractual agreements, because when you went to record you used union musicians. They all get paid and there are limitations to how much you could reuse—whatever the union designated."

In the early 1970s, a specified percentage of music written for one production was allowed to be reused in other shows but, in time, pressure from the musicians' unions limited the studio's ability to do this. Some snippets of music cues were picked up in various *Columbo* episodes and, in fact, due to a tight schedule, one entire show—*Requiem for a Falling Star*—gave no composer credit, because it contained no original music; it consisted entirely of pick-ups, such as DeBenedictis' crime theme from *Étude in Black* and Oliver Nelson's bongo-heavy Columbo theme from *The Greenhouse Jungle*.

There was never an official "Columbo theme," although some composers—like Nelson—did write one. For *Prescription: Murder*, Dave Grusin introduced the detective with a low-key jazzy take on the title music. On *Ransom for a Dead Man*, Billy Goldenberg intentionally wanted no music when Columbo first appeared. "There are characters in films that you do not musicalize," Goldenberg explained. "They do it all for themselves. You can't make Columbo funny because (Falk) is doing it already in the acting. There's too much of the intellectual in Columbo to write music (for). He is his own music."

Ironically, Goldenberg—the one *Columbo* composer who swore off giving the detective his own music—later became the one composer credited for a "Columbo Theme." In 1974, Norrie Paramor and His Orchestra wanted to record an album of crime show theme songs, and Universal offered up the music Goldenberg wrote for the helicopter ride in *Ransom for a Dead Man*.

Gil Mellé composed the first Columbo cue, a droll, bouncy tune for tuba and strings, when he introduced the character in *Death Lends a Hand*. The music fit the character so well, Mellé repeated it in his three other *Columbos*, usually at the close of lighter moments featuring the Lieutenant, such as just before a commercial break or the end credits.

But it was Peter Falk who inadvertently came up with the song that would become most associated with the character, while filming the second show of Season 3, *Any Old Port in a Storm*. During a scene in a bar, Columbo goes to a payphone to call the local newspaper to find out when it last rained. While pretending to wait on hold, Falk instinctively thought to fill the time by humming a children's tune that had always tickled his fancy: "This Old Man." In the next episode, *Candidate for Crime*, he hummed the ditty again while waiting in the suspect's campaign office and the murderer later hums it as well. Falk enjoyed the song so much, he added it to Columbo's regular bag of quirks, and the composers took note.

DeBenedictis said, "Columbo didn't have a theme, but Peter Falk loved the song 'This Old Man,' so whenever he was on camera, I would try—especially in humorous situations—to employ a little flavor of 'This Old Man.'"

Eventually, the producers and writers began writing the song into just about every episode, reaching its apex with Season 7's *Murder Under Glass*, in which Columbo is treated to a glorious feast served by a stream of waiters who parade out accompanied by a full orchestra playing a grand arrangement of "This Old Man."

8
The Strike

By late 1972, Dean Hargrove had completed all eight Season 2 *Columbos* and was simultaneously finishing up six *Madigans*. Falk was off filming *A Woman Under the Influence* for Cassavetes and had agreed to head to Philadelphia the following spring to co-star with him in Elaine May's gangster buddy picture *Mikey and Nicky*. Falk suspected that May's deliberate style of moviemaking would almost assuredly cut into the next summer's start of production on *Columbo*. So he agreed to shoot the first two episodes of Season 3 in the early spring and then return at the end of the summer to shoot the other six. At NBC's insistence, half of the eight shows were to run two hours.

At the same time, the Writers Guild appeared to be on the verge of going on strike. So, Hargrove decided to start transitioning showrunner duties on *Columbo* to Doug Benton, the writer-producer of *Hec Ramsey*, who previously shepherded *Ironside, The Girl from U.N.C.L.E.*, and *Dr. Kildare*. Benton also had done uncredited polish work on most of the *Columbo* scripts produced so far. He seemed to know the format as well as anyone, and would be assisted by Jackson Gillis as executive story consultant and Robert F. O'Neill, who had worked on all seven episodes for Season 1, as associate producer. Levinson and Link would read early drafts and identify inconsistencies and story points that could be improved.

Benton began assembling *Columbo* scripts late in the fall, knowing he had to have one ready to shoot by early February and a second about four weeks later. He narrowed his options to four proposals: one by Myrna Bercovici (a cosmetics queen kills a thieving chemist), two by "murder consultant" Larry Cohen (a winemaker suffocates his brother in a wine vault, and a Senate candidate bumps off his campaign manager), and one by Robert Specht (a think tank scientist murders to protect his son). Benton assigned all four to writers whom he thought could quickly crank out shootable scripts. Drafts for the first two came together the fastest.

Lovely But Lethal

Jackson Gillis took on the cosmetics story, *Lovely But Lethal*. He set the first scene in a laboratory, opening on chemist Dr. Murcheson—illuminated by eerie infrared lights—nervously scraping his scalpel across a patient's cheek. The chemist's assistant tries to calm him by noting "how many years Dr. Frankenstein must have spent on his research." Murcheson scoffs—Dr. Frankenstein only made one monster and "didn't live in our jungle. He didn't *have* to succeed...." The analogy inspired producer Benton to make the entire episode a tribute to Universal monster movies. He hired horror film/*Night Gallery* veteran Jeannot Szwarc to direct and instructed Dick DeBenedictis to compose a spooky score. He cast Vera Miles (*Psycho*) as cosmetics queen Viveca Scott, and Vincent Price (*House of Wax*) as her rival, David Lang. The role of Lang's pretty young secretary who wants to emulate Viveca went to Sian Barbara Allen, who had just appeared in the thriller *You'll Like My Mother*. Allen played the part heavy on the creepiness, gazing longingly at Viveca, and turning what was scripted as an impulsive kiss on Viveca's cheek into an extended, uncomfortable embrace.

Eager to keep his star happy, new producer Benton also cast several of Falk's acting buddies on the show. John Finnegan played Columbo's sidekick sergeant, Bruce Kirby was used as a custodian, and Cassavetes cohort Fred Draper played Murcheson.

Vincent Price reveled in the role of sharp-tongued David Lang, making audiences wish he were on-screen far longer. But instead of lengthening his part, the producers made it slightly shorter. One of his scenes—Lang begrudgingly offering his secretary a $10 raise after she covers for him in front of Columbo— was trimmed. Another was deleted. After killing the assistant chemist, Viveca must flee her victim's house when there's a knock on the door. At the door— though cut from the final print—was Lang, arriving with a payoff for the victim.

In fact, considerable changes were made to Gillis' first draft, even though filming was slated to begin in mere weeks. Gillis had originally plotted Columbo's primary interrogation of Viveca while she's out for a horseback ride at her "fat farm," forcing Columbo to awkwardly ride alongside and try to keep up. But the scene contained so much key information, it proved more practical to film the exchange on foot, with Viveca leading calisthenics and then being followed by Columbo to the treadmills.

In its first draft, *Lovely But Lethal* was supposed to end with Viveca desperately trying to stash the incriminating jar of Miracle wrinkle cream just as the police arrive. She was to find a split-second to grab the jar from her purse and flip it into the shrubs. But the jar would end up rolling down the hill and shattering at the bottom. The jar is reduced to fragments, its contents splattered. Columbo walks over, stoops and picks up the jar's telltale octagonal base, intact. "Boy," he enthuses. "*That* was sure a miracle!"

As originally written, Columbo was to spend most of his investigation agog at Viveca's celebrity, similar to his adoration of Nora Chandler in *Requiem for a Falling Star*. Yet Vera Miles played Viveca as tougher and colder, perhaps leading Falk to portray Columbo as far less fawning than the script suggested. The filmmakers even trimmed Gillis' second ending, with Columbo apologizing to the killer: "So I guess you know how bad I feel, Miss Scott. You've… you've been like one of my family for so many years…."

Although *Lovely But Lethal* would not rank among the best entries of the year, its star-studded cast, including a young Martin Sheen as the victim, convinced NBC to schedule it as the Season 3 opener.

Any Old Port in a Storm

Among Benton's three remaining options, the winemaking story seemed to have the most promise. But at three pages long, it was also the least developed. He needed someone who could turn out a script in a hurry. Benton remembered Stanley Ralph Ross, who'd written for *The Man from U.N.C.L.E.* at same time as Hargrove, and while Benton was on *The Girl from U.N.C.L.E.* Over two seasons, Ross had churned out two-dozen scripts for *Batman*.

Benton and O'Neill called Ross to say they were stuck and needed a script right away. They had a messenger deliver him Cohen's story. Ross looked it over and agreed to the job, not letting on that he'd never seen the show. He quickly called his secretary and asked, "Describe *Columbo* for me."

"Well," she replied, "he's a schlepper, he wears this raincoat, and he walks out of the room." Equipped with a few more details, Ross started writing the script that afternoon. He finished it one week later and had it messengered to the studio. Two hours later, the phone rang and his secretary handed Ross the receiver. "Is this Stanley Ralph Ross?"

"Yes."

"This is Peter Falk."

Ross didn't believe him, thinking it was impressionist Rich Little. Falk said to call him right back, and left the number for his office at Universal. Ross dialed the number, and sure enough Falk himself picked up the phone. "Do you believe me now? Anyway, I saw your script. It just came in by the messenger. I went in the bathroom to read it. It's wonderful. It's really wonderful. Listen. We have to get together and we have to work on the script before the producers come back and screw it up."

That night, Ross went to the Falks' home for dinner, and the next night Falk visited Ross' office. Falk didn't mess with the plot or the dialogue; he spent the evenings picking Ross' brain, just trying to understand the characters' reasons for everything they did and everything they said.

Ross had written the role of murderer Adrian Carsini for his friend Victor Buono, who played the villain King Tut in *Batman*. The producers had no interest in Buono. They took the script to Robert Shaw. Ross recalled, "Robert Shaw's best friend was Donald Pleasence. They had a reciprocal trade agreement whereby one could read a script for the other one and commit. Shaw committed for Pleasence. Pleasence had never read the script. They phoned Pleasence in England. He showed up (the next) Monday."

Any Old Port in a Storm was set to begin filming March 7, 1973. But on March 6, the Writers Guild went on strike. Benton and Gillis, as guild members, had to step away from *Columbo*. Universal was not so understanding. They eliminated the position of executive story consultant—as well as Gillis' employment. The studio also warned Benton that, if he failed to report for duty, he would be sued for breach of contract. Benton refused. Universal fired him. O'Neill—a line producer who did no writing himself—was promoted to producer.

None of the turmoil affected Falk. He was delighted to work with Pleasence, and the actors played off of each other masterfully. Like their characters Columbo and Carsini, the men shared an admiration for excellence. Whereas Falk tempered Columbo's fawning over Viveca Scott in *Lovely But Lethal*, he played up his respect and fondness for Adrian Carsini from start to finish. The episode's closing moment, as Columbo idled the Peugeot in front of Carsini's beloved winery and offered him a well-chosen glass of dessert wine, proved one of the series' most touching.

Although much of the action took place at Carsini Wineries, a real winery was used during only the first day of shooting. The crew rented the Brookside Winery in Guasti (near the Ontario Airport) to film in the aging cellar, bottle/label room, vat room, lab room, and wine shoppe, as well as a quick establishing shot of the winery exterior. All other interior scenes—including the various offices, tasting room, lounge, wine vault, restaurant and bar—were filmed on Universal soundstages. The other exterior shots of the winery, entry gate, and garage were taken the following week at the Harold Lloyd Estate in Beverly Hills.

After completing *Any Old Port in a Storm*, Falk was ready to begin *Mikey and Nicky*. Elaine May was not. Filming finally started nearly two months later, in May. But with the writer/director constantly changing her mind about scenes and ordering endless retakes, there would be no end in sight.

Meanwhile, as summer approached, *Columbo* was still without a writer-producer and a story editor. Hargrove consented to return for the remainder of the season, aided by his mentor and friend Roland Kibbee. Hargrove met Kibbee, whose writing credits dated back to the Marx Brothers' *A Night in Casablanca* (1946), as a fellow staff writer on the original *Bob Newhart Show* in the early 1960s. On *Columbo*, they would share the title of executive producer, but Hargrove handled most of the production duties; Kibbee primarily helped oversee the scripts.

On June 24, the 16-week-long writers' strike ended, and the two producers could begin scrambling for scripts for the remaining six shows.

Falk, however, was in no hurry to return to Los Angeles. *Mikey and Nicky* was wildly behind schedule and he had no idea when it would finish. To buy time, Falk announced that he was quitting *Columbo* and henceforth would appear only in movies. Universal had seen this act before. The studio viewed it as a purely financial negotiating ploy. They resolved to hold Falk's salary at $45,000 per episode. NBC, though, recognized *Columbo* as the key to making the Sunday wheel roll. Its Wednesday night wheel was a ratings disaster, and three new shows were being developed as replacements. Universal submitted Falk's agent a final bid: a three-year contract for six episodes per season at $100,000 apiece, in addition to the two shows already shot. Universal would pay $45,000 of his salary, NBC the rest. And to seal the deal, NBC offered a $300,000 signing bonus.

Falk, still stuck filming in Philadelphia, hadn't expected the studio and network to cave in to his demands so quickly. He continued to stall. At first, he said doctors had advised him to retire because the work was too hard on his one remaining eye and they feared for his sight. Falk then continued to ask for finer and finer points of creative control. He wanted to see all scripts well in advance and be given the time for him or his people to rewrite them to his content. He also wanted all episodes shot in between his movie commitments, meaning shows needed to be ready to be produced back-to-back-to-back. Falk finally signed at the end of August and, soon after, headed back to L.A., leaving *Mikey and Nicky* unfinished. He promised Elaine May he would return when he got his next free break, presumably at the end of the year.

Candidate for Crime

When Hargrove and Kibbee resumed work on *Columbo* they had two six-month-old scripts left over from Benton, both of which needed considerable work. With the original authors no longer available, Kibbee and Hargrove ended up making so many changes themselves, they were given a writing credit on the two episodes.

Benton had assigned the script in the closest shape, *Candidate for Crime*, to one of his most reliable *Ironside* freelancers, Irving Pearlberg. After the first draft, consultants Levinson and Link had already pointed out about a dozen easy fixes. They noticed there was nothing suspicious early on in the script to give Columbo any reason to suspect candidate Hayward. In addition, the script didn't explain Hayward's motive for killing his manager until long after his victim was dead—leaving the audience unnecessarily puzzled for most of the show. Originally, just one cop was assigned to watch over Hayward's hotel room on the night he has his campaign manager switch clothes with him and drive off in his car, so Hayward can elude his police detail and slip out of his room. Levinson and Link thought staging the masquerade was too elaborate a ploy just to elude one cop. They suggested adding a swarm of reporters that he also has to get past. As well, they advised against having Hayward talk about busing or any other "emotion-charged" issues that might bring up "irrelevant vibrations. Fake an issue or be vague about specifics." They too had problems with the idea that in the final scenes Hayward truly feared for his life, if he were to cavalierly head off to dinner on election night (so he can hide the fact that he's shot a bullet in his hotel-room wall).

First off, Hargrove and Kibbee changed Hayward's motive and made it clearer. Instead of his campaign manager vaguely threatening to expose Hayward stealing campaign donations to keep his wife from divorcing him, Hayward kills the manager for demanding he dump his mistress because it will hurt him in the election. The change was more in keeping with the seedy campaign manager's character and made the wife more sympathetic.

In the early draft, Hayward shoots into the victim's car and strikes a dashboard clock, which he resets to a fake time of death. The time clue was tweaked to have Hayward slip a new watch onto the victim's wrist, smash it, and reset the time—oblivious that the delicate watch is a not a model that a rougher man would normally wear.

Hargrove and Kibbee also switched Hayward's reason for leaving his bullet-bearing hotel room on election night to being called away to vote with his wife, and added a nifty clue to prompt Columbo to search the room: the candidate said he went into the room to make phone calls, but no extension buttons ever lit up on the other phones in the suite.

One problem, though, was that the original script already ran a tightly paced 89 pages, and would have to be cut to about 83 pages to fit into a 90-minute episode. Kibbee and Hargrove's changes made the script even longer, so they opted to tack on several new, extraneous scenes to expand it to a two-hour show. Added were a long, drawn-out traffic stop followed by an even longer visit to a mechanic.

The original script ended with a nailed Hayward wandering, distraught, out onto the balcony. Columbo moves near, to make sure he doesn't jump. Hayward finally reenters the room to be led away, but Columbo pauses to turn on the TV set just in time to learn that Hayward has lost the election. The finale was changed to Columbo telling Hayward he's under arrest, as a TV newscaster announces, "And according to our computer projections, it's still too close to call...."

Double Exposure

Another script literally dropped into Hargrove's lap. The godsend was submitted by a young Stephen J. Cannell, who in the coming years would create series such as *The Rockford Files, Baretta, The Greatest American Hero, The A-Team,* and *21 Jump Street*. For the last two years, Cannell had been the primary writer and story editor for *Adam-12*, helping craft 49 half-hour installments. He was a huge *Columbo* fan, but always had another assignment in the way—until the writers' strike. Suddenly with time on his hands, Cannell remembered his college thesis on subliminal cuts in advertising and thought it would make a great gimmick for *Columbo*. He wrote a full script and, as soon as the strike ended, swung by Hargrove's office to drop it off, stressing that he had written it for his own amusement.

Hargrove loved the plot: Bart Kepple, an expert on subliminal advertising, blackmails clients into purchasing his motivational films by having a sexy woman seduce the boss and taking incriminating photos. When one client, Vic Norris, threatens to expose him, Kepple shoots him with his .38, using a "caliber converter" to make it look like a .22. Kepple then tries to pin the murder—as well as the later slaying of his suspicious projectionist—on Norris' wife.

Cannell had Robert Culp in mind when he created Kepple, a character he described as "a slim, well-dressed, dynamic type in his 40s," adept at suppressing his fury below the surface. Hargrove was on the same wavelength, bringing Culp back for a third time. Culp played off Falk's ad-libs expertly and, like Falk, would paraphrase many of his lines, rather than stick to the letter of the script. "It's the only show I've done where you get time to properly work on a scene," Culp said. "Pete gets to the heart of the scene and you follow his lead."

Cannell named Kepple's mystery woman "Tanya Baker" after his daughter (Tawnia) and his mother's maiden name (Baker). He'd later reuse the name Tawnia Baker in an episode of *The Rockford Files* and as a recurring character over two seasons on *The A-Team*.

His script was a slight departure for *Columbo*, concentrating more on the crime and the cover-up rather than progressing through a gradual clue-by-clue resolution of the mystery. *Double Exposure* was filmed, edited and scored to run two hours, but in the eleventh hour, the producers opted to cut it back for a 90-minute timeslot.

In addition to trimming most sequences to remove nonessential dialogue, entire scenes were excised. As originally filmed, the show opened with Kepple visiting the home of Vic Norris, where his victim-to-be informs him that he's done being blackmailed into buying his films and will confess his dalliance to his wife, the board of directors, and the D.A., solely because he despises him. "No, Vic," Kepple answers. "You're buying the film tonight, whether you like it or not, and you're picking up the option on our contract—and we both know why." Norris pulls a .22-caliber pistol from his desk drawer, points it at Kepple, and cocks the trigger. Kepple doesn't blink; he knows Norris doesn't have the nerve to shoot.

Kepple immediately heads to the apartment of sultry Tanya Baker. He lies to her, saying Norris' wife found out about her, is hysterical, and "there's no telling what she might do." He urges her to skip town for a few weeks and gives her the money to fly to Lisbon. "If you're a good girl," he says, "maybe I'll join you there." He then begins preparing to kill Norris, where Hargrove's final cut of the episode would start.

Serious cuts came from the middle of the story, as well. Although it never made it on-screen, after Kepple shoots the projectionist with Norris' gun, he telephones Mrs. Norris from the projection room, pretending to be the projectionist. "I was hired by the killer to strand you on that street corner the other night so you wouldn't have an alibi," Kepple says. "He's trying to frame you for your husband's murder, but I don't want any part of that." He says he'd be willing to help her, if she comes to meet him. As soon as she hangs up, she calls the theater and is patched through to the projection room, where Kepple answers. His story seemingly confirmed, Mrs. Norris hastily leaves for the theater.

Mrs. Norris, in fact, is still at the theater, lingering out of sight, when Kepple returns with Columbo. After a police sergeant announces that the gun belonged to Norris, Columbo reluctantly tells him to go pick up the wife. "That won't be necessary," she says, standing at the door to the projection room. "I was here—I panicked when I saw him like that—and ran." Columbo briefly questions her,

A DELETED SEQUENCE from *Double Exposure* had the murderer trick Mrs. Kepple (Louise Latham), the wife of his first victim, into traveling to the scene of his second murder. *[Credit: NBCUniversal]*

then introduces her to Kepple, hoping she will recognize his voice.

The abridged version of *Double Exposure* is quicker paced, but the cuts do make it a little harder for the audience to follow. How did Kepple know to use a .22? How did he know where to find Norris' gun? Arlene Martel, the actress who played Tanya Baker, was cut completely from the show, but the changes were made so late, her name remained in the credits (albeit misspelled as "Martell").

Another story lead came from Steven Spielberg, who had worked for Hargrove on *The Name of the Game*. Spielberg called Hargrove to say that a friend named Brian De Palma was out of work and needed a job. Would he consider hiring him to direct a *Columbo*? Hargrove had seen De Palma's earlier low-budget comedies *Hi, Mom!* and *Greetings*, found them droll and amusing, and called De Palma in for a meeting.

At the meeting, De Palma announced that he not only wanted to direct an episode, but that he was already co-writing it with Jay Cocks, movie critic for *Time* magazine and frequent collaborator of Martin Scorsese. The idea, De Palma relayed, was that Truman Capote kills Johnny Carson live on *The Tonight Show*. "O… kay…," Hargrove nodded hesitantly.

As De Palma excitedly explained, "Since it's Truman Capote, I want to shoot the first eight minutes on video from a height of 4-foot-9." Hargrove was game and gave the go-ahead to write a full script titled *Shooting Script*. He contacted diminutive actor/composer Paul Williams (*Smokey and the Bandit*) about playing the Capote character.

"So we're chugging along and we get a script in, and the script is okay, but it needs some work," Hargrove recalled. "It had some problems from a format standpoint for *Columbo*, but they were not things that couldn't be addressed. So we're ready to go and I get a call from De Palma. He said, 'I hate to do this, because I know you were doing Steven a favor, but I've just gotten the money to do a picture I've wanted to do for a long time called *Phantom of the Paradise*, which is *Phantom of the Opera* done in a rock-and-roll opera, so I'd really liked to be freed from the assignment. But I've got a replacement. In fact, he's got a picture that's just coming out. We've arranged for you to go take a look at it at Warner Bros. You can see his work.' I said, 'Okay, and how do you spell Scorsese?' So I go over and I look at *Mean Streets*, which nobody's seen. I thought, 'This guy's really something!' So now Scorsese comes into my office, and he talks real fast, like this: 'Now don't worry about anything!' And I said, 'Well, Marty, these are 10-day shoots.' And he said, 'Don't worry about it. I did *Boxcar Bertha*.' So he signed on to do it, and as we worked on the script somewhat, we sent it over to Peter. And Peter read the script (during pre-production), which was always somewhat of a surprise. And he asked to have lunch with me. Now I'd had five scripts come out without a peep and we sit down to have lunch and he said, 'Well, I don't know about this script.' So I said, 'I know there are some problems, and I can tell you what I think they are and how we think we can address them.'

And he said, 'No, it's not that. It's not that.' And I said, 'What is it?' He said, 'I don't think we want two colorful characters in our show,' meaning the Truman Capote character was something that might diminish him. Because if you look at *Columbo*, it's usually Robert Culp or some rich, successful guy or woman, and he just felt that this was wrong for the show. Now I felt that, in the long run, he was right. You shouldn't do that. But that, having Scorsese and this whole project, it was just so interesting, and I said, 'I know it's not perfect, and we can fix some of the problems. But this director….' I did a whole pitch about this, but he wouldn't relent. So that was the end of that."

Publish or Perish

A few months earlier, Steven Bochco had passed along to Hargrove a finished *Columbo* script from young writer Peter S. Fischer. At the time, Fischer was toiling away on Lorne Greene's short-lived cop show *Griff*, and had written a *Columbo* on spec simply because *Columbo* was his favorite TV show. "It was like a rainbow when that script arrived," Hargrove recalled. "It was always very difficult to find someone who understood the mystery form. Not that they weren't good writers. Oftentimes the writers were better than the form. But there just weren't any mystery shows on television, so people hadn't done it before. The only mystery show before this one of any prominence was *Perry Mason*. And so you're looking around and bringing in guys who really don't understand the form, it's not that they weren't good. Like I said, some of them were real, real good writers who just couldn't quite get it in terms of the form, because these were very formulaic mystery shows by definition. And somehow it didn't work."

Although the story wasn't one they could use, the talent behind the writing, with tight plotting and ingenious clues, was unmistakable. So, later that fall, Hargrove and Kibbee called Fischer in to discuss a possible story idea of theirs: a book publisher kills his best-selling author just before the writer quits to join the competition, and frames the competitor. The conference, Fischer recalled, "took about a half-hour or so. We worked out the big pieces of *Publish or Perish*, and I went off and wrote it."

When Falk saw the script, he flipped. A few days later, he ran into Fischer in a stairwell at the studio and said he wanted him to be the new *Columbo* story editor. Fischer had to reluctantly decline, since he was tied up with *Griff*—despite knowing that the series was lousy and wouldn't last long. He said he hoped the offer would still be open when he was finally free. Falk was steamed—at Universal. He took it as a personal affront that the studio would rather have an elite writer working on a bad new show than his established hit.

Some weeks later, *Griff* got the axe and Fischer told Falk he was available. According to Fischer, "My agent, Sylvia Hirsch, called me and said, 'Oh my gosh, do you know what's going on? They're talking in The Tower about getting you on staff of *Columbo*….' I said, 'Sylvia, hang on a second. Do *you* know what's going on?' She said, 'Uh, no… what is it?' I said, 'Peter Falk is up there right now screaming and yelling at the guys that he's going to quit *Columbo* if I don't join them as story editor. That's what's going on.' They were ready to give me anything I wanted just to come on board. So I didn't hold them up. I said, 'Look, I could learn a lot on this thing. I'd get doors opened to me that weren't open before.' So we made a nice little deal. It was a good deal, but it wasn't an overly good deal, but the studio thought it was terrible. They wanted to get out of it as soon as possible. They were paying me extra for the scripts, they were paying me so much a week, and then scripts were all extra, onward and upward. After about three months, they said, 'How do we get out of this deal?' I said, 'I guess you don't.'"

Fischer's script for *Publish or Perish* was so fast paced and tightly packed that it could barely be contained within 90 minutes. Director Robert Butler cleverly thought to portray the murder in a three-way split screen, simultaneously depicting the publisher, the victim, and the hired assassin methodically moving in for the kill. The editing technique not only saved several minutes in running time, it made the sequence that much quicker and more suspenseful.

Fischer had created the part of the sleazy publisher with Jack Klugman in mind. But the producers, who thought Columbo played better off of stuffier personalities, chose Jack Cassidy from Season 1's *Murder by the Book*. As the victim, they wanted an actual author who was recognizable but not overly colorful like Truman Capote. They approached Mickey Spillane, whose Mike Hammer novels had sold 155 million copies.

Spillane recalled that the producers "said, 'Go as you are.' But when I got there, some idiots took me down to Rodeo Drive and bought a thousand dollars' worth of nondescript clothes!"

He later added that he'd "always wanted to play a corpse. The only scene I had with Peter Falk is with me dead as a doornail."

Mind Over Mayhem

The producers were still hoping to salvage the last Doug Benton script. Benton had had Steven Bochco write two drafts of the think tank drama, *Mind Over Mayhem*, before it was shelved. The main story was solid: Dr. Cahill, the head of a prestigious institute, murders a chemist who has proof that the doctor's son, Neil, stole his award-winning theory of molecular energy. Columbo discovers Neil is in love with the dead chemist's wife, Margaret, so he makes a show of arresting the son to force the father to confess.

From the first draft, Levinson and Link had spotted the story's primary weakness: dullness. In their memo, they called it "too straight-line, with no twists or surprises. The story seems to stop after the first act and doesn't really begin progressing until the last act." The only scenes with any life "verge ever so slightly on soap opera."

Among their suggestions were building some twists into the overly talky exchanges, cutting most of the long scenes with Margaret that went nowhere, and—after three years of stately mansions—switching the setting from an old-fashioned institute to a stark, ultra-modern facility.

They questioned why Columbo immediately suspects Dr. Cahill. From their first meeting, Levinson and Link advised, "there should be something very clever that puts him on the right track." They thought the ending didn't work as well as it could have because Columbo told Cahill he was going to arrest his son for murder on made-up charges while Neil and Margaret stood by. "Columbo runs an incredible risk that one or the other of them will blurt out the truth," they warned.

Hargrove and Kibbee addressed Levinson and Link's criticisms by building more excitement into the story and adding better clues. As a first clue, Cahill absentmindedly leaves a match at the murder scene that has been burned almost to the end—the sure sign of lighting a cigar. "I was looking for a cigar smoker," Columbo later explains to Cahill, "and there you were."

For the finale, instead of Columbo telling Cahill he was going to arrest his son while Neil and Margaret looked on, they had Columbo tell Neil he was to be arrested while his father looked on. Neil and Margaret could protest their innocence, but that only added to the drama. Cahill offered to confess once he and Columbo were alone. Mimicking the lovely last shot of Columbo sharing a sip of wine with Carsini, Columbo and Cahill sit in a stairwell, as the father agrees to confess and the cop kindly offers him a last cigar.

As a subplot, Bochco wanted to bring back Dog, who was last spotted in Season 2's *The Most Dangerous Match*. Sadly, the original canine actor had since died of old age. The producers found a suitable replacement—smaller, younger and cuter, with fewer wrinkles—but then had to add gray powder to the pup's face to make him look older. Falk would joke that the new dog delayed filming because while Falk was speedily in and out of Makeup, the pooch needed 20 minutes of primping before he was ready.

Swan Song

After the success of *Any Old Port in a Storm*, Stanley Ralph Ross was asked to write a second *Columbo*. He turned in a short story about a country gospel singer who takes his nagging wife/manager in his private plane, drugs her, and parachutes to safety just before the plane crashes. When the writers' strike ended, Ross was asked to expand it into a full script, but Ross, unwilling to write for Hargrove and Kibbee, refused.

Falk brought in David Rayfiel, the renowned movie script doctor who had penned Falk's 1969 war comedy-drama *Castle Keep*. The script was tailormade for Johnny Cash, country music's "Man in Black." Cash had done a little dramatic acting over the years, primarily in westerns. "We had this idea, and it's hard to get musical performers to do these shows because they get so much more money when they're out on tour than they could possibly make as a guest on a television show," Hargrove said. "We gave the script to Cash's manager, and we had a lunch meeting with them at the Beverly Hills Hotel. When the waiter came up and asked, 'Would you like a cocktail?' Cash said, 'No, I don't drink. I break out. I break out in Memphis. I break out in Dallas….'"

Cash had already performed over 100 concerts in 1973, but the filming schedule appeared to fit perfectly between the dates on his current tour. He would be flying into California for three concerts in mid-December, with his last tour date of the year set for December 19 in Bakersfield. The performance could be filmed for use in the episode, and then Cash was free until a series of shows January 9, 10 and 11, 1974, in Binghamton, Syracuse and Niagara Falls, New York.

The singer had originally announced that he would compose new music for the episode, but in the end decided to perform covers of Hank Williams' "I Saw the Light" and Kris Kristofferson's "Sunday Mornin' Comin' Down."

Although the producers preferred refined, sinister types as their murderers instead of down-to-earth nice guys like Cash's Tommy Brown, Falk and Cash gelled perfectly. Falk played Columbo more polite, embarrassed and deferential than ever before. He seems almost pained to have his suspicions confirmed. And, fittingly, the episode closed once again in the vein of *Any Old Port in a Storm*, only this time, after catching Tommy Brown trying to make off with the incriminating evidence (his parachute), Columbo has just the two of them sit in a car, exchange words of regret, and then flip on the radio for one last chorus of "I Saw the Light."

Cash so enjoyed the process that his manager began working with CBS on the possibility of him starring in the pilot for a detective series in which he'd play the good guy. It never came together.

One challenge for the episode was having to work around the holidays. More problematic, Falk's leisurely pace of filming had set the production back a couple of days, jeopardizing the concerts Cash had booked in New York. Worse, Cash was needed for retakes of the opening number, which had been filmed both on a soundstage and during the concert in Bakersfield, to get shots of a live audience. Due to technical problems, none of the footage shot in Bakersfield was usable. Hargrove had just days to figure out how to pull together a concert with a full audience.

When Cash's manager got wind of the delays and the juggled schedule, he barged into Hargrove's office. "You know," the manager said, "you're not going to finish this show for another five days, and two days from now Johnny's supposed to be in Upstate New York doing a gig."

"But you don't have a stop date," Hargrove responded.

"Stop date?" the manager replied, growing increasingly upset. "What do you mean?"

Hargrove explained, "They don't give stop dates on a television show because you never quite know when it's going to end. This really has nothing to do with me, it has to do with the studio. You made a deal with the studio and they didn't give you a stop date, so they're going to keep him here to finish out this episode. We'll do everything we can to move the schedule around to get him out as early as we can, but he's the guest star. We can't just move him out."

The manager stormed out of the office, to report to Cash that Hargrove was acting unscrupulously, had lied to them, and was taking advantage of them. Soon after, Hargrove remembered, "I ran into Cash and did something I normally wouldn't have, but this guy really got to me because it was questioning my professionalism. I said to Cash, 'Listen, I know there's a problem with you going to New York State and I have to explain why.' And I told him about a stop date and he just sort of nodded and didn't say anything. The next thing I know he went to Binghamton, where he had a (concert) date, and because we were short of having an audience for his performance in the show that we shot, on his own he hired a crew from a local television station to shoot one of his performances. We intercut it with the one we'd shot of his performing. It was amazing. He was a really nice man and a thorough professional. I really liked him."

For *Swan Song*, as well as the next two *Columbos*, Hargrove's longtime associate producer, Edward K. Dodds, would get producer credit. Hargrove explained, "Eddie Dodds had been working for me for a very long time at the studio, back since *The Name of the Game*, as a matter of fact. Eddie was a friend of mine and he came to me and said, 'Hey, can I get a producing credit?' And I thought, 'Well, why not?' So I went to Peter (Falk) and said, 'Hey, Eddie would like a producing credit.' Nothing was going change in the operation of the show, because he was like the unit manager or the production manager. Peter said, 'Yeah, okay.'"

Dick Irving, in particular, was pleased with the appointment since Dodds was a company man to the core, who could now provide a direct pipeline to everything that was happening during production.

A Friend in Deed

By the time Peter Fischer was able to join the *Columbo* staff, Hargrove and Kibbee had completed scripts for all but one of the season's shows. So they asked him to write the final episode and then assume the title of executive story consultant at the start of Season 4. As a starting point, they gave Fischer the idea of the murderer being Columbo's superior at the police department. "I can do something with that," Fischer replied.

To direct, Hargrove hired Falk's pal Ben Gazzara, who had directed for him on *The Name of the Game* and earlier on Gazzara's own series, *Run for Your Life*. Hargrove recalled, "I'd known Ben and I said, 'It's a 10-day show,' and he said, 'Yeah, I heard.' Now this is a guy who's Peter's good friend, who Peter looks up to, and the first take I saw, before Ben could say, 'Print,' Peter held up his hand and raised a finger. So I said if he's going to do that with Ben, it's going to happen all the time, and it did."

Fischer got a taste of what it would be like as story editor, with Falk on him constantly for revisions. Worse, Falk had given the studio a firm deadline, to allow him to return to Philadelphia to finish *Mikey and Nicky*. *A Friend in Deed* was completed "under tremendous pressure," Fischer said. "(Peter) had a stop date that he had to be finished by, so I had to work very hard on the script. As it turned out, we got it finished in plenty of time. Out of all the *Columbos* I did, this was my favorite one."

The show was supposed to run 90 minutes, but Fischer packed his script so tightly with gems that it spilled over to two hours.

Gazzara gave *A Friend in Deed* a darker, grittier feel than other episodes. It has more scenes without background music, and the score is less jaunty. Its only marginally lighthearted sequence is an extraneous, belabored one, added to pad the length to two hours, in which Columbo can't start his car and tries flagging down passing motorists.

Columbo's ratings remained strong through the third season, but not as consistent as during Season 2. ABC had moved up the start time of its Sunday night movie to 8:30 to go head to head with the *NBC Mystery Movie* and the strength of each movie greatly impacted how the wheel fared. *Hec Ramsey* was canceled after its second year. Yet *Columbo* remained a cultural touchstone, an audience favorite, and a Top 10 regular. The Johnny Cash episode, in fact, was the top-rated show for the first week of March 1974—the first time *Columbo* had ever reached number one in the Nielsen ratings.

Levinson and Link, however, did not seem impressed by the continued high ratings nor did they agree with conventional wisdom that the quality of the show had never been higher. In fact, interviewed two weeks after *Swan Song* aired, they were quoted as saying that if it were up to them, *Columbo* would have retired from TV after year two. They felt the writing was not up to par. Levinson called the previous episode, *Mind Over Mayhem*, "terrible," adding "it never should have been on the air."

While Levinson was usually unconcerned about *Columbo* being overly "realistic," the trickery in that episode galled him. "Columbo used entrapment," Levinson said. "The case could never have been brought to court. There's really no excuse for using a script like that. But *Columbo* stories are hard to find. After three seasons on the air, it's almost impossible to find six or eight new ideas. This year we had the problem of the writers' strike and that threw everyone off schedule. We had to start grabbing what we could find."

Nonetheless, the show was nominated for an Emmy Award in a new category, Outstanding Limited Series, facing off against *McCloud* and *The Blue Knight*. Falk was also nominated as best actor in a limited series.

"I almost didn't go to the Emmy Awards because in its first year (*Columbo*) won everything except Best Show," Hargrove recalled. "So we got nominated and I almost didn't go because I figured this show's been on a few years. After (reconsidering), I called (Benton and O'Neill) because all they'd really done was come in and do a couple of shows. I said, 'You know, I understand you guys are going to be nominated. We're all nominated. On the slim chance that we win, Kibbee and I would like to pick up the award rather than going up as a committee. I think it's enough that you guys got yourself an Emmy nomination for only a couple of shows.' So Doug said okay, but then I got a call back and he said, 'Well, the problem is that Bob's parents who live in Oklahoma are going to be watching the show, so we want to go up too.' And if they're going up, of course Eddie Dodds has got to go up. So I'm sitting there saying, 'Well, we're not going to win anyway.' So then, to my amazement, we won. We go up, I make the remarks, Kibbee says a little something, and as (O'Neill and Benton) step up to the microphone, the orchestra plays them off. So his parents in Oklahoma never got to hear him, which I thought was justice."

Season 3 – 1973-1974

Lovely But Lethal
Working Title: *Beauty Is As Beauty Dies*
Filmed: February 1973
Stars: Peter Falk, Vera Miles, Martin Sheen, Sian Barbara Allen, Vincent Price
Director: Jeannot Szwarc
Producer: Douglas Benton
Teleplay: Jackson Gillis
Story: Myrna Bercovici
Air Date: Sept. 23, 1973
Nielsen Ranking: #18 (21.3 points, 33 share)

Any Old Port in a Storm
Working Titles: *Any Old Port, Any Port in a Storm*
Filmed: March 7 – 20, 1973
Guest Stars: Donald Pleasence, Joyce Jillson, Julie Harris
Director: Leo Penn
Producer: Robert F. O'Neill
Teleplay: Stanley Ralph Ross
Story: Larry Cohen
Air Date: Oct. 7, 1973
Ranking: #7 (24.4 points, 37 share)

Candidate for Crime
Working Titles: *Candidate for Murder, Candidate for a Crime*
Filming Completed: October 1973
Guest Stars: Jackie Cooper, Joanne Linville, Tisha Sterling
Director: Boris Sagal
Executive Producers: Dean Hargrove & Roland Kibbee
Teleplay: Irv Pearlberg, Alvin R. Friedman, Roland Kibbee & Dean Hargrove
Story: Larry Cohen
Air Date: Nov. 4, 1973
Ranking: #4 (29.8 points, 45 share)

Double Exposure
Working Title: *Motivation for Murder*
Filming Started: October 1973
Guest Stars: Robert Culp, Robert Middleton, Chuck McCann, Louise Latham
Director: Richard Quine
Executive Producers: Dean Hargrove & Roland Kibbee
Teleplay: Stephen J. Cannell
Air Date: Dec. 16, 1973
Ranking: #4

Publish or Perish
Filmed: November 1973
Guest Stars: Jack Cassidy, Mickey Spillane, Mariette Hartley
Director: Robert Butler
Executive Producers: Dean Hargrove & Roland Kibbee
Teleplay: Peter S. Fischer
Air Date: Jan. 18, 1974
Rating: (37 points)

Mind Over Mayhem
Filmed: December 1973
Guest Stars: Jose Ferrer, Lew Ayres, Robert Walker Jr.
Director: Alf Kjellin
Executive Producers: Dean Hargrove & Roland Kibbee
Teleplay: Steven Bochco, Dean Hargrove & Roland Kibbee
Story: Robert Specht
Air Date: Feb. 10, 1974
Ranking: #11 (35.7 points)

Swan Song
Filmed: Dec. 1973 – Jan. 1974
Guest Stars: Johnny Cash, Ida Lupino
Director: Nicholas Colasanto
Executive Producers: Dean Hargrove & Roland Kibbee
Producer: Edward K. Dodds
Teleplay: David Rayfiel
Story: Stanley Ralph Ross
Air Date: March 3, 1974
Ranking: #1 (46.5 points)

A Friend in Deed
Filmed: Jan. – Feb. 1974
Guest Stars: Richard Kiley, Rosemary Murphy, Michael McGuire, Val Avery
Director: Ben Gazzara
Executive Producers: Dean Hargrove & Roland Kibbee
Producer: Edward K. Dodds
Teleplay: Peter S. Fischer
Air Date: May 5, 1974
Rating: (41.7 points)
Ranking: #7

9
The Scene of the Crime

As soon as Levinson and Link set the template of their sloppy sleuth playing off the societal elite, the show quickly established itself as the forerunner of *Lifestyles of the Rich and Famous*. Except for Jarvis Goodland's Colonial mansion in *The Greenhouse Jungle*, which was a front on the Universal backlot, the producers scoured the Hills of Beverly and beaches of Malibu in search of over-the-top opulence befitting a pretentious evildoer.

Most sites were initially identified by Universal's Locations Department. The staff was given a copy of the script and a breakdown of the needed interiors and exteriors. The Locations team would then search the Los Angeles area for matches—and call on agencies that represented clients willing to rent out their homes or buildings. Photos of possible locations were forwarded to the director and producer, who then might lead a team on a scouting trip of their own, to confirm that the settings would indeed work and to begin mapping out the action.

Columbo's producers preferred homes with large entrances, long hallways, big rooms, and panoramic views—all of which accommodated filming and lent the feeling of luxury. Sometimes, a script required a building with exacting features. The mansion in *Lady in Waiting*, for instance, had to have both a ground-floor bedroom with French doors and a canopied front door.

For Season 4's *Playback*, the home needed a private gate with guard shack outside, but inside a specialized, high-tech command center adjacent to a spacious living room, around the corner from an ornate staircase equipped with an elevating platform to carry a wheelchair. In the end, the team had to rent a

FOR *DEAD WEIGHT*, 2 Collins Island in Newport Beach *(behind center palm trees)* was used for the exteriors of General Hollister's waterfront home. The house was rumored to be owned in real life by Peter Falk—a tall tale almost certainly hatched by a confused guide giving tours of Newport Harbor. It actually belonged to Raymond Nemec, an executive with missile manufacturer Nemec Industries. The interiors were shot in Stage 16 at Universal.

Beverly Hills estate for the exterior shots and build the interior on a Universal soundstage.

During one scouting trip, executive location manager Ken Grossman was meeting with a woman at her multimillion-dollar home in Montecito, discussing his upcoming projects. When he mentioned that he needed an ostentatious "fat farm" for *Lovely But Lethal*, she suggested he take a look at her nearby "beach cottage" in Carpinteria. Grossman agreed to swing by, figuring at best he might be able to use it for another shoot. To his amazement, the complex, Grossman said, "was perfect—a castle with beautiful mosaics, an Olympic-sized swimming pool, and several guesthouses. We shot there for three days."

Cost was also a factor. For Season 4's *Negative Reaction*, the murderer's mansion in Glendale was selected primarily because it was luxurious—the plantation-style house was the inspiration for Tara in *Gone with the Wind*. But it also came cheap—it was owned by a missionary in Kenya who was unaware of the going

"The Scene of the Crime"   97

THE LOCATION manager on *Suitable for Framing* must have been attracted to the artwork adorning the exterior of this Bel Air estate while searching for a house for art collector Uncle Rudy. Statuary dots the grounds, including plaques of mythological figures on each side of the entrance gate. Interestingly, while the home used for Aunt Edna's isn't exactly located behind and down a wooded path from Uncle Rudy's house, it is nearby—just beyond and several blocks up the hill. *[Credit: Rebecca Koenig]*

TV rental rates. The director, Alf Kjellin, was also able to save about $10,000 in overtime pay and lighting expenses by staging a junkyard scene during the day, instead of at night. Similarly, he saved a few more thousand by switching a motel scene from night to day. Not all of the savings made it back to Universal—since Kjellin and the Locations team selected the finest restaurants in the area for their scouting meals.

Looks, availability and price were not the only criteria in selecting locations. Also to be considered: Were the doors wide enough to accommodate all the equipment? Were the rooms large enough so scenes could be shot from multiple angles? Was the neighborhood sufficiently quiet? And, did it offer enough parking for the caravan of cars bringing in the cameras, lighting and sound equipment, props and 70-plus cast and crewmembers?

A favorite among *Columbo* producers was the Enchanted Hill, the sprawling blufftop complex above Beverly Hills built in the 1920s by silent film western star

LOCATED 90 minutes from Hollywood, in the small oceanside community of Carpinteria, the Casa Blanca Estate was rented out by the widow of an oil tycoon. The complex's sprawling grounds, cliffside location, and tranquil white Moorish architecture were perfect as the "fat farm" in *Lovely But Lethal*. When Columbo first arrived, he was scripted to remark, "It looks like a resort!" But, after one look at his surroundings, Falk instead adlibbed, "It looks like a temple!"

Fred Thomson and his wife, screenwriter Frances Marion. The 120-acre estate, dotted with hacienda-style buildings, tennis court, stables, horse-riding rings, 100-foot swimming pool, and long winding drive, was used as Clifford Paris' compound in *Double Shock*, Nelson Brenner's hideaway in Season 5's *Identity Crisis*, and then again as Ward Fowler's home in Season 6's *Fade In to Murder*. For the Fowler's villa, art director Michael Baugh explained, "we wanted a gaudy, movie-star-type home, and this was the gaudiest."

More importantly, the property was the easiest to deal with. The owner lived in New York, so he wasn't around to interfere. He also employed his own private location scout to represent the property to studios and negotiate contracts on his behalf. It was regularly used for filming, including on episodes of *Barnaby Jones, Ellery Queen,* and *The Six Million Dollar Man*. The crew was intimately familiar with the property's layout, and appreciated its seclusion, ample private parking, and high, easy-to-light ceilings.

Once the sites were approved, the location manager took care of obtaining

BUILT IN 1922, the 5,698-square foot Mattison Boyd Jones house in Glendale was rented below market as the Galesko mansion in *Negative Reaction*. The cheap fees did not last long. In the 1980s, the home became a popular filming location for several TV series and the movie *National Lampoon's Christmas Vacation*.

contracts, filming permits, and consent forms signed by the residents. He also arranged for cast and crew parking, and hired needed security, police and fire personnel. Once production began, the unit production manager oversaw use of the property.

Estate rental fees for *Columbo* usually ran $1,000 to $1,500 a day, sometimes less if only the exterior was needed. The studio also insured each property for $1 million against injury to person or property. Floors and carpets were most at risk, so the crew typically laid down a special protective covering before rolling in the cameras.

Nonetheless, commonplace were dirtied carpets, floor scratches, banged walls, trampled flowerbeds, and the occasional broken window. Once filming was completed, a clean-up crew arrived to make any repairs to the owner's satisfaction. The Pasadena home used in Season 5's *Forgotten Lady* cost $2,000 a day to rent— plus another $30,000 to cover damages.

Pilferage wasn't a serious problem. There was actually a greater probability of

ENCHANTED HILL, the opulent hilltop Spanish Hacienda-style estate completed in 1925 by silent film power couple Fred Thomson and Frances Marion, was used in *Double Shock*, *Identity Crisis*, and *Fade In to Murder*. In 1997, the entire 120-acre complex was acquired for $20 million—and promptly leveled—by Microsoft co-founder Paul Allen. *[Credit: Los Angeles Herald Examiner Photo Collection, Los Angeles Public Library]*

GREENACRES, the 44-room mansion of early film comedian Harold Lloyd, doubled as the Suarian Embassy in *A Case of Immunity*. The library, replete with Lloyd's personal book collection, furniture and painting of Louis XIV above the fireplace, served as the First Secretary's office in the episode. *[Credit: Los Angeles Herald Examiner Photo Collection, Los Angeles Public Library]*

something getting stolen off a set at the studio. On *Requiem for a Falling Star*, a visitor carried off an expensive chess set right past the watchful eye of a backlot security guard. He had assumed the thief was authorized to take it.

The filmmakers encouraged residents to lock up any antiques or other highly prized items. Sometimes, the homeowners' actual furniture was used. Just as often, the set decorators brought in their own. For *Étude in Black*, a black baby grand piano was replaced with a white baby grand, which was thought to fit in better with the Maestro's tastes.

Other times, an entire room might be redressed. For *Double Shock*, the Enchanted Hill's owner approved of the crew repainting and installing new flooring in a back room to convert it into a home gym—all paid for by the studio, of course.

Universal's Prop Department held hundreds of thousands of furnishings, yet the *Columbo* team was typically drawing from the same requirements from one episode to the next. It wasn't unusual for multiple murderers to share the

ALTHOUGH the script called for a seaside winery, *Any Old Port in a Storm* made use of the now-abandoned Brookside Winery in Guasti, near the Ontario Airport in Southern California's Inland Empire.

same artwork, fireplace screens, and draperies. Even the iconic painting of Mrs. Melville from Ken Franklin's office in *Murder by the Book* was reused to adorn the walls of the Sigma Society in Season 7's *The Bye-Bye Sky High I.Q. Murder Case*.

To keep things fresh, beginning during Season 4, the producers looked for excuses to send Columbo to new settings, far from the manors of Bel Air. Yet the character always seemed to work best when, no matter where he was, he looked like a fish out of water.

10
Turbulence Ahead

Heading into 1974, decorated with another Emmy and riding high on strong ratings, *Columbo* was at the top of its game. Falk, too, had truly perfected the character. That spring, he finished shooting on *Mikey and Nicky* and returned to California in ample time to begin the show's fourth season.

An Exercise in Fatality

Peter Fischer, officially on board as story editor, had a finished script waiting. In *An Exercise in Fatality*, fitness celebrity Milo Janus murders one of his health spa franchisees who discovers that Janus has been overcharging his partners and diverting the cash to a Swiss bank account.

To play Janus, the script called for "a man of 58 (who) appears 20 years younger—lithe and trim" and who "has parlayed a set of Olympic gold medals some 30 years earlier into a career as an actor, entrepreneur and franchise operator." Robert Conrad (*The Wild Wild West*) agreed to take the part, even though he was rankled at the age of his character. In reality, Conrad was only 39. The script made him nearly 10 years older than Falk instead of 10 years younger. As a compromise, Janus' age was changed to 53.

Fischer turned in a solid script, but it did have to be stretched to reach two hours. Falk saw an opportunity to expand the running time in a scene in which Columbo goes to Tricon Industries looking for a possible witness who used to work there. As scripted, the clerk at the front desk was to input the name into a computer keyboard, and "Columbo watches *in fascination* as the machine starts to type out a resume as we see computer reels spinning in the background."

It reminded Falk of a scene in *Blueprint for Murder*, where he got good mileage out of barely controlling his frustration at being forced to wait in one long line after another at the building permit office. So instead of fascination, Falk feigned impatience waiting for the printout, drumming his fingers, rubbing his furrowed brow, pacing around, and badgering the clerk. Unfortunately, he milked the routine for three solid minutes.

In another scene more amusingly extended by Falk's mugging, Columbo questions Janus in his backyard following an exhausting run on the beach. Columbo doubles over trying to catch his breath, discovers sand in his shoes, and breaks a shoelace trying to retie them. According to the script, "his surroundings are so immaculate, it would be improper to dump the sand on the patio," so Columbo instead was to empty the contents into his raincoat pocket. Falk ad-libbed instead sneakily jettisoning the sand behind his back, into the flowerbeds.

The episode now contained so much padding, one cute scene had to be deleted, where Columbo would have visited a luxury-car showroom to check on Janus' alibi. The two well-groomed salesmen stare in disbelief when Columbo steps out of the Peugeot. "You think he's really a customer?" one asks.

"I don't know. That *car*...."

The conversation would have run just over two minutes, but was unnecessary since in the very next scene Columbo briefly recounts what he learned at the dealership. Just as importantly, Fischer had included a similar setup at a used-car lot in his previous script, *A Friend in Deed*.

On *An Exercise in Fatality*, Eddie Dodds retained the title of producer, but Hargrove and Kibbee knew that he was not a long-term solution. There was also suspicion that Falk was overdue for his annual contract tussle. So proactively they brought back Falk's friend and Season 1 producer Everett Chambers to produce the remaining five shows of Season 4. Universal insisted Dodds stay on as associate producer. To ensure a smooth start, Hargrove and Kibbee left Chambers with seven completed and approved scripts, plus 12 more story outlines, 10 of them by Larry Cohen.

Negative Reaction

Nearly ready to film was another Peter Fischer gem. In *Negative Reaction*, henpecked photographer Paul Galesko kills his wife and pretends that she has been kidnapped. Galesko then kills an ex-con, making it look like self-defense, so he can pin the kidnapping on him.

Upon returning to *Columbo*, Chambers soon realized that his decisions no longer had to be approved by just Universal and the executive producers. Now he also had to listen to NBC and, in particular, Falk. He faced immediate pushback

EVER SINCE he wandered into an art class during the Broadway run of *The Prisoner of Second Avenue*, Falk became fascinated with drawing, including while waiting between scenes of *Columbo*.

when trying to cast the hot-tempered Galesko. Chambers and NBC liked Anthony Franciosa; Universal did not. NBC wanted a more familiar face, like Bill Bixby, Darren McGavin, or Tony Curtis. Falk wanted Peter Sellers, but his $360,000 fee was impossible to meet. The show had never paid a guest star more than $20,000. Falk said he would reluctantly settle for Chambers' more interesting but less marketable suggestions—Robert Duvall, Maximilian Schell, Oskar Werner, or Patrick McGoohan. NBC countered with Glenn Ford or Omar Sharif, but either would have blown up the budget: Ford demanded $50,000; Sharif insisted on $100,000. Chambers also suggested Louis Jourdan, Christopher Plummer, or Martin Balsam. The only name Universal, Falk and NBC could seem to agree on was John Cassavetes, who wasn't interested. Ultimately, Chambers proposed a name everyone could back, even though he had never before played a heavy: Dick Van Dyke.

"I'd seen him in a movie where he played a recovering alcoholic (*The Morning After*), which he was, and he was very good. He'd just come off his show (*The New Dick Van Dyke Show*)," Chambers said. "He was a star. I knew he could act. He did a *Hitchcock (Presents)*, so I knew him to be a competent actor. And I thought it was a kind of a coup. Most people thought I was crazy. But he was very good in it."

Between takes, Falk spent much of his time on the phone yelling at the moneymen in The Black Tower. He felt underpaid. He thought the studio was skimping on the show's budget. He was unhappy with his transportation—including a car, chauffeured limousine, and motorized dressing room. He didn't like how most of the new scripts were being written for a two-hour timeslot. He wanted shows held to a tight 90 minutes. He also felt that *Columbo* had caused his movie career to stall. Falk was convinced that Jack Lemmon got the lead in the film version of *The Prisoner of Second Avenue* because producers couldn't see Columbo in the role. If he were forced to be unhappy, someone would have to pay him for the displeasure.

On the eighth day of filming on *Negative Reaction*, Falk's lawyers notified Universal that the studio had violated his three-year contract by habitually paying him late, in their eyes nullifying their deal. He had had enough. He claimed his $132,777 fee for *An Exercise in Fatality*, due two weeks earlier, still had not been paid. Universal promptly delivered his check, which Falk refused to accept. Three days later, Falk filed suit against Universal in Los Angeles Superior Court for breach of contract. He wanted out. As a favor to Hargrove and Chambers, he agreed to complete *Negative Reaction* before he left.

"Peter feels that working conditions have deteriorated so badly that he can't continue with the series," his attorney said. "They've always been five or six days late with Peter's checks, which is not an unusual situation at Universal. But this one was two weeks overdue."

The studio responded that the contract contained no such provision, and it was confident that Falk would return. Universal president Sid Sheinberg told reporters: "What are his chances of winning? You can quote me on this: his chances range from zero to minus zero percent." Sheinberg figured they could space out the two already-shot *Columbos* and make up the shortfall with additional episodes of *McCloud, McMillan & Wife*, and new entry *Amy Prentiss*.

The stalemate dragged on for over four weeks until, among other concessions, Universal agreed to increase Falk's pay by $45,000 per episode and to hold two of the remaining four episodes at 90 minutes long.

By Dawn's Early Light

The contract dispute delayed by more than six weeks the start of filming on the next show, *By Dawn's Early Light*. Howard Berk's script featured Colonel Rumford, the commandant of a military academy, killing the founder's grandson, who had planned to convert the all-male school into a co-ed junior college. After seriously considering Jack Warden and Richard Basehart, Chambers hired Ed Asner to play the murderous Colonel during a break from *The Mary Tyler Moore Show*. But Falk's delays angered Asner, and he dropped out.

With time short, Chambers thought this might be his opportunity to use Irish-American actor Patrick McGoohan, who had starred in two British spy series—*Danger Man* (*Secret Agent*) and the eclectic *The Prisoner*—and had been on Chambers' short list since Season 1. The producer met McGoohan for lunch. Chambers could tell that the actor was more interested in appearing in films than on television. So he proposed that starring in a prestige show like *Columbo* would raise McGoohan's profile in the U.S. and result in more movie offers.

NBC was against the casting, arguing that McGoohan was not well enough known in the States. Indeed, Falk would have the final say, but he had never seen *The Prisoner*. In fact, he didn't really know who McGoohan was. But Chambers was so insistent that he was perfect for the role, Falk consented.

All of the action took place at a military academy, so the locations team scouted four possible sites in Southern California. Ridgewood Academy in Woodland Hills didn't look sufficiently impressive. Southern California Military Academy in Long Beach had more pavement than manicured grounds. St. Catherine's Military Academy in Anaheim was a bit of a drive and had a mix of architectural styles. Harvard School for Boys in Los Angeles appeared to be the best match visually and geographically. But a deal couldn't be struck. Dick Irving had an

ON LOCATION at The Citadel in South Carolina, producer Everett Chambers *(left)* and director Harvey Hart *(right)* wait to resume filming *By Dawn's Early Light*. In the background, actor Burr DeBenning sits on the side of a forklift. *[Credit: Everett Chambers]*

idea. His wife's brother, State Senator James Waddell, had attended The Citadel, a state-supported military college in Charleston, South Carolina. The script fit perfectly with the academy's distinctive Spanish marsh architecture, replete with towers, turrets and massive fortress-like masonry, and its regiments of eyes-forward cadets. And the Senator had plenty of pull within his state to get the school to say yes.

The Citadel permitted the TV crew to take over the campus from early August until early September, shortly before classes were to resume for the fall semester. Universal paid the school both to rent the facilities and for permission to film the cadets.

Instead of directly compensating the cadets who served as nonspeaking extras, Universal made a "sizable donation" to the institution, which the school applied to the cost of 500 students going to Annapolis for the upcoming Citadel-Navy football game. The 227 cadets who participated in the filming traveled to the Naval Academy all expenses paid; the others paid $20 each.

A caravan of more than 60 actors, crewmen and production executives flew from Southern California to South Carolina, while a fleet of trucks and cars made the drive, carrying equipment and props, ranging from Columbo's Peugeot to his raincoat (and its four backups). They planned for 17 shooting days, from 7 a.m. to 6 p.m.

The crew had the full run of the entire campus. Even the academy president, Lt. General (Ret.) George Seignious, turned his office over to Universal, to use as Colonel's Rumford's quarters. Seignious took up temporary residence in a smaller space down the hall.

Shortly after arriving in Charleston, McGoohan asked Falk if they could discuss the script together. McGoohan had a habit of writing—or rewriting—almost everything he appeared in. He admitted that, as a guest star, he knew it wasn't his place to take over, but he thought the script was missing one scene crucial to the story and to his character. McGoohan wanted to illustrate how important—and twisted—Rumford's code of honor and justice was to him. The audience should see that the Colonel feels fully justified in his killing, even as he encourages Columbo to seek justice in arresting the cadet he has framed. McGoohan asked Falk's permission to write the scene and run it past him. Falk immediately sensed that McGoohan knew what he was talking about. Without hesitation, Falk gave his blessing and they worked the new conversation into a scene in the mess hall.

Falk was doubly reassured as soon as they started working together. "I remember the first time I walked on the set, and we started rehearsing," Falk said. "I was so aware of the presence of this other actor. He commanded your attention. He was formidable. You were vividly aware of him. That turns an ordinary encounter into something electric. Something that has tension. I was aware of that the first time he opened his mouth. I was surprised by it and taken off guard by it, but I was delighted by it! It excited me."

According to Chambers, McGoohan wrote additional dialogue for the scene in which "he and Peter were having dinner in the commissary. They had a long scene in which he added a lot of stuff; it was a little too expository for me."

Chambers also cast a buddy of his and Falk's from New York, Bruce Kirby, whom he had earlier considered using as the ex-con, Alvin Deschler, in *Negative Reaction*. Not only did Kirby get the part of Columbo's number two, Sgt. George Kramer, but his son, Bruno Kirby, was hired as a cadet. "I liked Bruce's deadpan character," Chambers said. "He always played a deadpan and it was a good foil for Peter." The producer would encourage the writers to work in Sgt. Kramer whenever possible.

Production proceeded relatively smoothly, despite small problems related to filming in a non-studio environment. The hum of fluorescent lights ruined more than one take. Another scene had to be reshot because the camera picked up a nosy secretary peeking through a window.

During the final days of shooting, the cadets began returning to campus from summer vacation and, seeing McGoohan in uniform, mistook him for an officer. "It was really quite amusing," McGoohan recounted. "Most of the returning cadets who weren't aware we were filming and that I was an actor, saluted when they saw me. But I just ignored them." The cadets in turn remained at attention. "A cadet can't bring his arm down from a salute until the salute is returned. All those cadets (were) just standing there, wondering why I hadn't saluted them."

When someone finally explained the military rules to McGoohan, he began returning the salute—and estimated he did so about 2,000 times over the remainder of his stay.

Playback

Once back in California, the team segued right into the next show. In *Playback*, electronics wizard Harold Van Wyck has been mismanaging his mother-in-law's corporation. He spends his time chasing women and the company's money splurging on high-tech gadgets, mostly to create a security fortress to protect his invalid wife. When her mother demands his resignation, Van Wyck plots to videotape her getting shot and play the tape over the security monitor once he's safely away at an art gallery reception.

Chambers and Falk quickly agreed on who should play the invalid wife—their mutual friend, Gena Rowlands. The producer's suggestion for Van Wyck, however, was more unconventional—Oskar Werner. Aloof and morose, the Viennese actor had risen to modest fame in the mid-1960s in such critically acclaimed films as *Ship of Fools*, *The Spy Who Came in from the Cold*, and *Fahrenheit 451*. But Werner's pickiness in choosing roles and his disruptive behavior on the set, usually brought on by his heavy drinking, had all but ended his career. Though just 51, Werner hadn't had a movie credit in seven years and had never appeared on series television. He was living as a relative recluse on his farm in Liechtenstein.

Undeterred, Chambers submitted a request through Werner's agent in Luxembourg. The following day, Werner himself called back and agreed to read the script. To encourage him to sign, Falk personally phoned the farm in Lichtenstein. "I told him I do not do TV," Werner recalled. "Generally, TV lacks something for me, the quality feeling, so I don't do it." But Falk was persuasive, offering several extra perks, such as having Universal provide him with a cottage at the Beverly Hills Hotel for the length of his visit in America.

On the Thursday evening that the actor was supposed to fly into Los Angeles

International Airport, Chambers got a call at home from an indignant Werner. "Where are you?" the actor demanded to know. "Where is the director? Where is the writer? Why aren't you here?"

Confused, Chambers asked, "Where are you?"

"I'm at the airport, waiting to be picked up."

Chambers had to break him the news: "Well, we don't pick up actors at the airport. Take a taxi."

After a dramatic pause, Werner concluded, "I'll see you tomorrow at my cottage at 8:30. Be there."

Chambers arrived on time—only to be dressed down by Werner. "I am not a prostitute!" the actor bellowed. "I am not a whore! You cannot treat me like this…," continuing on and on, until Chambers, himself boiling, interrupted: "I'm not gonna take this. You can go back on the plane and go home." Chambers stormed out. But by the time he made it to the hotel lobby, he realized the gravity of his mistake. Chambers quickly phoned Falk and the director, Bernie Kowalski, explaining how he had lost his temper and cursed out their guest star. "We're gonna lose the actor. Get to the Beverly Hills Hotel and kiss Oskar Werner's ass."

Falk and Kowalski hurried over to the hotel, just as Werner was getting into a car to drive off. "Oh, hello, Peter!" Werner greeted, cheerily. "I'll see you soon." And off he drove, as if nothing had happened a half-hour earlier.

Chambers recalled, "Oskar Werner was a very unique actor and that's why I wanted him, because I thought he was one of the best actors around. But he was a very strange person. He was an alcoholic. He used to carry a little bag with him that had two bottles of wine in it that he would drink."

Certainly, during the first few days of shooting, Werner seemed off. He had so much trouble memorizing his lines that the beginning of his first scene with Falk could not be filmed as an extended two-shot. The director had to yell, "Cut" after every line. Instead, the start of the scene had to be filmed as a quick series of medium shots of just Werner saying his line, then just Falk saying his lines, back and forth.

On about the third day of shooting, Chambers got an emergency call from Dick Irving in The Tower: "Your star is drunk on the set. Go take care of it." Chambers arrived to find Werner plastered, unable to work.

"Dick Irving was married to a notorious alcoholic," Chambers said. "He knew from a lifetime you don't 'take care' of alcoholics. I just went down and suspended shooting. There's nothing you can do. He's just got to go sleep it off and come back tomorrow. And I never said one word to him. I was married to an alcoholic. I know you don't handle it that way. You don't chastise him. That's just what they want. I never said one word to him. He never touched another drop again, just that one day. I guess he tested us. And, of course, that behavior when he arrived, he was probably loaded on the plane and got up in the morning half-stewed. He and I became friends after that. We partied at Jack Cassidy's house."

The episode, however, did fall several more days behind schedule because Falk decided he was displeased with the script as he was performing it, particularly a brief scene in which he visits an art gallery to confirm Van Wyck's alibi.

"Sometimes I'd get a call and I'd go down to the set because Peter was unhappy with what was going on," Hargrove said. "On *Playback*, Peter had a problem with one scene and I just couldn't get through to him. It was a short page-and-a-half scene, and he said, 'I've got a problem with this scene, I don't know what I'm going to do. Well, I'm gonna go home and think about it.' And then he came in the next day and he had a four-page scene to replace the one-and-a-half-page scene, and it went on and on and on. It was terrible. So we just let it go, because it was Peter, and Peter was running the show."

As scripted, Columbo was supposed to ask the art gallery manager to explain a painting to him. She responds that you can't explain art—"it's just something you feel." So he points out a framed object on the wall, and declares, "That other one I don't care for—but this one—well, it's very simple. Very easy for me to understand."

Stunned, the manager reveals that the "sculpture" is an air vent. Columbo shrugs, explaining that he doesn't see much difference between it and some of the "real" sculptures nearby.

Falk thought they were missing a golden opportunity. He instead had Columbo pester the manager for nearly three minutes, inquiring about and reacting to the names, meanings and prices of three different pieces of modern art. He notices a fourth piece on the wall doesn't have a title and is embarrassed to learn it's the ventilator.

Troubled Waters

The next script in line to be filmed was Steven Bochco's tale of a deadly dentist, *Uneasy Lies the Crown*. Ben Gazzara signed to direct, but Falk had reservations about building an episode around a dentist. Gazzara consented to film *Troubled Waters* instead. The idea of placing Columbo on a cruise ship was Jackson Gillis', inspired by a recent episode of *Hawaii Five-O* about a bad guy being pursued aboard a Pacific Far East Line cruise between Hawaii and San Francisco.

Gillis' treatment was expanded into a full script by Bill Driskill, a seasoned TV freelancer who cut his teeth on *Highway Patrol* in the late 1950s. At Falk's insistence, Peter Fischer then rewrote Driskill's script—over and over and over again. Since the story required the perpetrator to have a portable key duplicator, the murderer, Hayden Danziger, became a used-car dealer. Yet Used-Car Dealer lacked the gravitas of traditional *Columbo* murderers. So to give the role an extra dash of class, Chambers hired Robert Vaughn, best known for *The Man from U.N.C.L.E.*

As associate producer, Eddie Dodds contacted Pacific Far East Line about filming aboard one of their Hawaiian cruises. The cruise line declined. "After reviewing the script, I do not feel that it is compatible with the image we strive to establish for our ships," Pacific Far East's advertising manager replied. "I must add that we did have some anxious moments about *Hawaii Five-O* as well, but at least in that case the crime was not committed on the ship. Furthermore, the ship and company have just so recently been associated with this type of episode (*Hawaii Five-O*) that it does seem a bit much to have another similar one follow so soon."

Fortunately, British shipping and cruise company P&O had recently purchased the Princess Cruise Line and was looking to make a splash in the U.S. At that moment, its 760-passenger *Spirit of London* was docked in Vancouver and being remodeled into the *Sun Princess*. Its maiden voyage—a 12-day cruise from San Francisco to Mexico—was slated to depart at almost exactly the time the studio had hoped to begin filming.

In late September, three weeks before filming was to begin, Chambers and Gazzara led an eight-man contingent that flew into Vancouver to look the ship over, confirm it would work for their needs, and begin planning where each scene would be filmed. They realized everything checked out, except the cabins, which were too small to accommodate all of the crew and equipment. Instead, they would have a row of cabins that opened onto a fake corridor built on a soundstage at Universal and shoot all interior-cabin scenes in the days before the ship departed.

Universal and P&O quickly struck a deal—the TV crews would be permitted to film throughout the ship, so long as they didn't interfere with the trip's normal operations. The noise of Universal's large portable generators was not to bother the passengers. The cruise line should be promoted in the script and in establishing shots of the ship. The script should also be tweaked to prevent the audience from thinking that someone could easily break into their cabin. (As the Captain requested, "I would ask that the way in which Danziger obtains the master keys is by a method which must be nothing less than a miracle for we have had enough trouble with master keys in the past and I would hate the public to get the wrong idea!") In addition, the studio would be charged rack rate for 32 cabins to house the 50 members of the cast and crew. The two largest suites were

Cruise to Mexico from San Francisco on the Sun Princess.

She leaves Oct. 17.

A great lady—the Spirit of London—becomes a Princess. The Sun Princess. Along with her new name, she's decked out in Princess style. You'll discover that the atmosphere and cuisine are decidedly continental. The registry and officers are British, and very anxious to make you feel at home.

The Sun Princess is ready to celebrate with a debut cruise to the Mexican Riviera. You can join the party for 12 days of fun.

You'll sample the many moods of Mexico. Jet-set resorts—like Acapulco. Sleepy, sunny villages—like Manzanillo. During the cruise, an episode for the popular "Columbo" TV series will be filmed. Peter Falk will be aboard to add drama to your sea adventure.

Can't get away Oct. 17? Take the 12 day cruise to Mexico Oct. 29. It departs—and returns—to San Francisco. Or sail from San Francisco Nov. 10, cruise to Mexico, then fly home from Acapulco or any Mexican port. On the November cruise, Harry James will be aboard to entertain you in Big Band fashion.

The Sun Princess is the only cruise ship sailing to Mexico from San Francisco this fall.

Last Inside Passage Cruise in '74.
For Oct. 12, we've put together a 5 day package. It includes: Your flight from San Francisco to Vancouver. A 3 day cruise to British Columbia's breath-taking Inside Passage. A city tour of Vancouver. Then a 2 day cruise back to San Francisco, arriving Oct. 17. Contact your travel agent now for more information.

Princess Cruises, 278 Post St., 20 Mezzanine, San Francisco, California 94108. (415) 421-8715
Please send me literature on ☐ Sun Princess to Mexico ☐ Princess Tours ☐ Caribbean/ S. America

Name
Address
City   State   Zip
My Travel Agent   N-97-9-15

PRINCESS CRUISES promoted the *Columbo* connection for the inaugural sailing of the *Sun Princess*.

held for Mr. and Mrs. Peter Falk and Mr. and Mrs. Robert Vaughn.

The cruise line immediately started advertising that travelers should book the Columbo Cruise. The passengers did have to agree to the possibility of becoming accidental extras, in the event the camera caught them in the background of a scene.

"We had to work around the activities of the cruise," Chambers recounted. "This was a plus for the people who were taking the cruise, but a difficulty for us because the (stage employees union) said you had to have your hours consecutive and then it's overtime after that. We always had to shoot things that were available—the dining room, the rec room, a bar, the theater, the deck, whatever, when it was not in use by the crew for the passengers. So we would shoot sometimes for three to four hours, and then stop for two or three hours before we could shoot again. So some of the crew would get paid for 20 hours with 12 hours of overtime."

During the return trip to San Francisco, as the ship made its way back up the California coast, a violent storm hit. Chambers said, "We were still shooting on a rocky ship. Half the crew got sick. Ben Gazzara got sick, but he kept going anyway."

Falk was among those who, once they finished their final scenes, spent the remainder of the bumpy voyage in their cabins, under the weather.

Early versions of the script contained a running gag in which the audience narrowly misses seeing Mrs. Columbo. The writers toyed with the idea of finally showing her in the last scene, but in the end opted to keep her unseen. In one draft, Columbo, having just solved the crime, decides to fetch his wife and explore the port. As he enters the cabin, his head down, there's a middle-aged woman in front of the mirror, brushing her hair. Before looking up, Columbo says, "Come on, honey, we'll go ashore."

"I beg your pardon," the woman replies, indignantly.

"Oh!" Columbo says, clutching his head. "Where's my wife? Isn't this C53?"

"This is the port side, C52."

Columbo apologizes and retreats sheepishly, as the woman stares him down. We cut to Columbo walking down the gangway amid a crowd of fellow passengers, when he sees a familiar face and waves. "Honey! Wait for me!" and the camera freezes on his wave.

In the final version, while we still never see Mrs. Columbo, the running joke was changed to Columbo constantly mixing up the terms "ship" and "boat."

Meanwhile, the *NBC Mystery Movie's* fourth season was off to a strong start in the ratings, despite threats that the competition would try to out-*Columbo Columbo*. The previous season, CBS had moved its highly rated series *Cannon* up an hour to 9:00 Wednesday nights to compete against *Banacek* and the rest of NBC's *Wednesday Mystery Movie* lineup. More impactfully, CBS followed *Cannon* with a new cop show clearly inspired by *Columbo*—*Kojak*. But whereas Falk's character was shaggy and unassuming, sucking a cigar, Telly Savalas' was bald, buttoned-up and intense, sucking a lollipop. *Kojak* was a sensation, regularly winning not only its timeslot, but becoming the highest-rated 10 p.m. show on television. In response, NBC tried moving its battered Wednesday wheel to Tuesdays, before finally pulling the plug.

For the fall of 1974, CBS had an even bigger target in mind. The network moved *Kojak* to 8:30 Sunday nights. Falk was unfazed by the news. He conceded that the competition would harm his ratings, but he fully expected *Kojak's* numbers to suffer even more. He said he was 100 percent confident that *Columbo* would be renewed. "You can make book," Falk said. "*Columbo* will survive the season. It'll do more than that. My deal calls for me to be back in the fall of '75—and I see no reason why I won't be."

As the season premiere, *An Exercise in Fatality* would face not only *Kojak* on CBS, but also the first run of *Fiddler on the Roof* on ABC. Critics predicted *Fiddler* would win the timeslot, followed by *Kojak*. *Columbo* won handily, ranking as the week's tenth most-watched program. *Fiddler* came in No. 15. *Kojak*? No. 32.

Week by week, though, *Kojak* did build an audience. By season's end, *Kojak* would on average outperform the *NBC Mystery Movie* wheel as a whole, but lose when it went against a first-run *Columbo*.

A Deadly State of Mind

As the calendar changed to 1975, Hargrove and Kibbee were ready to depart *Columbo*. They could see the show was in capable hands with Chambers. They had a TV movie (*Long Way Home*) and two proposed series (*McCoy* and *The Family Holvak*) lined up. In the years ahead, Kibbee would produce *A.E.S. Hudson Street*, *Dear Detective*, and *Barney Miller*. After joining Kibbee on *Dear Detective*, Hargrove would go on to create *Father Dowling Mysteries*, *Matlock*, *Jake and the Fatman*, *Diagnosis: Murder*, and 29 *Perry Mason* specials.

Once he became sole producer on the show, Chambers was comfortable with green-lighting the first script generated under his leadership—*A Deadly State of Mind* by Peter Fischer. In the tale, psychiatrist Marcus Collier has been using drugs and hypnosis to study the mind of his patient/lover Nadia so he can write a book. But when confronted by Nadia's husband, Collier and the man fight, and he kills him with a poker. Collier then concocts a story about burglars for Nadia to tell the police. When Nadia's lies start unraveling, Collier hypnotizes her into leaping from her fifth-story balcony.

Fischer created a tight, suspenseful plot, but had one big problem. He didn't know how to end it. Dick Levinson had an idea he had earlier suggested for *Any Old Port in a Storm* and other episodes, but it never quite fit in. What if there was an eyewitness to the crime who was blind? As the murderer fled the crime scene, he'd narrowly avoid hitting the blind man out walking his dog. After learning someone was almost struck by a speeding car about the time of the murder, Columbo would tell the killer he has a witness who can tie him to the scene of the crime. In walks the blind man's non-visually impaired brother. The murderer would then accuse him of being blind—something only the person fleeing the scene would have said. The pop worked perfectly for *A Deadly State of Mind*.

Falk was even more methodical than usual while filming the episode. Chambers recalled shooting Columbo's investigation of the suicide at a condominium complex in Redondo Beach on a night that Falk caused to go on forever. "We were shooting near the ocean on location at night, and it was colder than hell," Chambers said.

The episode, scheduled to film in 10 days, took 16, according to co-star George Hamilton, "because Falk is a perfectionist."

But *one* extra week? Falk was just warming up.

Season 4 – 1974-1975

An Exercise in Fatality
Filmed: May 15 – June 4, 1974
Stars: Peter Falk, Robert Conrad, Gretchen Corbett, Pat Harrington Jr.
Director: Bernard Kowalski
Executive Producers: Dean Hargrove & Roland Kibbee
Producer: Edward K. Dodds
Teleplay: Peter S. Fischer
Story: Larry Cohen
Air Date: Sept. 15, 1974
Nielsen Ranking: #10 (36 points)

Negative Reaction
Filmed: June 7 – 24, 1974
Guest Stars: Dick Van Dyke, Don Gordon, Larry Storch, Joyce Van Patten
Director: Alf Kjellin
Executive Producers: Dean Hargrove & Roland Kibbee
Producer: Everett Chambers
Teleplay: Peter S. Fischer
Air Date: Oct. 6, 1974
Ranking: #10 (36.8 points)

By Dawn's Early Light
Filmed: Aug. 12 – 31, 1974
Guest Stars: Patrick McGoohan, Burr DeBenning, Bruce Kirby, Bruno Kirby
Director: Harvey Hart
Executive Producers: Dean Hargrove & Roland Kibbee
Producer: Everett Chambers
Teleplay: Howard Berk
Air Date: Oct. 27, 1974
Ranking: #28 (28 points)

Troubled Waters
Working Title: *The Cruise*
Filmed: Oct. 9 – 30, 1974
Guest Stars: Robert Vaughn, Jane Greer, Dean Stockwell
Director: Ben Gazzara
Executive Producers: Dean Hargrove & Roland Kibbee
Producer: Everett Chambers
Teleplay: William Driskill
Story: Jackson Gillis, William Driskill
Air Date: Feb. 9, 1975
Ranking: #24 (28.7 points)

Playback
Filmed: September 1974
Guest Stars: Oskar Werner, Gena Rowlands
Director: Bernard Kowalski
Executive Producers: Dean Hargrove & Roland Kibbee
Producer: Everett Chambers
Teleplay: David P. Lewis & Booker T. Bradshaw (& Robert Presnell uncredited)
Air Date: March 2, 1975
Ranking: #11 (39 points)

A Deadly State of Mind
Filmed: January 1975
Guest Stars: George Hamilton, Lesley Ann Warren, Bruce Kirby
Director: Harvey Hart
Producer: Everett Chambers
Teleplay: Peter S. Fischer
Air Date: April 27, 1975
Ranking: #12 (43.3 points)

11
The Peacekeeper

The spring of 1975 lacked the usual fireworks and histrionics Universal had come to expect from Peter Falk. He had enjoyed cutting back to six shows a year during Season 4, and thought several episodes—*By Dawn's Early Light*, *Troubled Waters*, and *Playback*—were among the best he had ever done. Falk was especially intrigued by Patrick McGoohan's suggestion that, since Columbo was such an engaging character, he didn't need to be chained to a formula.

"It would be interesting to take him out of the mystery format," Falk mused at the time. "I think the appeal is in the character, and he would work in any situation."

His one complaint was the need for writing help. "We've got only one permanent writer, Peter Fischer. And it isn't enough," Falk moaned. "No one man can be expected to keep the show fresh and ingenious; to think of hard, original clues; to find delightful twists for the endings; and to come up with clever and formidable criminals. We need more writers and we need more money to hire them."

Privately, Falk knew that Universal had no intention of expanding his show's budget. In fact, at that exact moment, the studio was hatching plans to slash expenditures to the bone on every show it produced. Dick Irving was named vice president in charge of the newly formed Television Productions Controls Division, charged with making sure no production lost money. The studio spent about $240,000 for the typical one-hour drama, but recouped an average of $220,000 from the broadcast network. The studio lost money on every show that it couldn't later syndicate. And a typical episode of *Columbo* cost three times the average.

Irving vowed to cut down overtime shooting, eliminate limousine service for stars, and do away with unnecessary out-of-town shoots and chase sequences. "Luxury and waste will no longer be tolerated on any of our shows," Irving decreed. "Everyone connected with all the 41 hours of product we put on the air each week will be targets of our attack on waste. No show, no individual will be an exception."

The last point was specifically directed at *Columbo*, even though he had enjoyed a good personal relationship with Falk. "I didn't take on this job expecting to be the best-liked man at the studio," Irving said. "Artists, producers and writers will simply have to accept the fact that Universal is undertaking a stiff austerity program. I expect the rest of the industry soon to follow suit, if television is to survive."

The pronouncement, on its face, seemed either absurd or a death wish in light of the battles over *Columbo*. Every episode, every season seemed to get more and more expensive. So before making the announcement, Universal had forewarned NBC that if it were unable to hold *Columbo* to its budget, it would shut down production on the show. NBC knew that without *Columbo*, Sunday nights were lost. It could not risk a production freeze. The network agreed that it would repay Universal for every dollar spent above budget on the show. In the twinkling of an eye, Universal was suddenly freed from being the budget cop. That was now NBC's responsibility. As part of the deal, NBC would provide an on-site liaison who was in charge of making sure any overages were necessary. He would review stories, budgets and all other aspects of production to ensure the show was being produced as efficiently as possible.

NBC looked to Bob Metzler, a longtime screenwriter and production coordinator who since 1955 had volunteered his time to act as business manager for the annual Academy Awards ceremony. He was familiar with all aspects of production, and known as sharp, even-tempered and personable, especially toward superstars with big egos.

Metzler started on March 26, 1975, one week before the first *Columbo* of Season 5 was to begin filming. His first meeting was with Dick Irving, who provided Universal's insight into how things worked on the show, covering five points. First, forget Producer, Director and all the other titles. Peter Falk runs the show. Second, Everett Chambers isn't Irving's or Universal's choice as producer. He's there because Peter wants him there. Third, associate producer Eddie Dodds is the studio's man, secretly informing Irving how things are going during production. Fourth, story editor Peter Fischer is excellent. And fifth, $12,500 is the maximum Universal will pay for any guest star. Paying anything more is Metzler's decision, and NBC must fund the difference.

Irving then introduced Metzler to Levinson and Link, before sending him off to meet with Chambers, who filled him in on the reality on the ground. Chambers had his own list of points waiting for Metzler. First, Chambers said he had arranged to have a temporary office for Metzler on the second floor of his building. Second, he explained that filming a show in 10 days was impossible due to Peter's method of working. Third, Peter Fischer is excellent, but is being stretched too thin. Falk runs him ragged. Irving had already promised Falk and Fischer that they would recruit Bill Driskill as co-story editor. Fourth, Chambers requested a replacement for several members of his production team that had been assigned to him by Universal. And finally, Chambers handed Metzler copies of the three latest scripts to review. Metzler again found the meeting productive and positive, and promised Chambers that he would arrange to have both associate producer Eddie Dodds and the new production manager moved to other projects by the time they had finished their second episode together.

A Case of Immunity

Metzler then took out a red pen and began reviewing the budget for the first script, *A Case of Immunity*. Falk wanted Ben Gazzara to play the murderous Middle Eastern diplomat, and told Dick Irving that Bob Howard, president of NBC, was on board with his choice. But Gazzara wanted $20,000. Metzler knew if he didn't put his foot down on day one, he'd never be able to slow down the escalating costs. He insisted on instead using Hector Elizondo, who was willing to play the part for half the price.

A moment later, a second conflict arose. The script called for the Arab King to depart for the airport by taking off from the consulate in a helicopter. Chambers argued that it would play better, as "a proper farewell to the King," if instead he and his entourage boarded a Learjet at the Burbank Airport—for an additional $8,000 to rent the jet and $5,000 for more extras. Metzler refused.

Ominously, starting on the first day of production, stormy weather limited shooting through the first week at the Harold Lloyd Estate, which was being used as the consulate. Each morning that Metzler arrived at the location he discovered that shooting was also delayed because Falk arrived at his leisure and learned the script on the fly, then frequently broke off to discuss it with the story editor. On day one, Metzler learned that Universal staff had overruled him and allowed Chambers to rent the Learjet. Metzler was furious.

On day two, Irving called Metzler to inform him that Falk was refusing to work until 25 more extras were hired to fill out the crowd at a garden party scene. Metzler was again irate and insisted that "such unprofessionalism should be cause for suspension." He rushed to the set, where Chambers and Dodds did their best to try to calm him down, explaining that the request for more extras came from the director, Ted Post, not Falk. Metzler pulled Post aside and explained that there was no need for that many extras—all he had to do was change to a narrower camera angle. Post disagreed; he thought the scene needed more production value.

Eventually, other studio executives joined the argument, attempting to shift the blame back on Falk, complaining about how the actor constantly thought up new ways to slow down production solely out of spite toward the studio. But after watching Falk work those first days, the more Metzler heard, the less he believed. "I think (Falk's) meticulousness is being misinterpreted, plus (it's) character assassination by Universal," Metzler said. "Falk IS slow and meticulous, but I have seen no signs of vindictiveness. The 10-day schedule is unrealistic for him—but Universal wants to standardize all NBC shows."

Metzler requested that Universal compile a survey of all 90-minute shows for *Columbo's* first four seasons—budget vs. final costs, and schedule vs. actual shooting time. He believed that if *Columbo* had never come in on time and at budget, perhaps the problem was indeed unrealistic expectations by Universal. The report convinced him more than ever that there was no practical way to shorten the schedule; any cost-savings would have to come from spending less on a daily basis.

Indeed, as each day passed, the production fell another page or two behind schedule and another several thousand dollars over budget. Metzler wondered if some of the losses could be recouped by expanding the episode to two hours; brief scenes in a bank and travel office had already been cut from the script. Maybe they could be restored, and several new scenes written. But he quickly remembered that Falk had already had Fischer and Driskill revise the script 11 times since production began; this episode might never end if they were to suddenly introduce entirely new scenes. It would remain at 90 minutes.

Now You See Him

Everyone involved had higher hopes for the next episode, which had the unlikeliest of beginnings. With great idea men like Levinson, Link, Hargrove and Kibbee gone, Fischer was left to rely on freelancers for additional story ideas. "Writers came in and pitched stories to me," Fischer said. "But mostly I didn't get the kind of material from these freelancers that I wanted, so I ended up writing several (scripts) myself. It was basically like trying to pull teeth, because they didn't quite understand the concept and I thought it was so painfully obvious."

Out of nowhere, an agent dropped off a story outline from a young, unproduced Londoner, who had written the piece on a lark and was visiting friends in Los

Angeles. According to the young writer, Michael Sloan, "The agent attached a note to my script, indicating that I was a young writer visiting from London, that the agent did *not* represent me, nor did he have any interest in me as a client. But he had promised me he would send the *Columbo* story in to the studio, and he did. His good deed done for the day."

Fischer, to his own amazement, loved the story, which involved a magician who kills a nightclub owner who has been blackmailing him over his Nazi past. Sloan's final clue was particularly clever—Columbo discovers the killer's motive recorded on hammered-out keystrokes on the victim's typewriter ribbon. (The clue was so ingenious that it stayed lodged in the memory of a real-life police detective in Lancaster, Pennsylvania, who a few years later was investigating the disappearance of thousands of dollars from a business. He suspected the office secretary of stealing and forging checks, but had no proof. So he checked her typewriter ribbon—and found the incriminating evidence.)

Fischer called Sloan in, they spent several days working together on it, and then, with notes from Fischer, Sloan fleshed it out to a full script after returning to London.

Sloan recounted, "Ten days later, I sent my first draft teleplay across the Atlantic to Peter Fischer at Universal Studios. A week passed with no word. I was certain Peter *hated* the script and I would never hear from him again… until he called me to say that the teleplay worked great. He changed the title (from *Quicker Than the Eye*) to *Now You See Him*."

The project launched the prolific career of Sloan, who would write for dozens of shows and create several others, including *The Equalizer*. "His career got started," Fischer smiled. "It made me feel good because all us writers help other writers get along. This was my payback for all the people who paid me. It was wonderful."

Orson Welles was the top choice to play the murderous Great Santini by everyone—except Metzler. The cost was already forecast to exceed budget by $53,000, and it would be impossible to hire Welles for less than $20,000. Acceptable alternates were Donald Pleasence, Richard Kiley, Patrick McGoohan, and Jack Cassidy. Metzler volunteered, "I favor Cassidy—suave, svelte, good contrast to slob Columbo." What sealed the deal was Cassidy agreed to the role for half of Welles' rate.

They also hired well-known magician Mark Wilson to design the illusions and tutor Cassidy in sleight of hand. Unfortunately, the schedule allowed for only one day of rehearsals before filming began. Consequently, most of the magic tricks had to be relatively basic so Cassidy had time to learn them—perhaps not up to the level one would expect from a world-class prestidigitator.

The script featured a humorous subplot about Columbo's wife giving him a new raincoat, which he hates. He constantly tries to lose it, but his fellow detective keeps finding it for him. Bob Dishy was perfect for the role, returning as the overeager Sgt. Wilson from *The Greenhouse Jungle*. "Bob Dishy had done one before and I wanted him in this one because the overcoat was a good schtick, good for him to play it," Everett Chambers said. Dishy and Falk played off each other so well that Falk on the spot would rewrite and expand their scenes together.

What didn't make the final cut was Sloan's proposed ending. After the murderer is led away, Columbo grimaces in pain and has to sit down. "Cramps, sir?" asks Wilson. "No, my feet. When my wife took back my raincoat, she traded it in for a pair of new shoes," Columbo says, as he leans forward to remove one of his shiny new patent leather shoes, "and they're killing me."

Also deleted was the Nazi magician's attempt to frame the Jewish singer who is romancing his daughter, by leaving one of the crooner's handkerchiefs at the murder scene.

Metzler insisted that the entire production be filmed on the backlot, including construction of an elaborate nightclub in Stage 43, inspired by Hollywood's Magic Castle, complete with theater stage, bar and grand staircase. Chambers had requested shooting a scene where Columbo visits a magic shop on location. Metzler said no, reasoning, "the added expense doesn't warrant the so-called additional production values." Filming the scene on the lot cost $2,200 vs. $4,500 on location.

Two days before filming began, Peter Fischer accepted the offer to produce Levinson and Link's new series, *Ellery Queen*. No one wanted to tell Falk. He had constantly been complaining that as talented as Fischer was, he needed writing help, and here he was about to lose Fischer. It took five days before Dick Irving finally broke the news to Falk over lunch in the commissary. Falk went ballistic. He returned to the set so angry, he could not continue and headed for Chambers' office, where he proceeded to rant and rave about Fischer being arbitrarily removed as story editor.

Falk then stormed off to Metzler's office. He entered, but was so upset he refused to speak. No matter what Metzler said, Falk just stood there, boiling. Falk finally left, and Metzler hurried down to the kitchen set on Stage 34 to find out what had happened. No one on site knew why Falk was seething. Soon after, Falk arrived, walked up to Metzler and, with his voice quavering in anger, said, "Somebody should care for this show." He then stalked through the set, so mad he didn't know what to say or do, before finally beckoning Metzler to join him outside the soundstage.

In the street Falk became hysterical, red-faced, screaming: "This show needs a story editor!" Metzler told him that he was as surprised as anyone that Universal promoted Fischer, but that he was sure Bill Driskill would be a worthy replacement. Falk continued to scream, "You can't treat this show that way!" Metzler reiterated that he had nothing to do with the switch; it was made without his knowledge. Falk paused, took a deep breath, and nodded. He knew Metzler was not involved with the move, but he could not tolerate this treatment.

Aware that Falk's anger had already delayed shooting for nearly two hours, Metzler attempted to calm him down with reassurances that he personally would become involved in making sure he was happy with the story editor situation. His composure regained, Falk returned to the set to start rehearsing a scene with Bob Dishy. The scene, which covered just half a page in the script, was supposed to be shot that morning. Falk stopped production, with a full crew standing by, to personally rewrite the scene and make it five times as long.

As the actors rehearsed and the set was relit, Metzler walked over to talk to the director, Harvey Hart, who had been in the commissary when Mount Peter first erupted. Hart correctly thought that Falk's sudden "uncontrollable anger" may have been stoked by his conversation with Irving, but it was just the "top of the iceberg." Losing Fischer was a blow, but Falk appeared to be most upset with how unimportant *Columbo* seemed to be to Universal.

The next morning, Falk's anger returned. He stormed into a meeting between Chambers and Metzler, resuming the previous day's hysterical ranting and insisting that they accompany him to see Irving. The diatribe continued in Irving's office. The executives promised him more writing help. They revealed that Fischer had agreed to stay on part-time as co-story consultant and that Fischer's payment for *Columbo* would be billed to *Ellery Queen*. Falk didn't seem to be buying it.

The next day, May 1, Metzler resolved for a fresh start with Falk. He knew that if he were going to make any headway on speeding up production and bringing down costs, he would have to make sure Falk viewed him as neither an enemy nor a doormat. That afternoon, he stopped by Falk's office. He noticed on one wall a plaque that read, "Give them quality—whether they want it or not."

Metzler sat down and, rather than rush into his arguments, first let Falk vent on some of his points of contention, such as the $12,500 ceiling on guest stars. Falk still could not reconcile the fact that they ruled out Ben Gazzara for *A Case of Immunity* "for a measly $7,500."

"NBC has to adhere to some kind of a production policy and $12,500 is an arbitrary and firm top," Metzler explained. "There is nothing I can do about it, and there is nothing I should do about it in view of the fact that Hector Elizondo did a magnificent job. Jack Cassidy is doing a good job for $10,000. You can buy a lot of good talent for $12,500."

"But you can't get Orson Welles."

Metzler agreed that Welles possibly could have been the one exception to the price cap, but "I know we couldn't have had him for $20,000, so why consider him at all?"

"But think of the publicity. Peter Falk and Orson Welles."

"That's YOUR publicity," Metzler answered. "However, I grant you that his name could conceivably help the ratings."

"And Ben (Gazzara) would have, too," Falk added.

"I don't agree. He is a good man, but his name with yours would not have meant any more to the show than you with Hector Elizondo."

"I don't agree with you, but I guess you're entitled to your opinion."

Metzler then tried to patch up their rift and to reassure Falk that NBC was fully behind getting him writing help that he approved of. Falk didn't believe him. "All I get are words from (NBC in) New York," he retorted. "Everyone hopes the problem will go away. No one intends to do anything."

Metzler tried to side with Falk; maybe the head office in New York was all talk. "That's not unusual," Metzler nodded. "But NBC in Burbank intends to deliver. However, Burbank must approve our eventual choice of a writer."

"It's going to cost money…," Falk warned.

Metzler conceded that money had not yet been discussed, but the figure needed to be reasonable.

Falk remained unconvinced. "Universal used to promise me writing help, but I never got it until I MYSELF found Peter Fischer. Then I couldn't have Fischer because he was working on *Griff.* When *Griff* was canceled, I expected to get Fischer, but no. I had to raise Cain until I finally got him. Peter Fischer was a mountain. Why should NBC-New York or Burbank be any different from Universal? Promises are cheap."

Metzler answered, "NBC, both New York and Burbank, want to maintain the highest quality of the show and the only way to achieve that is to restore Peter Falk to being a contented man who without anger and hysterics can do the job he was hired to do."

Falk felt that poor, unfinished scripts and the absence of a story editor had in the past forced him to be the one rewriting on the set.

"Do you WANT to write?" Metzler asked.

"No. I want to act out lines I can believe and then get the hell out of here. I planned to work three months on *Columbo* and then do pictures. I have had several offers I have had to turn down. I spend seven months a year on *Columbo*."

It finally occurred to Metzler that streamlining production was in both of their interests—lower costs for NBC and more time for the actor to make movies.

He proposed, "Would you try some things with me, some radical, never-before-attempted efforts to speed up shooting?"

"I am listening."

"First," Metzler said, "let's drop the back-to-back operation."

"Wait a minute," Falk protested. "I asked for that so I could do pictures. It is in my contract."

"You have got it, but you are still not doing pictures."

"Okay, I am still listening...."

Metzler continued, "Drop the back-to-back operation for only a couple of days between pictures, then with me and with the director go over the action on the sets, become familiar with the geography of the sets. That way we can avoid reshooting because there were two different concepts of the action."

He cited the example of three days earlier, on *Now You See Him*, when the director, Harvey Hart, thought the murder should be played one way and filmed the body falling and lying a certain way. When Falk arrived on the set, it didn't look right to him. He insisted that the body be moved. Four shots had to be restaged, relighted and re-filmed.

"Hold it. Hold it," Falk cut in. "Harvey is as good a director as we will get."

"I agree, but you and he did not confer about how the action should be played. He shot it his way and you didn't like it. So it was reshot. NBC paid for it twice."

"Right," Falk mused. "I see your point...."

Metzler added, "Let's keep this time flexible. Call it 'rehearsal time,' call it anything you like. It will be only enough time between pictures to let you relate the script to the set. Before we shoot, you and the director should be in agreement on how the action is to be played."

"Sounds reasonable."

"But this walkthrough is of no value if you don't read the script—the ENTIRE script—beforehand."

Falk reacted uncomfortably, as if he had been trapped. "I may have to do a little rewriting," he said.

"Maybe," Metzler nodded, "but let's decide to keep it to a minimum. You don't want to write. You want to play Columbo delineated by a writer in whom you have confidence."

Just then, Falk's secretary, Carole, broke in to request that Metzler attend a production meeting in Everett Chambers' office to discuss the next picture. Metzler told her to have them start without him; Falk was reacting favorably to his suggestions and he didn't want to leave until Falk was on board with his terms. Falk smiled, seemingly pleased that Metzler preferred to continue their conversation rather than drop it in favor of a production meeting.

Metzler repeated his desire to hire a writer whom Falk trusted. Falk still wasn't sure: "That's easy to say, but where is he? Sometimes when I know a thing is wrong, I have told Peter Fischer and even HE couldn't fix it. Usually he could. But sometimes he would come back with a rewrite that was worse than the original."

After several minutes of back and forth, Falk finally consented, "Okay, if I get the scripts in time, let's try it, but I still need writing help with Bill Driskill."

"The way is clear for that help," Metzler said. Chambers had promised to compile a list of possible writers. Metzler suggested Al Aley, a former story editor on *Ironside* who was looking for a new project.

"Who's Al What's-His-Name?" Falk asked dismissively.

"Al Aley. He worked for me, and I think he might have what we need for *Columbo*."

"Well, let's start talking to these guys."

Metzler said, "Everett is the producer and should put this into motion."

"The sooner the better."

"We'll take only as much time as it takes to get the right man. Once we get him, I would like to have you try my two suggestions. Read the complete script. Then walk through the action on the sets, whether they are finished or not, with me and with the director."

"And with a writer," Falk inserted. He then started to grouse about a previous complaint by Metzler that the last script doctor they hired wasn't worth the money, before talking himself into agreeing with the point. "Actually, I think you are right about Larry Cohen," Falk admitted. "We paid him a hell of a lot of money for what? We could have gotten a lot more out of him for that kind of dough."

Falk then pivoted to Metzler's earlier complaint of continuing to pay Levinson and Link as consultants. Again, Falk came to agree with Metzler: "And we ought to look into Levinson and Link. Why are we paying them for their memos?"

"We may be committed to them by contract, but we will look into it."

Metzler rose to leave. Falk said, "Look, Bob, I don't know what the hell they are handing me out of New York and Burbank, but I think you are sincere. Anyways, I will know in a couple of days."

"You sure will, and I don't think you will be disappointed. Burbank has assured me that we will get adequate writing help."

"Okay," Falk smiled, "and thanks. We will see."

As Metzler exited to head for the production meeting, he felt that they had finally turned the corner. Following a relatively calm, 90-minute discussion, he was convinced he had found common ground with his star. Certainly, there had to be smooth sailing ahead.

12
Bon Voyage

W ork resumed on *Now You See Him* at the same glacial pace it left off, albeit with Falk in a considerably better mood. Bob Metzler arrived on the set to witness the actor inserting a quick bit of business for his buddy Mike Lally. Instead of Lally just sitting as a nameless extra at the bar, Falk had Santini recognize him and walk over: "Michael Lally! The greatest wire act, he and his brother. You should have seen them. How is he?" Lally mumbled in response, "Well, he's still working. I gave up the act. I got a little bit too old, Mr. Santini."

Metzler was incredulous. The bit appeared to have no purpose, except to bump Lally up to Screen Actors Guild pay.

Metzler, though, held his tongue. He was determined to do everything he could to keep Falk positive and the production moving, namely making sure Chambers was pushing ahead identifying writing help for Bill Driskill. He knew that although Peter Fischer would continue to get credited as—and paid for being—story editor, his active involvement with *Columbo* had ended. More than anything, Fischer was kept "on staff" to pacify Falk. Fischer admitted, "I wasn't doing much. Bill Driskill was doing it all. I had left him two or three scripts so he didn't have to start off with an empty plate. He had a head start, and I had nothing to do with it because I was too busy on *Ellery Queen*."

After a week of no progress on the writers front, Falk submitted two names he wanted: either Len Deighton, the author of *The IPCRESS File*, or Tom Mankiewicz, who had helped script the last three James Bond pictures and developed a reputation as a fixer. A Universal rep contacted Mankiewicz's agent to see how much he would charge to read a *Columbo* script and give his thoughts. The agent said $5,000. The actual screenwriter was only getting $7,500. "You're out of your mind," the rep replied, and hung up on him. Metzler couldn't believe Universal had botched the deal and demanded they call right back. The rep again phoned Mankiewicz's agent, this time proposing, "All right, $7,500 a script. Take it or leave it." The agent accepted, later joking to Mankiewicz, "If we'd turned them down again, we might have gotten 10."

After Mankiewicz signed on, Falk met him for lunch on the day of the Emmy Awards. Falk was nominated, but said he was leaning against attending, because they had reduced the number of nominees in his category. Mankiewicz couldn't understand why he would stay home, since everyone figured he was going to win.

"Yeah," Falk explained, "but I'm only up against Dennis Weaver for *McCloud*. It's just the two of us, so if I win, I just beat Dennis Weaver."

So Mankiewicz suggested, "If you win, come up and say, 'Sorry, Dennis, it came up tails,' and they'll love you."

"That's not a bad idea. I'm going."

Falk went to the ceremony, won, and delivered the line, to terrific laughter and applause. So he began his acceptance speech by thanking Mankiewicz. Later that evening, friends walked up to congratulate Mankiewicz on his writing for *Columbo*, forcing him to explain that the shoutout wasn't for *Columbo*—it was for the joke.

A Matter of Honor

Falk understood that Mankiewicz wouldn't be at his beck and call to rewrite on the set. He told him, "I want somebody on this show to look at the scripts and to make sure that everything is right. That the clues are at the right time. Independent—not our staff."

The first script Mankiewicz received was *A Matter of Honor* by Brad Radnitz, who made a career out of mostly one-offs for dozens of series including *Mission: Impossible*, *Ironside*, *McMillan & Wife*, and *Hec Ramsey*. Although it was a rather dull script, the action took place south of the border, and NBC loved it when the show moved to a new, marketable location.

NBC requested that Mexico and the local people be portrayed in a positive light; even the villain, a proud bullfighter who can't tolerate that his longtime assistant witnessed him showing fear in the ring, was to kill not out of greed, money, or lust, but to protect his honor.

Just as in *Troubled Waters*, the local authority in *A Matter of Honor* pulls Columbo away from his vacation—and his unseen wife—to help investigate a curious crime. Radnitz even worked a shoutout to *Troubled Waters* into his script, by having the constable sharing how all of Mexico has adored Columbo ever since the newspaper reports of him solving the murder at sea.

Everett Chambers researched the possibility of filming in Mexico or New Mexico, but quickly ruled out the latter because he needed a bullring. The Locations team zeroed in on the Hacienda Vista Hermosa near Cuernavaca, about an hour-and-a-half south of Mexico City. The 450-year-old stone fortress turned five-star, 100-room hotel was basically the *Columbo* Villain Mansion of Mexico, the go-to place when Mexican films and TV needed a lush, gorgeous, multimillion-dollar, luxurious backdrop. A handful of American films had also been shot there, most notably the ending of *Butch Cassidy and the Sundance Kid*. To cap it off, the estate had its own bullfighting ring.

"Originally, Bernie Kowalski was going to direct," Chambers recalled. "So he and I and some of the production staff went to Mexico to find a bull arena. We went there, surveyed and arranged hotels. When we came back, Bernie was offered a year-to-year contract to executive produce and direct *Baretta*. That was a big deal. I let him go."

Chambers immediately pivoted to another director he knew Falk would approve of—Ted Post. But Post, knowing he had the studio "over a barrel," negotiated for a considerably higher fee and perks to accept the job. Universal agreed to pick up the difference, rather than stick NBC with it, since they had inadvertently caused the switch. Post then traveled down to Mexico with Bill Driskill to review the locations, while Chambers stayed behind to cast the episode.

The lead was simple to cast since, at the time, Ricardo Montalbán was one of the few Mexican actors well known enough in America to fit the part. Chambers also wanted to use Jorge Rivero, the "Robert Redford of Mexico," but Rivero wanted $2,000 per day and guest billing along with Montalbán. That was fine with Chambers, since he mostly wanted him for his name. He just gave him a miniscule part. As the victim, Chambers and Falk both wanted Emilio "El Indio" Fernández, the legendary Mexican actor who was revered in his country and played iconic roles in American films, such as General Mapache in *The Wild Bunch* and El Jefe in *Bring Me the Head of Alfredo Garcia*. Fernández's role wasn't much larger than Rivero's, but he wanted a flat $6,000 for the job. NBC scoffed. Metzler suggested substituting Pancho Córdova, who recently did a guest shot on *McCloud*.

Chambers pleaded his case for using Fernández, arguing that the money would be worth it because the role turned out to be larger than originally planned. In addition, Fernández had directed a number of films, so he could be of great help to Post. Most important of all, Falk was dead set on Fernández. Metzler conceded: "After listening to his reasons for hiring Emilio Fernández, I agreed that we should have him—principally to accommodate Peter." He knew the union wouldn't allow the actor to assist the director. So he gave Chambers the okay, if he could get his price down.

Chambers convinced Fernández to accept $500 a day. But that night, according to Metzler, Fernández "got drunk and demanded the original $6,000."

Once on site, other costs continued to mount. The set decorator was unhappy with the Vista Hermosa's furniture, which they had originally planned to use, so new furnishings had to be rented.

The team optimistically budgeted to shoot for 14 days, meaning they would have to film about five pages of script per day to stay on schedule. After three days, they found themselves a half-day behind. They figured they were in passable shape until that evening, when they started to view the footage. They had originally gotten permission from the union to use a half American crew, half more affordable Mexican crew, but as soon as they started viewing the dailies, in "el teatro" at Vista Hermosa, they knew the sound was "miserable." Granted, listening to the tracks in the stone theater, with its six hard surfaces—floor, ceiling and four walls—made for terrible acoustics. Chambers still needed better sound recording. He immediately called Universal to send down a professional mixer and a boom man.

On day four, during the filming of a scene in the bullring, Falk fell on a wooden post and landed on his backside, bruising his posterior. The production shut down for the day.

On day seven, one of the crewmembers, Tony, was driving through town when he accidentally sideswiped another car. Inside, a female passenger had had her arm dangling out the window. The woman lost her arm, and Tony was arrested and put in jail. By the next morning, Tony was released. The authorities assured the film crew that there would be "no stigma attached to the *Columbo* company." Nonetheless, Tony was removed from the production.

Back on the set, Post was supposed to spend day eight filming the action scenes involving the bull. By nightfall, he had little usable footage. Post said it was because the scene was inherently difficult and slow, and he needed three days to shoot it, not one. Others blamed Post for showing up on the set unprepared, the technical advisor and the matador's double for doing a bad job, and the bull for being too big and too slow to charge convincingly.

Each day, often hampered by an afternoon rain, the production fell further and further behind. Worse, no one was happy with the script and Driskill had to continually rewrite it as they went. At times, the production crew was frozen, literally waiting for his revisions before they could go on.

After 12 days, only half of the script had been shot. Film and lab costs were way over budget. Metzler had hoped to make up some of the overages by stretching the picture out to two hours. But the schedule and script were such a mess, he knew they'd be lucky to make it work at 90 minutes. Metzler reported the bad news to his bosses: "At this late date it is perfectly obvious that this script was not ready to go. Everett Chambers admits this, but gets off the hook by saying, 'But NBC okayed it.' There MUST be more consideration given to obvious production problems by (NBC Story Department's) Pat Betz and Len Hill on ALL scripts… not just those that are shot on foreign locations and not just those shot in the studio. Both Post and Hart agree with me that the script should be good—*quality*—and tight—*logical and playable*—BEFORE we go into production. *Matter* is NOT a good script… neither is it tight."

During the next three days, the company was able to complete the allotted number of pages. But then came the scenes in the busy marketplace. Shooting under difficult conditions and unable to quiet the crowds of onlookers pushed behind boundaries, the crew found live sound recording almost impossible. Filming crept along slowly over the next three days, even though Post knew that every line of dialogue would have to be looped in later.

A Matter of Honor ended up taking 20 days to shoot and exceeding its budget by more than $250,000.

Forgotten Lady

A Matter of Honor's late finish delayed by one week the start of the next episode, *Forgotten Lady*. Inspired by MGM's smash retrospective *That's Entertainment!*, Bill Driskill had aging musical star Grace Wheeler kill her doctor husband after he refuses to fund her return to Broadway with her former partner, Ned Diamond. Grace did so unaware that she was suffering from a terminal disease and her husband was just trying to protect her health. When Columbo cracks the case, Ned takes the rap to spare Grace from spending her final days in prison.

Typically, Falk was not a fan of shows with a female murderer, but Grace was a sympathetic character. Up until that point, only five of *Columbo's* 38 murderers had been women. "Peter didn't like to do shows where the heavy was a woman," Chambers confirmed. "He didn't want to bring down women. We eventually ran out of males."

Since the script hinged on Grace obsessively watching her old musicals, it was imperative that the murderer be an actual movie musical star whose old film clips could be shown. Everett Chambers was determined to sign Fred Astaire and Ginger Rogers to play the leads "regardless of cost." NBC loved the idea of an Astaire-Rogers reunion and offered to pick up the stars' salaries beyond $15,500. They knew the costs—already predicted at $143,000 over budget—

would skyrocket, but figured it was worth it if the episode could be stretched to two hours and could kick off the fall season.

One concern among the executives was that Ginger Rogers, despite winning an Academy Award for *Kitty Foyle* (1940), typically played wisecracking roles and wasn't a strong enough—or at least sympathetic enough—actress to pull off the role of Grace. They pushed for Angela Lansbury, who proved unavailable, or Cyd Charisse. Rogers, as it turned out, was also unavailable, and Astaire was not interested.

Chambers then moved to his Plan B: Janet Leigh, who with Donald O'Connor had starred in a 1953 musical produced by Universal: *Walking My Baby Back Home*. "Janet Leigh was a friend of mine and I wanted her for it," Chambers said. "She and her husband Bob Brandt and I had a company together. He was a stockbroker who became a producer. We did a series and a movie together. I thought she'd be wonderful for the part. I also wanted Donald O'Connor, because Janet and Donald O'Connor had made a movie together, and I wanted to use the footage from that movie, which was a Universal movie. I called Donald O'Connor and he'd just booked a state fair in some town, and he couldn't do it."

NBC and Falk, however, preferred Leslie Caron to play Grace. Caron was living in Paris, so NBC would have to pick up roundtrip airfare and living expenses. But Falk said he would extend the show to two hours if they could get her—but only if they could get her. NBC agreed. Caron agreed. But then Universal discovered that MGM was preparing a *That's Entertainment, Part II* and likely would not allow *Columbo* to use any Caron footage. Leigh got the part, with the proviso that she would make at least $12,500 and no less than the actor who played Ned.

With O'Connor unavailable, options for the male lead were down to Louis Jourdan or Dan Dailey. Dailey asked for $15,000. He ultimately got the job when he agreed to drop to $12,500. The next morning, Dailey arrived in Wardrobe looking a little under the weather. As Metzler reported: "He has rheumatic fever. Can't move, much less dance. Search is on for a replacement."

Metzler suggested pulling out of retirement John Payne, the *Miracle on 34th Street* star who had made a series of Fox musicals in the 1940s. The other last-minute candidate was Dick Van Dyke, who had co-starred with Leigh in *Bye Bye Birdie* (1963). His price tag, though, would be at least $20,000. Chambers perked up. He thought Van Dyke had been terrific in the previous season's *Negative Reaction*. If Van Dyke said yes, Chambers would get creative and find a way to "bury" $7,500 in the Universal budget, so NBC wouldn't be on the hook for the overage. Chambers still would have to come up with another $7,500, since Leigh would also get a raise. They made the call anyway. Van Dyke declined; his agent said that although he was personally fond of the actor, he did not wish to again "play second fiddle to Peter Falk." John Payne got the role, which would prove to be his last.

Using footage from *Walking My Baby Back Home* actually turned out to be more difficult than Chambers had anticipated, because Janet Leigh was on loan-out from MGM when Universal made the picture. The two studios had to work out the rights before they could figure out what to charge *Columbo*. But striking a deal did get Donald O'Connor into the episode—he can be seen in several clips from *Walking My Baby Back Home* and heard in another.

The plot also required the use of footage from *The Tonight Show*, since Grace's butler establishes what time he had checked in on her by noting the Johnny Carson show had just ended, so it had to be 1 a.m. NBC was okay to license the footage—taken from the episode recorded just before filming began, so long as it didn't contain any of the *Tonight Show* theme music.

Forgotten Lady's script opened at the premiere of a *That's Entertainment!* knock-off called *Song and Dance*. To save money, NBC ruled out filming the scene where the script detailed: outside of Grauman's Chinese Theatre. It would also cost a pretty penny to rent their second choice and fill its courtyard with extras, so the scene was filmed instead at the theater on the Universal backlot's New York Street.

The production did cost Falk his battered brown shoes, which he had worn in every episode since *Ransom for a Dead Man*. A stuntman was wearing them for a scene in which he dangles from a tree and then drops about 10 feet. When he hit the ground, the stunt man broke his ankle.

"It was a compound fracture," Falk said. "So in order to get the shoe off, they had to cut it with a knife. That's why I couldn't wear those shoes anymore."

Fortunately, his scuffed-up backup pair were a near-identical match.

Forgotten Lady's schedule stretched from 14 days to four weeks, yet Falk remained adamant that it and the next episode be completed in time for him to shoot back-to-back movies. Consequently, the *Columbo* team juggled their schedules so that Falk spent the last week of production filming *Forgotten Lady* in the evenings on Universal soundstages, and the daylight hours filming the next episode on location.

Identity Crisis

That next episode, the secret-agent caper *Identity Crisis*, was in danger of starting even later, due to a squabble over who would direct. Falk and Chambers were pushing for Patrick McGoohan, a natural after his work on *Danger Man* and *The Prisoner*. McGoohan was amenable to directing—for $20,000.

Falk also thought the script was long and should be trimmed to 90 minutes. NBC proposed a compromise: they'd pay McGoohan $12,500 if he supplied a 90-minute show and $20,000 if he supplied a two-hour show. Falk did not want McGoohan's pay tied to the length of the show. He said if they paid McGoohan $20,000, he would not ask that the script be cut, but equally he would not guarantee a final running time of two hours until after he saw the final edit.

The dispute went on for a full week before the top brass at NBC-New York, headed by recently named VP of programming Marvin Antonowsky, decided to drop in on the Universal lot. The NBC bigwigs first met with Metzler, impressing on him that from here on in every *Columbo* was to run two hours or it was not to be made. At the end of the day, the entourage headed down to the *Forgotten Lady* set to meet Falk. Upset that NBC was playing games with the McGoohan negotiations, Falk refused to meet Antonowsky, calling him "a blackmailer."

Finally, 10 days past the date a director should have been hired, McGoohan signed on to star and direct. Metzler quickly pulled McGoohan aside, knowing that he was itching to rewrite the script, but there were mere days before cameras had to roll. Without telling Falk, Metzler and McGoohan made a secret deal: McGoohan, according to Metzler, would "beef up the script for his purposes and guarantee a two-hour script for my purposes."

McGoohan began furiously rewriting. When Chambers asked for his input on casting, the director didn't want to be bothered. "You cast it," he said. Chambers did slip his eldest daughter, Alicia, in as a youngster at the arcade. The only comment McGoohan would make about casting was directed toward Leslie Nielsen—Chambers' choice to play the victim, a rough-and-tumble "operator." McGoohan asked cryptically, "Why *Leslie Nielsen*?"

McGoohan could be both prickly and capricious. Without warning, he would decide to change locations. Two days before *Identity Crisis* was supposed to begin filming, he switched the opening arcade scene, planned for Magic Mountain, to the Pike amusement area in Long Beach, forcing a one-day delay. For the first week of shooting, the crew had to film entirely on location, since *Forgotten Lady* was still scrambling to finish and Universal refused to block out additional space for *Columbo* on the lot.

Although McGoohan didn't have time to create many entirely new scenes, he did leave his mark on existing ones. He included a few nods to *The Prisoner* (such as the catchphrase "Be seeing you") but seemed most intent on stretching the Columbo character in new directions. He didn't believe Columbo was really humble or polite. To him, that was an act, which the detective could turn on or off as the situation merited. Falk trusted him implicitly. When Columbo arrives

DURING THE production of *Identity Crisis*, Falk allowed director Patrick McGoohan to take his character in new directions. *[Credit: NBCUniversal]*

at the murder scene, late at night under the pier, instead of inconspicuously beginning his investigation in his normal low-key manner, McGoohan introduced Columbo dramatically approaching from the distance, emerging from the dark in an atmospheric swirl of cigar smoke. Columbo promptly barks at the photographers huddled around the body to scram, establishing his character as running the show and unconcerned with what others think of him. He's all business, until he kneels down in the sand, leans over to examine the body, and affably greets a fellow detective: "How you doin', Cliff?"

Falk adored McGoohan's unpredictability, particularly when the audience expected a scene to play one way and then realized its purpose was something entirely different. For the scene where Columbo and Sgt. Kramer visit a club to question the bartender, McGoohan had Columbo walk in and become immediately transfixed on the floorshow—a belly dancer. Kramer has to physically pull him away from the floor show to talk to the barkeep—and even then Columbo remains preoccupied, all but ignoring the interview as he gazes at the dancer. As they finally exit, Columbo shares that he was so obsessed with the woman not for her belly, but for her eyes, which betrayed that she was really shy. Falk was delighted that an otherwise boring interrogation had been turned into something layered and unexpected—even if it did portray Columbo completely out of character, as distracted and rude.

During Columbo's first encounter with murderer Nelson Brenner at a conference center, McGoohan had Brenner try to brush off the detective, repeatedly telling him he was in the wrong room. He established immediate tension between the two. He also had a speech that Brenner dictated earlier—which contained the final clue to the mystery—being recited during the confrontation.

Watching the dailies, Metzler was satisfied with the quality of the footage but alarmed by the quantity. McGoohan and Falk shot scenes over and over and over, and piled on the overtime. There were also reports of McGoohan's drinking, although he looked in total control on film. Consequently, McGoohan the director was put "on notice," but not McGoohan the actor.

McGoohan "was a very mercurial person," Chambers confirmed. "He was an alcoholic, and a couple of times he was off on benders when I should have had him in the office."

Despite the slow progress, all scenes without the star were saved for last, so that Falk could finish in time to meet his movie's start date. To make the deadline, Falk had to work his last day until 4:00 in the morning. The overtime cost NBC an additional $38,000. McGoohan one-upped his star. He filmed for one more week, finishing his last day of shooting at 5:30 in the morning.

As Falk headed off to begin work on the TV movie *Griffin and Phoenix*, NBC began scheduling episodes week by week for the fall. On Sunday nights, the *NBC Mystery Movie* would have Hargrove and Kibbee's *McCoy* as a fourth spoke and their *Family Holvak* as a lead-in. ABC would continue airing first-run movies in the slot starting with *Cabaret*, while CBS would follow *Kojak* with *Bronk*, starring Jack Palance as a tough-but-sensitive, pipe-smoking L.A. police detective.

Because of the episode's star-studded cast, NBC opted to have *Forgotten Lady* kick off the 1975-1976 season. It thought *Identity Crisis* was especially strong, so it would air during sweeps week in November. In between, NBC planned on airing *A Matter of Honor*, but Falk thought *A Case of Immunity* was stronger and should be the season's second *Columbo*. So when he was called to re-record dialogue for *A Matter of Honor*, Falk's agent said he was unavailable "due to his present feature shooting schedule" on *Griffin and Phoenix*. Miraculously, once NBC agreed to air *A Case of Immunity* first and delay *A Matter of Honor* until February, Falk suddenly became available.

Forgotten Lady opened the season getting beaten badly by *Kojak* and *Bronk*.

Although *Bronk's* popularity was more likely curiosity, cratering each successive week, ratings for the *NBC Mystery Movie* were not much better. Even *Columbo* struggled all season to crack the top 20. *The Family Holvak* lasted just 10 weeks. Its replacement, *Ellery Queen*, lasted 13 shows. *McCoy* was gone after four.

Sunday nights—NBC's lone bright spot—were now in disarray. The network renewed efforts to expand all *Columbos* to two hours. *Now You See Him* was shot as a 90-minute show, but it was very tight. In fact, the rough cut had clocked in at 18 minutes too long, so if they did a minimum of tightening, they'd just need about seven or eight additional minutes to fill a two-hour timeslot.

Falk, surprisingly, was more than agreeable; in fact, he had planted the bit about Mike Lally at the bar knowing Santini from their younger days precisely in case they needed more footage. Driskill was put to work writing a new scene for Columbo to question Lally about Santini's past, followed by a scene with Columbo sharing the revelations with Santini.

Falk finished filming his second movie, Neil Simon's *Murder by Death*, one week before Christmas and was now available to shoot the added scenes, to be directed by Everett Chambers. Jack Cassidy was in New York appearing in a play, so the crew had to fly to him to film his sequence in a restaurant. The scene with Lally was shot in Los Angeles, but tougher to pull off since Lally had no interest in doing it and felt he was tricked into it. Lally hated being saddled with a lot of dialogue; he preferred one-liners or, better yet, no-liners, milling around in the background. Although he'd been acting for 45 years, he had had no professional training.

The scene turned out to be a beauty: Columbo visits the aging wire performer in his rundown flat and, while milking him for info on Santini, spends more time asking about his modest furnishings, including a hotplate and the communal bathroom down the hall. Columbo displays real interest in the man, Lally shows his natural self-effacing personality, and their exchange is genuinely touching.

Last Salute to the Commodore

After the calendar turned to 1976, Falk was ready to start work on the final episode of Season 5. From all indications, it appeared as if it would also be the final episode of the series. Throughout the fall, Falk and his attorney Bert Fields had not been subtle about his intention to make Season 5 his last. Falk confirmed that he had had it with the grind of series TV, and needed more time to make movies and work on his relationship with his estranged wife, Alyce.

During the fall, the creative team had to choose between three highly unusual options for a fitting finale—two whodunits (a "marina story" by Jackson Gillis and "Orient Express in the Air" by Steven Bochco) and *Roar of the Crowd* by Howard

Berk, in which a circus lion is used as a murder weapon. Falk liked Bochco's idea the best, but it had story problems that couldn't be resolved and Bochco's time was limited due to other obligations on the lot. *Roar of the Crowd* was expected to be too expensive and difficult to cast, and Metzler found it "full of holes" and lacking an ending. That left the marina story, *Last Salute to the Commodore*. Gillis' ingenious setup showed Charles Clay cleaning up after the slaying of his naval architect father-in-law. But halfway through Columbo's investigation, prime suspect Clay turns up dead and the Lieutenant has a traditional multi-suspect whodunit on his hands.

NBC wanted Robert Day to direct, but Falk wanted McGoohan back. NBC shuddered. McGoohan had done a good job with *Identity Crisis*, but was slow and expensive. Yet NBC was in the heat of negotiating with Falk's agent over the possibility of one more year of *Columbo*. Chambers called Antonowsky and was able to sell him on how hiring McGoohan would help his cause. McGoohan it was.

What NBC didn't know was that Falk had given McGoohan a story commitment to write his own teleplay. After taking a few brief stabs at it, McGoohan realized he couldn't "lick the ending" and agreed to film *Last Salute to the Commodore*. Only, McGoohan wanted to film *his* version.

NBC feared the worst, estimating filming would require 22 days instead of the predicted 14 and the budget would be $800,000 to $900,000, with a final cost "well over $1 million" and an expensive cast headed by Anthony Hopkins, Gena Rowlands, and O.J. Simpson.

Hopkins was offered the part of Charles Clay for $12,500; he declined, and Chambers got Robert Vaughn for $17,500. The choice was inspired because, seeing a past *Columbo* murderer, the audience would be further convinced that Vaughn was the culprit—and doubly shocked when, 60 minutes in, he ended up dead.

Metzler, figuring this was the last hurrah, declined the studio's offer to put him up in a Newport Beach hotel near the harbor, where most of the filming would take place. Instead, he'd watch the dailies and drive down from Los Angeles once every few days to check in on McGoohan and Falk, who kept assuring him "that their radical departure from the script will play."

With McGoohan rewriting on the fly, filming took a full month. Among his most significant alterations, McGoohan preferred Columbo showing the ropes to a young, wide-eyed apprentice, instead of working alongside old stalwart Sgt. Kramer, as specified in the script. McGoohan would make up the role as he went along; he just needed Chambers to find him a fresh-faced kid who could improvise. The producer thought of comedic actor Dennis Dugan.

Chambers recalled, "I knew Dennis. He was married to Joyce Van Patten. I had seen him in a movie of the week. He was a very funny guy. So I got Dennis to do that part. He wasn't a character in the script. There was no dialogue (written beforehand). But he appeared through the whole thing. Patrick (McGoohan) improvised all that stuff with him. Some of it's funny, some of it worked, some of it didn't." (It definitely worked for Dugan. The appearance helped him land his own pilot and series, *Richie Brockelman, Private Eye*, and guest shots as Brockelman in *The Rockford Files*.)

But the biggest departures came from McGoohan as director in his instructions to Falk. McGoohan noted that after five years, it was now or never to try to stretch the character and "try something different." Falk was game. First, he encouraged Falk to show a wider range of deliveries. He had him play Columbo's first scene quietly, almost mumbling, as if he's heavily medicated. In other scenes, he screamed at the top of his lungs, particularly during a Q&A with a boatyard foreman that the director staged over the earsplitting roar of sawing and drilling. Most of all, McGoohan was tickled when Columbo annoyed those around him—especially his suspect. Whenever possible, he had Falk invade Vaughn's personal space, constantly leaning in too close, putting his arm around him, grabbing his arm, even patting his leg. For one added sequence, McGoohan crammed four people into the tiny Peugeot, with Columbo nearly sitting on Clay's lap, as the newbie Mac circled the driveway. Later, Columbo got downright creepy when he interrupted a young lady's yoga session, cozying up inches away and having her try to move his legs into the proper position. Falk didn't stretch the character—he snapped it. But after years of carefully constructing every syllable to fit an established template, he loved the experimentation.

Gillis' original script closed with a traditional drawing-room mystery reveal. Columbo gathers all of the suspects in a room, explains how he solved the mystery, and identifies the culprit: freeloading nephew Swanny. Gillis had had Swanny reset the Commodore's timepiece one hour ahead, to give himself an alibi—unaware he was changing it from April 30 to April 31. All of the other suspects had identical "calendar watches" and would have known to move it up to May 1.

McGoohan's "improved" resolution was to have Columbo simply hold a ticking timepiece up to each suspect's ear and tell them it was the Commodore's watch. All are oblivious except Swanny, who replies, "Tisn't"—because he was the only one who knew the murderer had smashed the Commodore's actual watch. The entire, ridiculous denouement, in which Columbo lets Mac run key parts of the proceedings, is painful to watch.

As a coda, McGoohan tacked on an additional scene, where Mac (a play on the

British nickname for a raincoat) has taken to carrying around his own raincoat, and Columbo jumps in a rowboat and begins paddling out to sea, somehow whistling "This Old Man" while smoking a cigar.

Falk, though, had such a blast shooting the episode that he began having second thoughts about ending the run. So he made sure to include a hint that kept the door open for a possible return. After spending the episode trying to give up cigars, he lights one up before entering the rowboat. "I thought you were going to quit," Sgt. Kramer notes.

"Not yet," Columbo smiles. "No, not yet, Sergeant. Not yet."

Two weeks after the airing of *Last Salute to the Commodore*, Falk took home his third Emmy, as best actor in a drama series. One can only assume voters submitted their ballots before watching this most recent performance. Asked backstage if his series would be returning in the fall, Falk was crystal clear: he was done negotiating. He had multiple films lined up. They had seen the last of *Columbo*.

Season 5 – 1975-1976

Forgotten Lady
Filmed: June 30 – July 29, 1975
Stars: Peter Falk, Janet Leigh, Maurice Evans, Sam Jaffe, John Payne
Director: Harvey Hart
Producer: Everett Chambers
Teleplay: Bill Driskill
Air Date: Sept. 14, 1975
Nielsen Ranking: #19 (31.8 points)

A Case of Immunity
Filming Started: April 3, 1975
Guest Stars: Hector Elizondo, Sal Mineo, Kenneth Tobey
Director: Ted Post
Producer: Everett Chambers
Teleplay: Lou Shaw (& Howard Berk uncredited)
Story: James Menzies
Air Date: Oct. 12, 1975
Ranking: #20 (36 points)

Identity Crisis
Filmed: July 24 – Aug. 22, 1975
Guest Stars: Patrick McGoohan, Otis Young, Val Avery, Leslie Nielsen
Director: Patrick McGoohan
Producer: Everett Chambers
Teleplay: William Driskill
Air Date: Nov. 2, 1975
Rating: (33.8 points)

A Matter of Honor
Working Title: *A Matter of Bravery*
Filmed: May 26 – June 18, 1975
Guest Stars: Ricardo Montalbán, Pedro Armendariz Jr., A Martinez, Jorge Rivero
Director: Ted Post
Producer: Everett Chambers
Teleplay: Brad Radnitz
Air Date: Feb. 1, 1976
Rating: (30 points)

Now You See Him
Working Title: *Quicker Than the Eye*
Filmed: April 25 – May 15, late Dec. 1975
Guest Stars: Jack Cassidy, Bob Dishy, Nehemiah Persoff, Robert Loggia
Director: Harvey Hart
Producer: Everett Chambers
Teleplay: Michael Sloan
Air Date: Feb. 29, 1976
Rating: (28 points)

Last Salute to the Commodore
Filmed: Jan. 5 – Feb. 5, 1976
Guest Stars: Robert Vaughn, Wilfrid Hyde-White, John Dehner, Dennis Dugan, Diane Baker, Bruce Kirby, Fred Draper
Director: Patrick McGoohan
Producer: Everett Chambers
Teleplay: Jackson Gillis (& Patrick McGoohan uncredited)
Air Date: May 2, 1976
Ranking: #9 (38.8 points)

13
The Meltdown

Once post-production wrapped on *Last Salute to the Commodore*, all of Team *Columbo* disbanded for new jobs, certain the run had come to an end. Falk's representatives did continue to take calls from the studio and the network, negotiating in generalities rather than specifics. Privately, Falk was softening yet his preference was to make one or, at most, two specials a year. Patrick McGoohan seemed to have broken him out of his rut, and was busy writing his own *Columbo* script, in which the Lieutenant investigates the kidnapping of his never-seen wife.

NBC was interested in continuing the wheel, minus *McCoy*. As a replacement, Universal offered Jack Klugman as crime-solving coroner *Quincy, M.E.* Dennis Weaver reupped for a seventh year of *McCloud*. Rock Hudson agreed to a sixth season, but his co-star Susan Saint James didn't, so *McMillan* lost his *& Wife*. The only mystery left was *Columbo*. Universal figured that if they met Falk's price, he would be back. "It happens every year," said one executive. "He says he is leaving and we offer him half of California, and he comes back."

Universal actually offered $250,000 each for up to six episodes, meeting the dollar figure floated by Falk's agents. So in mid-April NBC renewed the wheel for the fall. Universal called back Everett Chambers, after about two months with another studio, as well as Bill Driskill, and charged them with readying six scripts to begin shooting in the summer. Falk, though, hadn't signed anything—at least with Universal. He had inked a contract to star in Robert Altman's *The Y.I.G. Epoxy*, to begin filming in August, immediately followed by Ingmar Bergman's first film in Hollywood, *The Serpent's Egg*. He was also developing a film with Arthur Penn about the Attica Prison riot, which he planned to do third.

Falk intimated that, at best, he might be willing to slip in one *Columbo* during the summer and perhaps "one *Columbo* a season for the rest of my life... Columbo is a tough character to retire. I don't care where I go—Paris, Belgium, Alaska—they know him. It makes it very difficult to just walk away."

Just an occasional *Columbo* was not a problem for Universal, which assured NBC that it could fill up the wheel with extra episodes of *Quincy*. The news did not go over well with NBC.

After four months of wrangling, Falk agreed to four episodes, two to be shot during the summer and two in the late winter or early spring, depending on when he finished his string of movies.

Fade In to Murder

In the meantime, Driskill had come up with six scripts to consider. Howard Berk's *Roar of the Crowd* was still in play. Peter Fischer submitted a Shakespeare-flavored "museum story." Bob Metzler turned in *Solo for the Bowstring*, about an orchestra member who commits murder with a bow and arrow. Ken Kolb's *The Lesser of Two Evils* featured a psychiatrist who makes money off murderers by certifying them as insane once they're convicted and then diagnosing them as sane after they're imprisoned. And Lou Shaw's *Fade In to Murder*, about a fictional TV detective who kills his producer, had been kicking around since Season 4.

To make the season special, Chambers proposed filming one episode in Japan, arguing Columbo would contrast well with such a reserved culture. The producer got the immediate backing of Metzler, who was obsessed with miniature bonsai trees. "He was a bonsai maniac," Chambers recounted. "When I came up with the idea of Columbo going to Japan, (Metzler) was all for it. He helped manipulate it, because (if green-lit) he would follow us (to Japan)."

When *Fade In to Murder* was selected to start the season, Chambers suggested changing the backdrop from Hollywood to Japan. Writer Alvin Sapinsley agreed to make the changes. But Metzler didn't think the story was strong enough to merit the extra expense nor did it make any sense to send on location a production tailormade to be filmed entirely, and affordably, on the backlot.

Falk's first choice of director, McGoohan, was unavailable—off in Canada appearing in *Silver Streak*. In desperate need of guidance, Falk called on Elaine May without notifying Chambers. "Somewhere along the way Peter lost confidence in me as his backup," Chambers shared. "When I came back, Peter was in a snit. His wife had kicked him out of the house. He was really upset. So I came into like a beehive. And Peter was a very insecure guy. He always had to have a guru, somebody that he could depend on, and that's what he had in me,

"The Meltdown"

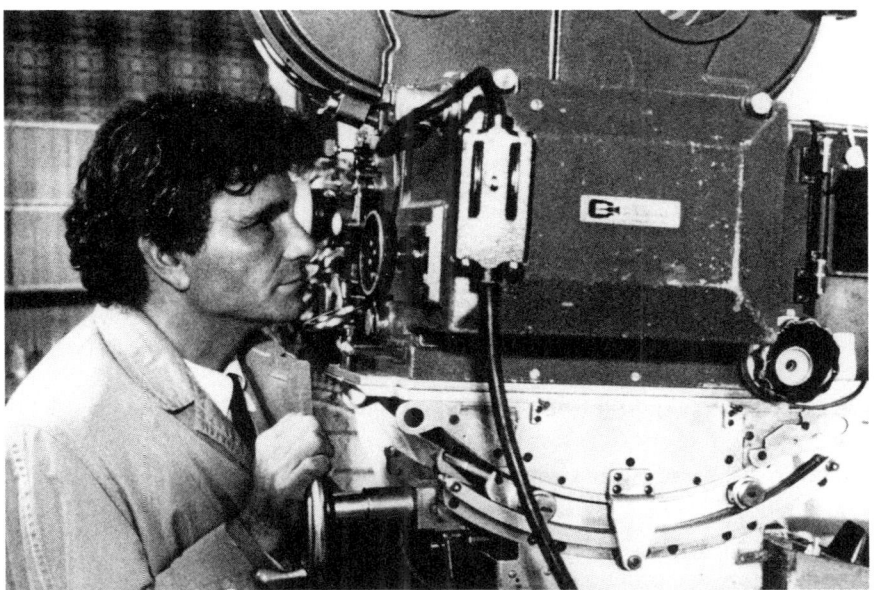

FALK RETURNED for a sixth season determined to provide even greater input behind the scenes.

he felt. I stayed on as long as I did because there was a camaraderie and I was on his side, not the network or Universal's side."

May was holed up in the Beverly Wilshire Hotel, doctoring *Heaven Can Wait* for Paramount. She said she didn't have the time to help *Columbo*. Falk was insistent. He promised a huge payday from NBC and said he would kick in the rest of the money she needed to purchase the rights for the troubled *Mikey and Nicky* from Paramount. May said yes, but she didn't want credit. She also wanted assistance from—and payment for—her friend and fellow script doctor Peter Feibleman.

For *Fade In to Murder*, the writers took extreme delight in playing with Falk's real-life contract battles—as the studio executives rage against the demands of *Detective Lucerne* star Ward Fowler, played to the hilt by William Shatner. "Who does Ward Fowler think he is?" "Paying an actor that kind of money is insane!" "Fowler's not the first actor to win an Emmy, and he's already one of the highest-paid performers in television. If we give in to him now, it's going to be worse next year, and the year after that." But the execs ultimately conclude, "Without Ward Fowler, there won't be next year for this show. Because of Ward, *Detective Lucerne* is the highest-rated show on television... Ward Fowler *is* the show."

As an inside joke, once Shatner was hired to play Lt. Lucerne, his *Star Trek* comrade Walter Koenig (Chekov) was brought in to play a cop investigating the murder scene. Koenig's one scene was shot in a day and without Shatner. "I didn't work with Bill (Shatner)," Koenig said. "Bill was in other scenes. I remember we took a little trolley, a go-kart together to go to lunch and that he didn't talk to me. It was a time between the (*Star Trek*) series and the movies, and I don't think he remembered my name."

Once filming started, Falk uncharacteristically called for few changes to the script. The handful of deviations helped to keep the action moving and to limit the episode to 90 minutes. Cut was Columbo having Fowler handle a police sketch of the masked killer, so he could get the actor's fingerprints to compare them to prints not on the murder weapon, but on the blanks inside.

Snipped from the final scene was Columbo, after hearing Fowler's confession, admit that he was bluffing about the fingerprints on the blanks. "Do you know how hard it is to raise a fingerprint off a bullet?"

Condensed was a scene in which the victim's husband, in need of an alibi, has his secretary confess that they spent the night together. The producer was supposed to say he and the secretary were going to be married, and he was about to ask his wife for a divorce. His mistress would then add that her beau had lied only to protect her child.

Similarly deleted was a scene in which Columbo raids the producer's apartment to search for a tweed jacket to match a thread Fowler planted on the murder weapon. In the filmed version, the suspected garment—changed to a blue mohair sweater—and the producer were brought to Columbo during the next scene, in Fowler's apartment. The secretary came along too, perhaps less for story purposes than to get more screen time for the actress—Falk's real-life girlfriend, Shera Danese.

Danese had just finished a brief shot on Bill Driskill's new mystery series *The Feather and Father Gang* on the Universal lot. According to Danese, "Peter said one of the producers of *Feather and Father* came to him and said, 'We had this fabulous actress on our show. You should use her on your show.' And it turned out to be me. Now that's what Peter told me, that the producers on *Feather and Father* knew the producers on *Columbo*. Maybe he didn't want me to think I was getting the part because I was at that time dating him."

Fade In to Murder's shooting schedule ballooned to 22 days, including working through the night on the last day. Filming wrapped at 7 a.m. The cost went more than $300,000 over budget. Worst of all, the crew was nowhere near ready to start on the next episode.

Old Fashioned Murder

Originally, Chambers had hoped to use *Roar of the Crowd* as the second episode. He paid freelancers Les and Tina Pine $7,500 for a rewrite, but their revision, now titled *A Lion in Season*, was unusable. "It's worse than before… and absolutely the worst *Columbo* script ever submitted," Metzler reported.

Instead Chambers defaulted to Peter Fischer's *In Deadly Hate*, inspired by Shakespeare's *Richard III*. Fischer envisioned Burgess Meredith as an aging, Shakespeare-quoting curator of his sister's medieval museum, who's fearful that his profit-minded nephew intends to take over. The uncle schemes to kill the nephew and make it look like the work of his other nephew. The script was conventional *Columbo*. In fact, it reused the motive of *Any Old Port in a Storm* and the Shakespearean trappings of *Dagger of the Mind*. It even borrowed the "calendar watch" clue that was excised from *Last Salute to the Commodore*.

Falk did not want something conventional. During the production of *Fade In to Murder*, he gave *In Deadly Hate* to May and Feibleman, without notifying Chambers or Universal. "Peter cut me out," Chambers said. As Bob Metzler reported to his bosses at NBC: "Elaine May is in complete control… she won't talk with Everett because she doesn't know who he is." Falk actually had gone directly to NBC to secure the writers' pay—$23,000 to May and $15,000 to Feibleman. Universal's Dick Irving had to hear about their hiring thirdhand.

When Chambers saw their first revisions, he realized that May and Feibleman were completely overhauling the plot and the characters. And until he had a somewhat "final" version, he couldn't begin casting. Falk told him not to worry about it. The only thing he needed Chambers to take care of was finding the right director.

Chambers recounted, "Peter said, 'Get me a director who will do everything I want him to do,' which meant everything *Elaine* wanted him to do. I got a friend of mine, Bob Douglas, who did *Baretta* with Bobby Blake. So I knew he could stomach it. I said, 'It's a credit, take the money and run.' He said okay. He was okay with somebody else telling him what to do all the time."

The same night that the *Columbo* crew was working until the wee hours of the morning to finish filming *Fade In to Murder*, Falk's assistant, Carole Smith, was keeping the same late hours with Elaine May, rushing to type up her notations and scribblings on what used to be *In Deadly Hate*. That Friday afternoon, she delivered the revised script—half-typed, half-handwritten—of the newly renamed *Old Fashioned Murder*. The production meeting planned for the next day was postponed until the following Monday, to give everyone the weekend to read the new script.

Most everyone who read it was left aghast. Everything had been turned on its head. Most of the lead characters were changed from men to women. The murderer was changed from the bitter, sharp-tongued uncle to a colorless spinster, Ruth Lytton. She tries to pin the killing not on a nephew, but on a niece—who may secretly be Lytton's own illegitimate child. By the end of the episode, Lytton has an abrupt change of heart and agrees to confess to spare her niece's feelings. Also added for unsuccessful comedic touches was a sister prone to fainting. Even Columbo's quick trip to question an old Italian barber became a visit to an effeminate male hairdresser at an upscale salon, where Columbo ends up getting his hair oddly styled.

The moneymen were equally apprehensive. The episode was predicted to go $500,000 over budget, the sets hadn't been built, and Falk was scheduled to leave for the Altman film in less than three weeks. "Do not shoot it!" warned one exec. "Dump it! You'll have to shut down in the middle of shooting."

Unbeknownst to Chambers, May had begun casting the episode. She hired her daughter, Jeannie Berlin, to play the niece; her friend Joyce Van Patten as the murderer; her collaborator Feibleman as the guard; Berlin's ex-boyfriend Jon Miller as a cop; and Feibleman's typist to play the jewelry salesman. Poetically, May suggested that Chambers appear as the primary victim, even though the producer hadn't acted in decades. He declined.

Come Monday, the production meeting consisted of Falk, May and Chambers. Story editor Bill Driskill wasn't invited because no story ideas were being solicited. Chambers, though, insisted on bringing up the holes in the script. "There were so many *Columbo*-type mistakes," he recalled. "It was a robbery of a private museum with millions of dollars of artifacts in it, and the bad guy broke in by digging a little hole outside the entrance. The alarm went underground and he cut the wires. I said, 'Elaine, you can't do that. That's too simple. You've also put a telephone booth in a place where there wouldn't be a telephone.' If anybody had a problem, she just wouldn't change. Peter backed her up. She and I didn't speak."

Filming finally got underway one week later. Against Metzler's wishes, the first scenes were shot on location—at a gas station, 40 miles north of the studio in the town of Piru, and at a jewelry shop and a hair salon. Because the gas station scene was shot out in the open instead of on the backlot, trucks and other background noises got on the dialogue track, necessitating the actors loop in their lines later. Shooting also ran seriously behind, so the salon scene was only half-finished. But the salon they chose was only available for filming on Mondays. They would have to continue paying the actor playing the stylist $1,000 a day until they could complete the scene a week later.

The next day, Falk arbitrarily decided he wanted a set changed from a bedroom to a sitting room. The set had to be redecorated and then Falk called Feibleman to come check it out, causing Falk to miss his appointment in Wardrobe.

Feibleman and May continued rewriting the script as they went. It was only day two but Metzler could see where this was headed. He called his bosses at NBC and recommended the production be shut down until a completed script was in hand. NBC, not wishing to antagonize Falk, said to keep going.

Falk's natural indecisiveness intensified since, after production started, May returned to the East Coast and he had to get her input by long distance. "Elaine May was calling in from a phone booth in New York," Chambers recounted. "She would tell Peter, 'This shouldn't be a dolly shot,' and Peter would go back to the director and have him change his shot."

May also had her daughter, Jeannie Berlin, stand behind one of the cameras and use hand signals to coach the other actors.

Script pages were being swapped out so quickly that the actors had insufficient time to prepare and memorize their lines. The production shot six days a week, so Falk reconvened the cast on a Sunday to rehearse the next day's scenes, without any of the crew and without permission from Universal or NBC. He kept them on the set until 10:30 at night, denying the actors the required minimum of 12 hours between work sessions.

"We have no intention of paying for this rehearsal," Metzler stated. "Actors cannot accept calls from other actors." The Universal Labor Relations Department was called in to investigate.

Since NBC was picking up the overages, Universal cared less about the increased costs than about the hassle of having to work around other shows' production schedules, since they had little idea when *Columbo* would actually finish up on one stage and begin work on another. They were also burning through film. Rather than save the best take from each scene, Falk insisted on printing multiple copies of each. One day's rushes totaled 110 minutes of film.

Dick Irving was livid. He called Metzler—twice—to go off on tirades. Irving was adamant: "Enough is enough!" Metzler confirmed that NBC didn't want to confront Falk, because they were afraid he would walk out before the show was finished. Irving, however, would welcome that, since they'd be able to place him on suspension.

Chambers had still hoped to film an episode in Japan and planned a scouting trip there for the end of August, after *Old Fashioned Murder* was supposed to have wrapped. By September 1, barely half the script had been shot. Chambers was happy to have an excuse to leave town. He and writer Ken Kolb flew to Japan for two weeks to research story ideas, assuming that shooting—and the Elaine May experiment—would be completed by the time he returned.

Soon after, Falk's film with Altman fell through, and he pulled himself out of the Bergman film since they could not meet his salary demands. His schedule suddenly wide open, Falk was even less motivated to complete *Old Fashioned Murder* in a timely fashion.

At the time, the press interviewed Celeste Holm, who played the overly dramatic sister, to ask about the ongoing project. She said she was unable to share what the episode was about—but not because she was sworn to secrecy. She simply didn't know. Holm said we "rehearsed it one way and then (Falk) had us film it 27 different ways. God only knows what the editor will do with the finished product; he can make it into anything he wants. Falk's a compulsive perfectionist, and it drives everybody crazy."

As for her character, she said, "Damned if I know! I think it was a sad, rich, lonely, self-destructive and very foolish lady. I had heard strange tales about Falk, but until now had no idea of what they meant."

The mounting delays and expenses would have been problematic even if they were making a masterpiece. Metzler could see they were far from that. He was growing increasingly concerned watching the dailies. He went to Stage 5 and, during a pause in shooting, pulled Falk aside. He resolved not to mention May by name, to avoid aggravating the situation. "Peter," Metzler said, "the footage is *bad*."

Falk disagreed. "Everyone says it's bad. How wrong can they be?"

"Are you sure they are wrong?"

Falk had no response and returned to filming. Then suddenly, in the middle of one take, he stopped and turned to Metzler. He asked if he thought he was defending a bad situation. Metzler shot back that Falk was in a better position to answer that question than he was. The two held up production for several minutes, barking back and forth at each other.

During this time, Metzler had been keeping Peter Fischer in the loop on *Columbo*, since Metzler also oversaw Fischer's mini-series *Once an Eagle*. They both were horrified at, according to Metzler, "the destruction of *In Deadly Hate*."

"They made such a mishmash of it that I took my name off of it," Fischer said. "It was awful." Fischer instead had his story credited to "Lawrence Vail," the playwright character in Kaufman and Hart's *Once in a Lifetime*, who is driven to the nuthouse by the ineptitude of a Hollywood studio.

Chambers returned from Japan on September 16, to discover the production far from finished. Finally, on day 30, everything came to a head. "Today," Metzler reported, "is the day that all hell broke loose." The day before, NBC had finalized the deal with Falk to ensure two more episodes would be filmed before the season was finished. So, with his signature in hand, they figured that—after four years of buckling to his every demand—they could at long last stand up to Peter Falk. NBC was finally prepared to join Universal in presenting a united front. Herb Schlosser, the newly named president of NBC, instructed Dick Irving to "shut down *Columbo*." Chambers was told any last scenes had to be finished that day, under authority of both Universal and NBC, and that Falk was to be barred from post-production.

Metzler headed for the set to calm down Falk. He expected him to be fuming. Instead, Metzler discovered "he was genuinely stunned... and then not-so-genuinely played the part of the martyr who has just been wounded by the 'injustices' of NBC and Universal. The 'offense' that hurt most was (the) retraction of his right to edit the film. Jeannie Berlin was her usual repulsive, drama-coaching self who was finally banished by Everett Chambers. Despite Peter's protests, the picture wrapped at 10:40 p.m."

Six days after finishing shooting *Old Fashioned Murder*, Falk flew to New York to personally meet with new NBC president Herb Schlosser and his predecessor, Bob Howard. The bigwigs stressed how they hoped the relationship could continue, but things had to run more smoothly and efficiently. Falk blamed Universal, citing their resistance to Elaine May. Howard reminded him that the studio held the right to resist her: "If Universal doesn't want Elaine May, Universal doesn't have to have Elaine May." They could not tolerate another month-long shooting schedule. Falk promised that he would shoot the next show in 12 to 15 days.

Chambers had settled on *The Lesser of Two Evils*, featuring a psychiatrist who intentionally leaves incriminating evidence at a rare coin shop. He then has a thief steal coins for him from the shop and, on his way out, trip the alarm at the exact moment the psychiatrist is across town committing murder. That way, when the intrepid Sgt. Wilson (Bob Dishy) ties the psychiatrist to the robbery, he is establishing an alibi for the murder.

The day after Falk returned from New York, he had Carole Smith call Chambers to have him both send the latest script to Feibleman and notify *Old Fashioned Murder*'s editor, Stan Frazen, to be available to work in the cutting room with Falk over the weekend. Chambers complied.

The following Monday, Metzler met with Chambers to discuss his two "tactical errors": first, sending the script to Feibleman and second, permitting Falk to edit. Both moves undermined the firm stance presented at the New York meeting that the companies had been promoting all week. Chambers thought Metzler was fooling himself. "The combined NBC-Universal decisiveness and strength was good for one day only—last Friday, when we wrapped the picture,"

Chambers said.

Shortly after their meeting, Chambers received a call from Falk. Both men knew the working relationship was fractured beyond repair. Falk finally asked, "Do you resign or do I have you fired?" Chambers, reading the writing on the wall, had been looking for a new job, but hadn't found one yet and knew that if he quit he'd void the remainder of his Universal contract. He declined. Falk fired him.

When Dick Irving got the news, he said Chambers wasn't going anywhere. He stressed to Falk's lawyer, "Peter cannot fire a Universal employee." Irving, backed by NBC, wanted Everett Chambers to remain. "Now if Everett doesn't want to stay on, that's a different matter."

Following the meeting, NBC scrambled to review Falk's contract, to make sure he wasn't granted any "extra concessions" that would allow him to dismiss the producer. To their relief, the contract stated that Chambers was in charge of selecting the scripts and Falk was obligated to shoot them, according to Universal's schedule and budget, or Falk would be in violation. Emboldened, Irving also relayed to Falk that his request to have his personal assistant receive associate producer credit was denied.

The next day, Metzler and Irving confirmed with Chambers that they were behind him, and wanted him to stay. He should start planning the next show. Chambers then called Falk to tell him they had chosen *The Lesser of Two Evils* for the third show, and it would be done without Elaine May or Peter Feibleman. Falk curtly replied, "Thank you very much," and hung up.

The united front began to crumble once Falk and his lawyers started turning the screws on NBC. Ten days later, Irving called Chambers into his office. Universal was letting him go and paying off his contract for the two remaining shows. *Columbo* had no producer, and Falk had no other projects lined up—for the first time since the series started.

14
The Fixer

NBC's Sunday night wheel returned to begin one final go-around on October 3, 1976. But for the first time in *Columbo* history, another *NBC Mystery Movie* series had the honor of opening the season. The hotly anticipated *Quincy, M.E.* got the nod and drew such good ratings that the second episode was scheduled the following week, right after *Columbo's* debut with *Fade In to Murder*. Slipping past ABC's *The Six Million Dollar Man* but crushing CBS's *Sonny and Cher Show* and *Kojak*, *Fade In to Murder* was the third most-watched show of the week, with *Quincy* fourth. The network decided to piggyback the third episode of *Quincy* after *Old Fashioned Murder*, during November sweeps.

Prospects for Sunday nights looked great—until NBC decided to begin mixing up its scheduling. Part of the reason was necessity—*Columbo* had completed only two shows and would get, at most, two more. *McMillan* and *McCloud* cut back to six apiece. So NBC began regularly doubling up all four series, burning through its original episodes and leaving most Sundays with a movie, a mini-series, or a rerun. Over the season, original mysteries aired on just 15 of the 34 weeks. From week to week, viewers now had to consult a *TV Guide* to know if the *NBC Mystery Movie* was even on. Ratings plummeted. NBC blamed the wheel itself. After four original episodes, *Quincy* was spun off as its own weekly one-hour-long show. Its replacement in the rotation, *Lanigan's Rabbi*, would last four episodes.

Nearing the end of 1977, Falk still owed Universal two more *Columbos* for Season 6. But with no producer, work halted. One hindrance was that NBC considered it Universal's responsibility to find a new producer and Universal considered it NBC's.

Talks with Harvey Hart, Bill Blinn (*The Rookies*), and Bill Sackheim (*Once an*

Eagle) went nowhere. Dick Irving observed, "No one with any self-respect will take the job."

The key was finding someone whom Falk trusted and would listen to. Since Falk's primary complaint was with the material, ideally it would be a writer-producer who could do any rewriting himself, yet would not indulge in the excesses of someone like Elaine May or Patrick McGoohan. What they needed was a return to the iron-fist rule of Levinson and Link.

One name made particularly good sense: Richard Alan Simmons, the force behind Falk's Emmy-winning *The Price of Tomatoes*. He was one of the few company men that Falk heeded. For *The Trials of O'Brien*, Simmons somehow had gotten Falk to complete 22 hour-long dramas in one week apiece. In the intervening 10 years, he had primarily been writing and producing TV movies.

Falk met with Simmons shortly after Christmas 1976. Simmons was available, but he wanted to make one thing clear: he wasn't a *Columbo* fan. He loved Falk's characterization, he just didn't care for the show. That didn't mean he wasn't up for a challenge—so long as he was allowed to make "improvements." Simmons suggested building more humanity, emotion, drama and tension into the program, without messing with the Lieutenant's character. Falk was sold.

Simmons asked for a bankroll. NBC balked. But time was getting short. As they weighed their options, Falk contracted to star in Neil Simon's *The Cheap Detective*, to begin filming in the spring. NBC knew Simmons' hiring would make Falk happy but, for a change, it wasn't because the men were social friends—they were colleagues who worked well together. Falk's previous appointees, like May and Chambers, were loyal to Falk first. Simmons prioritized the work. Hopeful that it might finally have found an ally on the inside, NBC consented to Simmons' terms.

Falk was pleased, especially after just having agreed to a $2.4-million divorce settlement with his ex-wife. Falk had his lawyer, Bert Fields, propose to NBC that, for $2 million, he would make four additional *Columbos* for the 1977-1978 season to be run as standalone specials, free of the wheel. NBC's official response: "Forget it." The wheel would definitely not return. But four independent specials were worth, at most, $1.5 million to the network. They figured they'd be lucky to just finish the current season and wanted to be sure Simmons would work out.

After signing the contract, Simmons swung by Metzler's office to pick up the two unproduced scripts still under consideration—*The Lesser of Two Evils*, which Feibleman had been massaging over the last few months, and Metzler's own "orchestra story," now called *Murder in B Flat*. Metzler quickly realized that Simmons was picking them up only as a courtesy. He wanted to generate his own scripts. Off the top of his head, Simmons threw out story ideas—*good* story ideas—left and right. What if Columbo squared off against a genius from Mensa? Or a gourmet chef? Or an obsessive orchid grower?

Simmons was enthusiastic about the job—not consigned to it. The errand to pick up two scripts he had no interest in turned into a deep two-hour discussion that flew by. As Simmons turned to leave at 7:15 p.m., Metzler jotted down in his notebook, "The prospects of a smooth-running *Columbo* show look good."

To get a true feel for the show, Simmons wanted to view *Columbo* at its best and at its most recent. He screened *Death Lends a Hand*, *Any Old Port in a Storm*, *Playback*, *Fade In to Murder*, and *Old Fashioned Murder*. Falk's portrayal amused him, but he found the shows themselves shallow and artificial. He thought they overly relied on clues. Simmons concluded that, since the show was basically about Columbo conversing with the killer, both of their characters should be better developed. He saw most of the villains as cartoons; he wanted more unique personalities, with insights into their personal lives, backstories and extenuating circumstances that impacted their decision to murder. Columbo's character was already well defined, but Simmons saw room to deepen it. Instead of just mentioning a relative, Columbo should tell stories about them—or about his own past—that resonated with his current case.

As well, Simmons thought that the adversaries' relationship should be more fraught with tension—from the go. Columbo shouldn't drift into the story, meekly searching for his lost pencil. The detective should make a more formidable entrance, with the killer dreading his arrival. The murderers should respect Columbo's skills, but still be confident that they can outsmart him. No longer should anyone think of Columbo as an idiot or a harmless pest. Even other detectives should look up to him—and no longer be buffoons themselves. In fact, Simmons created a recurring character, Sgt. Burke, whom Columbo could confide in and conspire with. Unlike the often-gullible Sgts. Kramer and Wilson, whom Columbo was always one step ahead of, Burke would work in lockstep with the Lieutenant. Simmons would feature Sgt. Burke in most of the episodes he produced, seemingly unconcerned that he cast different actors in the role from one show to the next.

The Bye-Bye Sky High I.Q. Murder Case

During his first days on the lot, Simmons narrowed his villains to four: the Mensa genius to star Robert Morley, an Agatha Christie-type playwright with Bette Davis, a gourmet cook, and a psychiatrist played by Hal Holbrook. He began fleshing out the main characters and the basic setups, then farmed out the most promising two—Mensa genius and Agatha Christie—to freelancers, expecting full scripts in two to three weeks. Simmons would then act as his own story editor, personally rewriting each script until it met his standards and he knew it was safe to turn on the cameras.

The producer was confident he could get the show back on track, but expectations needed to be realistic. No producer had come close to meeting a 10- or 14-day shooting schedule since Season 1. Supported by NBC, he demanded

---

Season 6 – 1976-1977

Fade In to Murder
Filmed: July 14 – Aug. 6, 1976
Stars: Peter Falk, William Shatner, Bert Remsen, Alan Manson, Lola Albright
Director: Bernard Kowalski
Producer: Everett Chambers
Teleplay: Lou Shaw, Peter S. Feibleman
Story: Henry Garson
Air Date: Oct. 10, 1976
Nielsen Ranking: #3

Old Fashioned Murder
Working Title: *In Deadly Hate*
Filmed: Aug. 13 – Sept. 24, 1976
Guest Stars: Joyce Van Patten, Jeannie Berlin, Tim O'Connor, Celeste Holm, Peter S. Feibleman
Director: Robert Douglas
Producer: Everett Chambers
Teleplay: Peter S. Feibleman
Story: "Lawrence Vail" (Peter S. Fischer)
Air Date: Nov. 28, 1976

The Bye-Bye Sky High I.Q. Murder Case
Working Title: *Bye Bye, Sky-High I.Q.*
Filmed: March – April 1977
Guest Stars: Theodore Bikel, Kenneth Mars, Sorrell Booke, Samantha Eggar
Director: Sam Wanamaker
Producer: Richard Alan Simmons
Teleplay: Robert Malcolm Young
Air Date: May 22, 1977

from Universal—and received—17 days for a 90-minute show and 22 days for a two-hour show.

For *The Bye-Bye Sky High I.Q. Murder Case*, Simmons let the plot flow naturally from what he pictured a murderous Mensa member would be like—a brilliant accountant who bullies his inferiors, has a beautiful wife who cares only about his money, and is so smart he can design an absurdly complicated, seemingly foolproof murder.

Simmons cast Robert Morley as the lead. Morley's agent agreed to the deal, but had to back out when he realized his client would be in a play by the time filming began. Second choice was Peter Ustinov, who wanted $20,000 plus expenses. NBC said yes, but Ustinov changed his mind and passed. Simmons quickly pivoted to James Mason or Rex Harrison, before settling on Theodore Bikel.

Try and Catch Me

The Agatha Christie tale was assigned to veteran TV freelancer Gene Thompson, who had recently optioned his first novel, *Lupe*. Thompson's *Columbo* teleplay came in on time, but Simmons found it largely unusable. Metzler noted the "script is a bomb. Gene Thompson's $400,000 picture deal based on his novel has paralyzed him." In fact, after *Columbo*, Thompson gave up television to concentrate on novels.

Simmons turned the script over to Luther Davis for a full-yet-fast rewrite, knowing Falk had just weeks before he was needed for his next movie. Immediately after *Bye-Bye* wrapped, production began on Falk's fourth and final contracted episode. In *Try and Catch Me*, octogenarian mystery novelist Abigail Mitchell suspects her niece wasn't really lost at sea in a boating accident, but was actually bumped off by her husband Edmund. So she locks him in her walk-in safe, where he suffocates, but not before stashing a dying clue.

As with most of the *Columbos* he produced, Simmons devised the basic premise, handed it off to a writer-for-hire, provided notes through the writing process, and—once a finished script was submitted—exhaustively rewrote it. Simmons detested stereotypes and preferred ambiguity and shading. So he thought the audience should have some uncertainty over whether Edmund really killed his wife.

Simmons removed some incriminating dialogue from Davis' script, such as when during a heartfelt conversation with Abigail on the pier, Columbo was to mention, "A few weeks before your niece died, she filed an assault and battery complaint against her husband. Then she withdrew the charges. You must've had some idea about that. And you still arranged to leave him your money."

Originally, when Abigail walks in on Edmund in her library, he was supposed to be examining some books, a glass of brandy in hand. Instead, Simmons had him pick up a photo of his deceased wife and smile.

In his initial treatment, Simmons had called Abigail Mitchell's hit play *Murder in Three Flats*. Metzler pointed out that the title was very similar to that of his own, *Murder in B Flat*. Simmons passed along instructions to change the title. The revised book title, "*The Night I Was Murdered* by Abigail Mitchell," became Edmund's dying clue. The victim tears off the first two words from the cover page, leaving "*I Was Murdered* by Abigail Mitchell."

As the character of Abigail developed from being a more intimidating character to a kindlier, less threatening character, Simmons changed his casting plan from Bette Davis to 5-foot-tall, 80-year-old Ruth Gordon. After a long career as a writer and stage actress, Gordon had found superstardom in her latter years with movies like *Rosemary's Baby* and *Harold and Maude*.

The moment filming was completed on *Try and Catch Me*, Falk reported to the set of *The Cheap Detective*. Yet Simmons was still embroiled in post-production on *Bye-Bye*; there was no possibility of completing *Try and Catch Me* before the end of the season. It would have to be held over for the fall. Falk, with no new TV contract, signed to begin filming a movie about the notorious Brinks robbery of 1950 that would keep him occupied until December.

In the meantime, Simmons finished *The Bye-Bye Sky High I.Q. Murder Case* barely in time for it to air before the summer hiatus. It finally broadcast on May 22, 1977, six months after the last original episode and long after most series had switched over to airing strictly reruns. Falk joked that it had been so long that "a lot of people thought Columbo was dead."

Despite not having Falk under contract, Universal had Simmons continue to do preliminary work on additional *Columbos*, including a new story about a real estate woman and another about a network executive. The producer had brought a semblance of control to the operation. Shows still went over budget—*Try and Catch Me* cost nearly $1.5 million and went two days over schedule—but not ridiculously so.

In mid-July, as Falk was finishing *The Cheap Detective*, news arrived that *The Brink's Job* needed a major rewrite and would not begin filming until after the start of 1978. A window opened, and NBC seized the opportunity. They agreed to meet Falk's previous terms: $500,000 per show for four specials—two at 90 minutes, two at two hours. What sealed the deal was an agreement between NBC and Universal. NBC would continue paying overages of $225,000 per show—but not a cent more. In exchange, Universal would not give NBC a rebate if the overages were less than $225,000. Whether *Columbo* went thousands of dollars over or under budget, the incentive to control expenditures once again returned to Universal. NBC could now project its final costs and no longer needed an agent on site questioning every expense. Bob Metzler was out of a job.

Make Me a Perfect Murder

Simmons had the next script ready to begin filming by mid-August. *Make Me a Perfect Murder* involved ambitious television executive, Kay Freestone, who murders her boss/lover when he bypasses her for a promotion. The subject matter allowed the writers to slip in some jabs against their meddling overlords at NBC. "Over at the network, all we get to do is pay for these pictures and try to let you know what we want—and how we want it," Freestone tells the producer. "Anything wrong with keeping you informed?"

Falk liked the first draft, but it spent considerably more time following the murderer than it did Columbo and it took even longer than usual to get the detective on-screen. Simmons suggested starting the show with Columbo's Peugeot getting rear-ended. Then he could wear a neck brace for much of the episode, giving him an added schtick to play with. As well, originally Columbo was supposed to get the final clue while sitting with Freestone at her home, watching her new pilot, *The Professional*. Instead, Columbo catches a bit of *The Professional* on his own, taking Dog to the TV repair shop.

The tense showdown finale was supposed to be shot during a light show at the Griffith Park Planetarium, but was switched to an arcade at the Santa Monica Pier.

Guest villainess Trish Van Devere found Falk's improvisations helpful in loosening up her own performance. "I go into things almost overly prepared," she said. "I can be too ready, too stiff. Peter Falk knew how to rectify that. He would give me a line out of context, or surprise me to get the reaction he wanted. It worked wonders."

At 77, Mike Lally turned in his final performance in *Make Me a Perfect Murder*, playing a security guard who, while making his rounds, stops to pick up a magazine off a table and sneak a peek at the centerfold. One day during production, Lally suddenly just stopped showing up on the set. After about a week, Falk had his secretary, Carole Smith, try to track him down. Falk finally reached Lally's son, who had been sworn to secrecy on why his father had quit. Lally Sr. had caught another of Falk's longtime cronies stealing. Lally wouldn't rat out the co-worker, but he couldn't work with him either. Lally Jr., though, promised only that he wouldn't tell Falk. He hadn't said anything about telling John Cassavetes, who passed the truth on to Falk. The dishonest crewmember was fired, but Lally was ready to be done.

Murder Under Glass

After a rare two-month break, Falk returned to film Simmons' gourmet chef story, *Murder Under Glass*. Under *Trials of O'Brien* writer Robert van Scoyk, the bad guy became a food critic, Paul Gerard, who poisons a restaurant owner who threatened to expose his extortion racket. Simmons' primary instruction was to ensure Columbo and Gerard didn't like each other, but did respect each other's talents. They were to suppress their mutual distaste, subtly showing it but not telling it, until the end, after Gerard unsuccessfully attempts to poison Columbo.

The directive played into Simmons' preference that Columbo be more confrontational and self-aware. To Simmons, Columbo had nothing to be modest about. Falk in turn began playing the character even brasher, bolder, bigger. His delivery became more measured, more dramatic, more labored, and his hand gestures more flamboyant. In one scene, Columbo bawls out a young, timid waiter for no apparent reason. Falk, in trying to stretch the character, was unwittingly turning his portrayal into a broad caricature, like a comic doing an impression of Columbo.

Falk insisted his fiancée, Shera Danese, play the villain's girlfriend. He also handpicked a young director whose career had suddenly gone cold. Jonathan Demme's first big-budget feature, *Citizens Band*, had just been released—and bombed. "What had been sort of a promising, budding career just hit a wall," Demme said. "I couldn't get arrested… until Peter Falk saw *Citizens Band* and invited me to do a *Columbo*, saving me." Shortly after *Murder Under Glass*, Demme was hired to direct *Melvin and Howard* and eventually *The Silence of the Lambs*.

As soon as filming was completed, Falk and Danese married on December 2, 1977, with his buddy and business advisor Wayne Rogers (*M*A*S*H*) as his best man and John Cassavetes, Ben Gazzara, and Bob Dishy as ushers. The couple had to delay their honeymoon until January, since Falk was due on the set for the next episode.

How to Dial a Murder

Simmons next planned to go with his psychiatrist idea, but he didn't have in mind a traditional shrink, like Columbo previously battled in *Prescription: Murder* and *A Deadly State of Mind*. Working with screenwriter Anthony Lawrence, Simmons made his killer a behavioral psychologist, patterned after EST founder Werner Erhard. He got inspiration for the criminal method from the recent *Doberman Gang* movies. In Lawrence's plot, self-help lecturer and movie buff Dr. Eric Mason discovers a colleague had an affair with his late wife.

WEDDING PARTY *(left to right)* included maid-of-honor Jennifer Austin, best man Wayne Rogers, Shera Danese, Peter Falk, and groomsmen Ben Gazzara and Bob Dishy.

So he trains his dogs—a Doberman pinscher and a German shepherd—to attack when they hear the word "Rosebud."

A subplot involving college student Cindi, who has taken up residence in Dr. Mason's guesthouse, had been planned to be much racier. The flirty co-ed likes the doctor, and the doctor likes her, but due to guilt over the mysterious death of his wife, when they are alone, he finds himself unable to, uh, rise to the occasion. According to an early draft, when Columbo comes to interview the bikini-clad Cindi at poolside, she was to start coming on to him, beginning with requesting he cover her with suntan oil.

"You can ask me anything you want," Cindi says. "I think you're cute."

"Look, I don't want to mislead you, Cindi," Columbo responds, while continuing to apply lotion. "Like I told you, I'm a married man."

"That doesn't mean you stop being human."

"The truth is I'm old enough to be your father," Columbo says. "Maybe not by much, but old enough."

"That's silly. You can't be over 35."

When Columbo finally gets her to talk about her relationship with the doctor, she says, "It isn't as if I didn't try."

"You mean, nothing ever happened between you...."

"It isn't as if HE didn't try...," she says.

"It just never worked out?"

"I mean, he REALLY tried... I thought maybe it just might be me. I got very upset. But he explained that it had happened to him before."

"I think I understand."

"You can stop putting oil on now."

Columbo sheepishly puts the oil down, then realizes he has put too much on. He tries to wipe some off with a towel but, as he leans in, she tries to kiss him. Columbo gingerly eludes her lips and exits warily, shaking his head.

Simmons again had the murderer make an attempt on Columbo's life—and originally he planned two attempts. After the Lieutenant learns of the doctor's performance issues, he was to visit Mason. The doctor is seated alone at a table on the rooftop patio of the university's psychology building, his work papers spread out in front of him. Columbo asks him for advice for a "friend" who is experiencing the same sexual problems. "Here's the problem... he can't be a man with the girl," Columbo says, "you know what I mean? He tries, I mean he REALLY tries, but he just can't."

The veiled innuendo enrages the doctor to the point where he is on the verge of pushing Columbo off the edge of the building—when another officer suddenly shows up.

In the originally planned finale, Dr. Mason is about to poison the dogs at the animal shelter, when Columbo interrupts him and joins them in the cage. The doctor closes the door, locks it, and commands, "Rosebud!" But instead of attacking, the dogs lie down, having been retrained by Columbo.

In the revised final script, Dr. Mason is about to strangle the college student to keep her quiet, when Columbo walks in. And the doctor's attempt to sic the dogs (now both Dobermans) on Columbo was relocated to a separate scene in his memorabilia-filled house where the first murder took place. The dogs do jump Columbo, but to show affection.

Although Dog makes a brief appearance in *How to Dial a Murder* at the obedience school, the hound was originally envisioned to have multiple scenes, including when Columbo leaves his encounter with the doctor at the university to head to the school. The Lieutenant was to open his car door to see Dog sitting in his spot behind the wheel. Columbo commands him to scoot over, but Dog doesn't budge. He finally pushes him out of the way. As he begins to drive, Columbo turns to his pet: "I was talking to this psychologist. He says dogs have been known to attack their masters without a reason. What do you think about that?"

Dog stares at him in silence.

"No comment, huh? Well, I'll tell you somethin'. Don't go getting any ideas. I'm ready for you. You hear?"

Dog regards him balefully, then turns to stare out the window.

The episode's biggest delay came from initially being headed by a first-time editor. "He unfortunately was not ready to be an editor yet," recalled Simmons' son David, who for about three weeks worked as his assistant editor on the show. "He just got an amazing break. It was a little bit of a nightmare for me. There was one scene in the show where the dogs attack and he spent about two weeks working on 15 seconds. You can't do that in television, you have to keep up the pace. Whatever was shot yesterday is cut by the end of today. I remember my father saying to me, 'Why didn't you tell me what was going on in there?' and I didn't have a good answer for him other than I was working for this guy. That ended very unhappily for him. They went on to another editor, who brought in his own assistant editor."

The Conspirators

As Simmons was preparing to begin production on *How to Dial a Murder*, he still hadn't decided on what to do for the final episode. Fortuitously, he happened upon a script for a proposed TV pilot by Pat Robison about Irish poet Joe Devlin, who preaches peace but is actually running guns for rebels in Northern Ireland. The idea contained a gem of a clue—Devlin shoots a crooked middleman and poetically rolls a bottle of his favorite whiskey, Tullamore Dew, next to the body. The bottle's label displayed the slogan "Give every man his Dew."

In early December 1977, Simmons handed the idea off to Howard Berk (*By Dawn's Early Light*) to adapt it for *Columbo*. Just before filming began, NBC insisted on not upsetting Tullamore by associating the company's tagline with execution. They preferred an imaginary brand name for the whiskey. It became Full's Irish Dew, and the slogan "Let each man be paid in Full."

Although this was the final episode of Falk's contract, he'd been down this road before. Guest villain Clive Revill, who had starred as Fagin in Broadway's *Oliver!*, recalled, "There was no sense of regret on the set that the show was ending. Peter and I had a lot of creative fun interacting with each other's characters."

That said, Falk's delivery came across as somewhat stilted, as if he had performed one take—or 10—too many. Press reports noted that on one of the last days of filming, the set was abruptly closed to visitors when Falk suddenly became so upset over a minor technical delay that he "hurled wooden cartons about the soundstage." Once he cooled down, he apologized to the director.

In truth, Falk likely did not expect it to be the last time he'd put on the raincoat. Unlike two years earlier with *Last Salute to the Commodore*, the filmmakers did not include numerous departures from the formula or clever on-screen nods to closing the book on a decade of sleuthing, apart from the villain's catchphrase: "This far and no farther."

There was no wrap party, no media farewell tour. Yet as Falk completed work on *The Conspirators* in February 1978, he still hadn't heard anything from NBC about returning for an eighth season. He chalked it up to the network's capriciousness—over the last couple of years, it seemed like one minute the programmers had cooled on *Columbo* and the next they couldn't live without it.

"I think the network likes to live dangerously," Falk said at the time. "I have a feeling they're going through some sort of trauma." He figured the call would come any day. It didn't.

Season 7 – 1977-1978

Try and Catch Me
Filming Completed: May 6, 1977
Stars: Peter Falk, Ruth Gordon, Mariette Hartley, G. D. Spradlin, Charles Frank
Director: James Frawley
Producer: Richard Alan Simmons
Teleplay: Gene Thompson, "Paul Tuckahoe" (Luther Davis)
Story: Gene Thompson
Air Date: Nov. 21, 1977
Nielsen Ranking: #15

Murder Under Glass
Working Titles: *A Taste of Eternity, Murder in Aspic*
Filmed: November 1977
Guest Stars: Louis Jourdan, Shera Danese, Richard Dysart, Mako
Director: Jonathan Demme
Producer: Richard Alan Simmons
Teleplay: Robert van Scoyk
Air Date: Jan. 30, 1978
Ranking: #14

Make Me a Perfect Murder
Filmed: Aug. – Sept. 1977
Guest Stars: Trish Van Devere, Laurence Luckinbill, James McEachin, Ron Rifkin, Lainie Kazan
Director: James Frawley
Producer: Richard Alan Simmons
Teleplay: Robert Blees
Air Date: Feb. 28, 1978
Ranking: #43

How to Dial a Murder
Working Titles: *Fangs for the Memory, The Laurel & Hardy W.C. Fields Citizen Kane Murder Case, Snips and Snails and Murderer's Tails*
Filmed: December 1977
Guest Stars: Nicol Williamson, Kim Cattrall, Ed Begley Jr.
Director: James Frawley
Producer: Richard Alan Simmons
Teleplay: Tom Lazarus
Story: Anthony Lawrence
Air Date: April 5, 1978

The Conspirators
Working Title: *The Murder-By-the-Case Murder Case*
Filmed: Jan. 9 – Feb. 1978
Guest Stars: Clive Revill, Jeanette Nolan, Bernard Behrens
Director: Leo Penn
Producer: Richard Alan Simmons
Teleplay: Howard Berk
Based on an Idea by: Pat Robison
Air Date: May 13, 1978
Rating: (27 share)

15
On Ice

NBC never canceled *Columbo*. It just declined to order new episodes. Granted, the specials were getting good ratings. But now that the show was no longer part of a weekly series locking down Sunday nights for NBC, the network no longer saw as much value in *Columbo*. It was no longer worth the expense and difficulty of working with Peter Falk.

Just as importantly, in January 1978 NBC hired a new president and CEO, Fred Silverman. A programming savant, Silverman had risen to fame in the early 1970s at CBS by replacing their stable of "rural shows" with edgier, more urban programs and spinoffs. In the mid-1970s, he took over ABC, boosting it from worst to first with young, hip, titillating fare like *Charlie's Angels* and *Three's Company*. Silverman would not start at NBC until June, but his predecessors were unwilling to make a commitment to *Columbo* until the new regime was in place.

The prognosis was not bright. The last of the "character cop" shows—*Kojak* and *Baretta*—had just been canceled. TV investigators would become private eyes with good looks and light humor, along the lines of *The Rockford Files*, *Hart to Hart*, and *Magnum, P.I.* Mysteries were all but dead.

Indeed, Silverman had no intention of bringing back *Columbo*. When he arrived at NBC, its cupboard was bare and just three months remained until the start of the new season. Of the previous season's 30 most-watched weekly series, NBC had two.

There was some discussion of continuing *Columbo* minus Falk. Universal executive Charlie Engel thought the idea absurd. "It was suggested we find someone else to play Columbo," Engel recalled. "I said, 'This is a waste of time.

Don't waste our money. Peter is Columbo.' When you say Columbo, everybody knows it's Peter Falk."

Silverman had a better idea, a spinoff: *Mrs. Columbo*. The character was never seen on *Columbo*, so they could make her anything they wanted, conforming her to contemporary tastes. And that way NBC could retain the *Columbo* audience, without having to endure the hardship of working with Falk.

Silverman brought in Dick Levinson, Bill Link, and Peter Fischer to set the format, with Brenda Vaccaro in mind for the lead. Despite their misgivings, the three mapped out the character of Mrs. Columbo—in her 40s, close to Falk's age, ethnic, warm, fun-loving, spends most of her time in the kitchen. They wanted Vaccaro, Maureen Stapleton, or Jean Stapleton. Fischer wrote a script. Silverman liked it. But once Vaccaro turned the part down, Silverman began insisting on casting a younger, sexier actress, like buxom blonde Carol Wayne. Shera Danese, Falk's 29-year-old bride, put her name in the hat, saying that if she got the gig, "I know I could get Peter to guest on the series—if I had to gag him and tie him up and drag him to the set."

Fischer had had enough. Levinson tried to dissuade him: "Well, my feeling is they're going to do it no matter what happens, so I think it's better that we do it rather than have some other stranger come in and do it."

"No, Dick, I don't think so," Fischer replied. "This was a lousy idea from day one. It cannot possibly succeed, and I don't want anything to do with it." As Fischer later recalled, "This was the one time where Dick and I really disagreed. He talked himself into it, and it was a terrible idea."

Silverman ended up casting 23-year-old Kate Mulgrew, who had originated the role of Mary Ryan on the daytime soap *Ryan's Hope*. The casting made it clear to Levinson and Link that the show could not possibly work. They dropped out as producers, yet were contractually obligated to review and offer notes on each script, as they had done for every season of *Columbo*.

Silverman first negotiated to bring in Dick Irving as producer, before settling on Richard Alan Simmons to executive produce a two-hour pilot and five one-hour episodes. Simmons quickly rewrote the pilot to accommodate the younger actress. He added as many ties to *Columbo* as possible—the dog, the car, her always expecting him to show up but him never arriving. Simmons cast Bob Dishy as the sergeant and Robert Culp as the villain in the first show, and Donald Pleasence for the second. Falk was invited to make a guest appearance, but he was so repulsed by the whole affair, he wouldn't even allow them to put his picture on Mrs. Columbo's mantle.

The *Mrs. Columbo* crew worked 18-hour days, seven days a week for six weeks, to complete the first two episodes. The network didn't receive the final prints

CRITICS considered Kate Mulgrew's *Mrs. Columbo* a real dog. *[Credit: NBCUniversal]*

until days before they were to be broadcast. The pilot, *Word Games*, premiered February 26, 1979, to a large audience (No. 18 in the Nielsens). Size did not translate into enjoyment. The heroine whom unwitting viewers encountered was nothing at all like the unseen wife Columbo had been gushing about all these years. She was neither ethnic nor eccentric, was 30 years younger than her unseen husband, had a 10-year-old daughter, wrote for the local weekly, and in the pilot was stalked by a psychopath.

The first weekly episode lost a quarter of the pilot's audience. The third show couldn't be finished in time and had to be pulled at the last minute and replaced with a *Quincy* rerun. Silverman announced that future episodes would air on time, but then the show would go on hiatus to be retooled. Privately, they realized the *Columbo* connection created false expectations for the audience and hampered an otherwise serviceable mystery series. The mission became removing any and all *Columbo* references, short of the new title, *Kate Columbo*. When that didn't help matters, they renamed it *Kate the Detective* and then *Kate Loves a Mystery*, but ratings continued to slip toward an inevitable cancellation.

With *Mrs. Columbo* floundering, discussions for reviving *Columbo* finally resumed in late 1979. But for a change Falk wanted to do more shows than the network did. "I can't imagine the network not bringing *Columbo* back," he said. "I wouldn't play Columbo every week, but I might do four specials a year."

NBC's Fred Silverman, however, said they were considering doing no more than one special annually. "He is such a perfectionist, it will take him a year to do one," Silverman explained, seemingly wanting the halo effect as the network of *Columbo* with minimal commitment.

Perhaps as a negotiating ploy, Falk suggested he retrieve his 20-year-old, threadbare raincoat from Universal. "I should get it back," he said. "It's mine. They keep it because at any time we could go back and do more *Columbos*. We used only one raincoat, though we had backups in case I got catsup on it. But I always went back to the original. That one felt good. I could always tell the difference."

As negotiations dragged on, Falk made it clear he was ready to don the raincoat again. "I'm ready to start doing *Columbo* again, all they gotta do is ask me," he vowed. As leverage, his team floated the possibility of Jimmy Stewart making a guest appearance, should NBC ever decide to restart the show.

Ultimately, the 1979 deal broke down over money. According to Perry Lafferty, NBC senior VP of programming, Falk wanted "an open-end deal which would give him the assurance there would be no time or budget limitations on the show." Universal was ready to proceed if NBC would again cover any overages. NBC said no.

In the meantime, *Columbo* never really went away—except in primetime. CBS had been airing occasional reruns on its late-night *CBS Late Movie* since 1976. Even though the episodes had to be harshly edited to accommodate twice the commercials, they enjoyed excellent ratings. In the fall of 1979, with no prospects for first-run *Columbos*, CBS began running an old episode every Thursday night. CBS moved the show to Tuesdays, then Mondays, back to Tuesdays, and finally back to Thursdays before its rights expired in 1985.

Yet Falk's feature film career was reaching new heights. His 1979 release, *The

In-Laws with Alan Arkin, premiered to great reviews and tremendous box office. Falk promptly signed a three-picture deal with Columbia Pictures to develop his own starring vehicles. During press tours for each movie, he was frequently asked about returning to TV. "I keep hoping *Columbo* isn't dead," he said during one interview. "Every year they keep threatening to bring him back. But they never carry out their threats."

In fact, Falk and NBC came close to a deal at least three more times: first in 1981, when he pitched five to eight specials a year; then in 1984, when NBC expressed interest in a trio of *Columbos* to go along with a trio of *Perry Masons* for the upcoming sweeps ratings periods in November, February and May; and finally in 1986, when Falk said he was willing to do from two to six specials a year. In each case, they came close but no cigar.

16
Second Life

On March 12, 1987, Dick Levinson—a three-packs-a-day smoker for over 30 years—died of a sudden heart attack. He was 52. Bill Link was devastated. Across four decades of show business, they had shared every professional moment together. For the first time in his life, Link stopped writing, unsure if on his own he even had the ability to continue.

Columbo would help him get back on his feet. Later that same year, ABC approached Universal about starting its own wheel. The dealbreaker: one of the segments had to be *Columbo*. Link said he was willing to consult if ABC was serious about reviving his most famous creation. But he made it clear that if he was going to be involved in a *Columbo 2.0*, there were to be no changes in the established format.

By the spring of 1988, Universal and ABC had hammered out the framework of a deal. The new wheel would be comprised of three mystery series, each producing six episodes. Burt Reynolds agreed to star as Florida P.I. *B.L. Stryker*. Lou Gossett Jr. would play crime-solving anthropology professor *Gideon Oliver*. Bill Link consented to executive produce the entire *ABC Mystery Movie* wheel. And Link said that Steven Spielberg was interested in directing the first *Columbo*.

ABC was willing to put up the money. They had everything they needed, except Peter Falk. He was in New York filming the wise-guy comedy *Cookie*. Falk said he needed five workable scripts before he would even consider reviving *Columbo*. So Link began brainstorming story ideas with past *Columbo* writers and then flying on weekends to New York to pitch them to Falk. Jackson Gillis suggested a 1980s take on one of his old *Perry Mason* twists—a gigolo shoots his lover twice, hours apart using different guns, so that if he's ever caught for the second shooting, he can prove he only shot a dead body. Robert van Scoyk (*Murder Under Glass*) wrote a treatment about a high-powered attorney who murders his best friend and frames the man's wife—his own jilted lover—whom he volunteers to defend in court.

The anticipated comeback was delayed when, on March 7, 1988, the Writers Guild of America went on strike again—halting the development of all TV series. Near the end of the five-month dispute, Falk finally agreed to one season containing six two-hour shows. He would get more power than he had had previously, along with the title of co-executive producer. Link also promised to consider a script Falk had begun writing during Season 1, in which a beautiful murderess tries to misdirect Columbo by romancing him, and he starts falling for her. That said, because of the writers' strike, Falk's was the *only* finished script they had. "It needs work," Link stated, before quickly adding, "Then again, they all need work."

Each episode would receive a more realistic schedule of 20 days and a budget of approximately $2.6 million, including Falk's salary of $650,000 for acting plus a producing fee. Although the budget was markedly higher than a decade earlier, inflation in production costs and salaries would actually force the revived series to take greater shortcuts, such as cheaper sets and fewer A-list guest stars. Whereas on NBC it wasn't unusual to have as many as four name stars on a single *Columbo*, the ABC shows would be lucky to get one or two recognizable guests.

One key for ensuring success was assigning *Columbo* to a Universal executive who could get the best out of Falk, through a constructive rather than combative relationship. The studio placed the show under Charlie Engel, a longtime vice president known for looking after James Garner and other "problem actors." Engel explained, "You might ask, how did I keep getting assigned to all of the 'troublemakers.' Now I use that in quotes and in small letters. I suspect it had to do with the fact that I had been there a long time and I learned very early in the business that the goal of the company was to make the shows successful, the goal of the company was to have relationships with the talent, so that the talent is happy and my bosses would be happy. And to do that you can't have an ego. Your success—my success, so to speak—was in the success of the shows that I was involved with and their success to the studio. I was the one who would sit down and fire people. I was the one who was assigned the troubled stars, and I had no problems whatsoever because I knew what the goal was, to know what the artist wanted and what they needed."

No longer would there be reports of Falk feuding with the studio or the network. Future delays or on-set tantrums would remain in house. Falk was given a spacious, ground-floor office in the Producers Building, with a sunlit patio off

WILLIAM LINK and Peter Falk reunited in 1989 to revive *Columbo* for ABC. *[Credit: NBCUniversal]*

the back looking out onto the commissary. And Engel would make sure Falk was granted the autonomy to do as he pleased. Falk had always gotten his way, so what was the use of fighting it?

To ensure there were minimal problems, Universal assigned an army of producers to the show, at one point crediting 10 different ones on *Columbo*. As co-executive producer, Falk would offer direction and hold ultimate veto power. Richard Alan Simmons was brought back as executive producer; as showrunner, he would write the final draft of scripts and creatively steward the show.

Bill Link became supervising executive producer, the creative head of the entire wheel who worked with each series' showrunner and participated in some story meetings. Simmons brought in a favorite collaborator since *The Price of Tomatoes*, Stanley Kallis, as line producer to oversee production. Supervising producer Philip Saltzman acted as writing producer. Coordinating producer Abby Singer served as unit production manager. Co-producer Peter V. Ware oversaw post-production, and associate producer Todd London ran post-production shot inserts and the second unit. Celebrated editor John A. Martinelli was given an associate producer title as an inducement to do the show.

The most critical hire was Simmons. Post-*Mrs. Columbo*, the producer's offers had been drying up. During the 1980s, he worked on all of two mini-series. He was anxious to get back to the regular grind. Falk expressed to him that, like Link, he was against messing with the successful formula. He wanted to revive the show, not reinvent it. Falk pulled out the original, fraying raincoat. The studio tracked down and refurbished one of the original Peugeots, and also found a replacement Dog. Simmons even resurrected the mysterious character Sgt. Burke.

Simmons promised "no major changes to *Columbo* except what would be organic during the 12 years that have passed. It's the raincoat, the car, the cigar, and the dog. One doesn't play tricks with that. The audience has made it very clear that they don't want any changes. You'll see the years have been added with Peter's use of glasses and his hair-color change. Yet this only adds to the richness of the character. Peter's really still the same."

There would be some concessions to modernity—namely 1980s-friendly music, costuming and guest stars. After all, the world had changed. "Columbo in 1989 is not thinking about giving up cigars," Falk mused. "He's just thinking, 'Gee, it's getting harder and harder to bum a match.'"

For his crew, executive producer Simmons insisted on using old-timers he had worked with before. He needed directors, writers and composers whom he trusted, since he would be spending the vast majority of his time away from the set, writing. "On the set my father just knew that a crew needs to know who to listen to and that person should be the director. So he didn't believe in hanging around the set a lot," David Simmons recalled. "It was his job to hire the right director, let that director have his set, and then go back in the editing process and recut the hell out of the guy. The crew knows who the executive producer is, and it's a distraction when the director's not the focus."

Murder, Smoke and Shadows

As he had done when he signed on to his first tour of duty in 1977, Simmons threw out all the scripts that were already under development—including Gillis', van Scoyk's and Falk's. He would originate his own. He decided to write the first script himself and assign his other story ideas to longtime TV cronies, while at least listening to ideas from others. Writers who pitched him on an ingenious setup, surprising clue, or clever way to commit a murder would be told that they missed the boat. "That's not it," Simmons would frown. "That's not it. That may be a factor, but that's not what we're doing. We're doing characters."

With Columbo's character set, Simmons was hunting for ideas of unique counterparts to play off the detective, ones that could trigger fascinating interactions. The murderer's profession should also inspire an interesting method of committing his or her murder. Since Steven Spielberg was rumored to be considering directing the first new *Columbo*, Simmons thought, "What if the first show had Columbo match wits with Steven Spielberg?" Spielberg became the model for his villain in *Murder, Smoke and Shadows*—a wunderkind director who electrocutes a boyhood pal who threatened to expose his role in a fatal accident on one of his films.

Being able to shoot on Universal's backlot was not only cheaper, it let the 65-year-old Simmons deal with age discrimination in Hollywood, which he had been experiencing firsthand. He gave the upstart director character an older secretary. She laments how the youth are taking over the business, but in the end outsmarts her dismissive boss.

The movie-studio setting also allowed Simmons to slip in fantastical flourishes he enjoyed, such as a "Crane Ballet Sequence," in which the hotshot director tries to get Columbo sick by taking him on wild ride on his aerial crane, set to "The Blue Danube." Likewise Simmons' ending has Columbo theatrically introduce the undercover agents who aided him, as they trot out for a bow under a spotlight and to canned applause. At the last minute, Simmons decided to have Columbo take his bow wearing a colorful ringmaster costume.

The fantasy elements are ridiculous, yet because Falk trusted him implicitly, he allowed Simmons' screenplay to be filmed with very few changes.

Columbo Goes to the Guillotine

Usually Simmons patterned his murderers after colorful celebrities and concocted plots that flowed from their personalities and positions. His latest target, however, came along with a built-in nemesis and historical feud. He would pit mindreading, spoon-bending psychic Uri Geller against James Randi, the one-time stage magician who made it his life's work to expose frauds, particularly Geller. The CIA had hired Geller as a consultant after he'd demonstrated his paranormal powers by replicating pictures being drawn in another room. "The Amazing Randi" offered psychics a million dollars if they could pass similar experiments under his watchful eye. The men had even appeared together on a recent TV special, *Exploring Psychic Powers Live*. Simmons envisioned his psychic, Eliot Blake, beheading the debunker.

As writer, Simmons needed someone who could dream up an elaborate con job. So he turned to William Read Woodfield, a hobbyist magician and veteran TV writer, best known as one of the leading creative forces on *Mission: Impossible*. Jackson Gillis also contributed clues and critiques as executive story consultant.

Columbo Goes to the Guillotine would become best remembered for its ending, in which—preposterously—Columbo lays down under the blade of a guillotine and asks the murderer to bolt down a collar around his neck, without knowing for sure if the safety mechanism is in place. After the murderer unsuccessfully tries to behead Columbo, Woodfield wanted the detective to apprehend the killer and take him out to his Peugeot. "That's my car right over there," Columbo points out.

"You may not believe this, Lieutenant," the fake psychic responds, "but somehow I knew that."

In the end, the closing was changed to a wild-eyed Columbo strangely pointing a gun at his capture, declaring that he has to "apply the penalty" for his crime, and pulling the trigger—shooting out a joke BANG sign.

As Falk got more comfortable on the set, he started returning to his profligate ways. Coordinating producer Abby Singer's job was to make sure the show came in on schedule and on budget—an impossible task. According to Singer, Falk was "probably the nicest guy in the world, the sweetest man, but when it came to shooting, he was crazy. We did a guillotine scene. We lit the scene and it took about an hour. We got it ready to go. He came into the set and said, 'The setup's lousy. Do it another way, my way.' So we did it. The next day, we came out of dailies, and he put his arm around the director and me, and said, 'You know, you guys are right. Let's go back and reshoot it.'"

For another scene, in which Columbo replicates the villain's mindreading stunt in a soundproof chamber, only two pages of the script were scheduled to be shot that day. Director Leo Penn asked Singer if he could convince Falk to take minimal detours. "Abby," Penn begged, "we only got two pages here. Ask him to take it easy." Singer relayed the plea to Falk. "Aw, no problem," Falk shrugged. "Don't worry about the company; they can afford it." For that one brief scene, Singer said they shot 25,000 feet of film: "He just didn't care."

Similarly, on the last day of production, only two pages remained to be shot. Yet guest villain Anthony Andrews had to fly back to England that evening to present an award with the Queen. Penn again called Singer over: "Would you speak to Peter and see if we can get it out by 5:00? The actor leaves at 5:00 sharp." Falk smiled, "Abby, it's a piece of cake. We'll be done in no time."

"Well," Singer recalled, "by 5:00 we'd barely shot a page. We had to send the actor to London and had to bring him back. And it was ridiculous, but Peter would say to me, 'Abby, to hell with the company. They can afford it.' And he meant it."

Singer lasted one more episode, then quit. Universal begged him to stay on. "You don't have enough money," Singer said.

Meanwhile, Simmons was making conditions equally unbearable for the editing team. "The problem with this picture is there is no time," recalled editor John A. Martinelli. "We start a movie, they shoot half of it, and Peter Falk doesn't like the ending. Throw it away. Start a new movie. Now a new one. We get this one done. We view it at midnight or something, because (Simmons) writes all day, he works all day, this guy is crazy. We run the picture. These people always hate the dailies, they always hate what the director does. I think it took about 127 hours of running that movie to get their notes, because if Columbo blinks his eyes wrong, 'Tsk, that's not Columbo. I bet he does that better in the other take. Let's reshoot.' They did a whole reshoot on a scene because they didn't like two line readings."

One night, Falk had to go in to loop a couple of unclear words of dialogue, like "Oomph" and "Oh." Martinelli said that after about four hours, Falk still hadn't gotten the Oomph or Oh that pleased him. The actor finally threw up his hands and went home, telling the editors to fix it. It was 2:00 in the morning.

Martinelli agreed to let Simmons' youngest son, Daniel, apprentice on the picture as one of his assistants, so he could get into the union. The good deed did not go unpunished. "The show was agony, just total agony, because there was no discipline," Martinelli said. "One night it's now 5:00 in the morning and (Simmons) says, 'Okay, let's get to the next act.' His son turned so red, I thought he was going to die there or kill him. And this was his son!"

Martinelli said he found himself getting home about two hours a day, seven days a week. His second *Columbo* would be his last. Universal tried to convince him to stay, but understood completely why he refused.

Sex and the Married Detective

The third show of the season originated with writer Jerry Ludwig, who had previously worked with producer Stanley Kallis on *Mission: Impossible*, *Hawaii Five-O*, and *Police Story*. "Stanley went over to *Columbo* and he invited me to come over," Ludwig recalled. "I'd been an admirer of Dick Simmons for a long, long time, so I thought that was fun. You've heard all about Hollywood pitch meetings. This was the easiest sale I ever had. They said, 'Do you have any ideas?' and I said, 'Well, I have one.' They said, 'What is it?' I said, 'Columbo meets Dr. Ruth.' They said, 'Go and write it.'"

In *Sex and the Married Detective*, a famous sex therapist seeks revenge on her cheating lover. The first thought to play the murderer was Linda Hunt who, like Dr. Ruth Westheimer, stood well under 5 feet tall. Ludwig's script, though, ended up calling for someone taller, younger and sexier. But even though the lead was a sex therapist, the episode contained no sex and few sparks, since "that's not *Columbo*." The producers did dare to use the word "Sex" in the title, a provocative move after seven seasons without any. "I think we promised more than we delivered with that one, though," Ludwig admitted. "It was her job category rather than the activity."

During pre-production, Falk suggested that it might be fun to include a whimsical moment where his character plays the tuba. Priding himself on his creativity, Simmons responded, "The opportunities are limitless. Anything you can say, I can work into a show, including playing the tuba."

As filmed, in one of the series' most bizarre detours, Columbo stops to watch a music instructor demonstrate the tuba to his students. The teacher inexplicably asks Columbo if he would like a turn. Columbo picks up a spare tuba and plays, as the water fountains outside dance to the music.

Ludwig did admire the crew's desire to take the time to do things right. "It was a very luxurious tempo there," he said. "Because Peter was very exacting, a perfectionist, it moved often at a glacial speed. Around the office, they used to say Peter's ideal would be to make one episode a year, but spend the whole year making it."

As work proceeded on the third episode, Columbo finally made his long-awaited return to television. The strike had pushed the wheel's debut into February 1989, so ABC decided to program it on Monday nights instead of Saturdays, taking over the slot vacated by *Monday Night Football*. Yet the reception for the first aired installment, *Columbo Goes to the Guillotine*, was underwhelming. That night, it came in a distant third in the ratings, trailing *Lonesome Dove* on CBS and a block of sitcoms on NBC. Falk's mood was further dampened one week later by news that his friend and idol John Cassavetes had died of liver disease at the age of 59.

The pressure to make *Columbo* a success weighed heavily on Simmons. At home, he would confess to his family, "I just can't get it out of my head that if I make a bad picture, that doesn't make me a bad person." He continued to tinker with each episode well past its deadline. For one show, Simmons was on a mixing stage fine-tuning the sound until 1 a.m.—one day before the episode was to be broadcast. A Universal executive pleaded with him to release the print. "But it's not right," Simmons answered. The exec continued: "Let your pain be your gift to me." Simmons relented.

Grand Deceptions

For the season's fourth episode, Simmons had Columbo take on a murderer inspired by Oliver North, the lieutenant colonel awaiting trial in the Iran-Contra affair. In *Grand Deceptions*, Colonel Frank Brailie would run a right-wing think tank with a paramilitary training camp, while on the side selling arms, skimming money, and sleeping with the general's wife. Threatened with blackmail, the Colonel commits murder when others think he's busy organizing an intricate tableau of miniature soldiers as a birthday present for the general. In truth, he had secretly set the toys up that morning. The early script drafts by *Mission: Impossible/Perry Mason* veteran and former 20th Century Fox president Sy Salkowitz took direct fire at the right.

Falk, however, avoided expressing political beliefs in public, not wishing to alienate any of his audience. He approved the premise, but certain sequences would not fly: the word "Conservative" was removed from the name of the Foundation. Deleted were multiple scenes of Columbo walking in on war strategy simulations, each of which ended with missiles headed for America or its allies. Also scrapped was a brief scene in which Columbo was to walk up to a chalkboard in the mess hall, where "DEATH" was written in large letters. He would erase it and write "LIFE."

On the set, Falk continued to add his own flourishes. When he visits the general's home, Columbo was to instruct Dog to watch the car. Falk embellished the moment by cuddling and gushing over the pooch.

When Columbo investigates the crime scene, the script had a policeman hand him a flashlight that was discovered under a rock—a place it could not have been thrown by an explosion. Columbo was to ask the officer what the object was and where he found it, while holding it high in the air, to catch the Colonel's attention. Instead, Falk as Columbo hollered for a photographer and had the 11 investigators circle around him as he took the flashlight in a handkerchief, held it up and, before depositing it into an evidence bag, dramatically announced to the group, "This object that I have in my hand is a flashlight. Is that right?" "Yes, sir," they reply in unison. "Do you all see that?" "Yes, sir," they repeated.

Grand Deceptions' final shot was also changed. It was supposed to close on Brailie, furious that he's been caught, slamming his fist down on the tableau. Instead, the Colonel surrenders without much of a fight and the camera pans across the miniature battlefield, stopping inexplicably on a toy-solider-sized Columbo.

Despite the slow start, *Columbo's* ratings crept up for the second and third episodes, before dropping on the fourth. ABC renewed the series, along with *B.L. Stryker*. Lowly rated *Gideon Oliver* did not make the cut. ABC hoped to fill its spot in the wheel with a revival of *McCloud* or a new series starring either Kirk Douglas or Roger Moore. They ended up with the return of Telly Savalas in *Kojak* and Jaclyn Smith in *Christine Cromwell*.

Season 8 – 1989

Columbo Goes to the Guillotine
Working Title: *Extra Sensory Deception*
Filmed: December 1988
Stars: Peter Falk, Anthony Andrews, Karen Austin
Director: Leo Penn
Executive Producer: Richard Alan Simmons
Producer: Stanley Kallis
Co-Executive Producer: Peter Falk
Supervising Executive Producer: William Link
Teleplay: William Read Woodfield
Air Date: Feb. 6, 1989
Nielsen Ranking: #26 (16.3 points, 23 share)

Murder, Smoke and Shadows
Working Title: *Murder, Smoke and Mirrors*
Filming Started: Nov. 7, 1988
Guest Stars: Fisher Stevens, Molly Hagan
Director: James Frawley
Executive Producer: Richard Alan Simmons
Producer: Stanley Kallis
Supervising Executive Producer: William Link
Co-Executive Producer: Peter Falk
Teleplay: Richard Alan Simmons
Air Date: Feb. 27, 1989
Ranking: #18 (17.5 points, 27 share)

Sex and the Married Detective
Filmed: February 1989
Guest Stars: Lindsay Crouse, Julia Montgomery
Director: James Frawley
Executive Producer: Richard Alan Simmons
Producer: Stanley Kallis
Co-Executive Producer: Peter Falk
Supervising Executive Producer: William Link
Teleplay: Jerry Ludwig
Air Date: April 3, 1989
Ranking: #12 (19.1 points, 28 share)

Grand Deceptions
Working Title: *Grand Deception*
Filmed: March 1989
Guest Stars: Robert Foxworth, Andy Romano
Director: Sam Wanamaker
Executive Producer: Richard Alan Simmons
Producer: Stanley Kallis
Co-Executive Producer: Peter Falk
Supervising Executive Producer: William Link
Teleplay: Sy Salkowitz
Air Date: May 1, 1989
Ranking: #28 (14.2 points, 23 share)

Murder, a Self Portrait

Simmons meanwhile immersed himself in the fifth episode, despite starting so late that everyone knew it would have to be held over until the following season. He proposed pitting Columbo against Pablo Picasso, the famed Spanish artist known for both his abstract paintings and his abusive womanizing. Rather than making murderous Max Barsini's art abstract, he suggested the clues be abstract. Columbo must decipher them through the recorded dreams of the murder victim.

Falk was tickled by the opportunity to make the villain an artist, as drawing had become one of his greatest passions, ever since he had started sketching nudes during his off-hours from performing *The Prisoner of Second Avenue*. He also backed his wife, Shera Danese, playing the role of Barsini's jealous second wife.

In her third *Columbo* appearance, Danese said she was inching closer to her longtime ambition—to one day play the murderer. "My first time on the show I was a secretary," she said. "The second time I was the killer's secretary. This time I'm the killer's wife."

The avant-garde nature of *Murder, a Self Portrait* compelled Simmons to pour in every bit of strength and creativity he had. The unrelenting hours and incredible pressure took a serious toll on his health. "My father was working himself to death," his son David confessed. "They had to bring doctors into the office because he wouldn't go (home). For health reasons, he could not continue."

Before the show was completed, Universal terminated Simmons, along with line producer Stanley Kallis and fellow writing producer Philip Saltzman. The three veterans were unceremoniously ushered into retirement. Unless something drastic was done, Lt. Columbo would soon be joining them.

17
Back to Basics

The tepid response to *Columbo's* return took everyone by surprise. Falk, Link and Universal refused to believe that pop culture had lost interest. What went wrong?

The studio surveyed viewers to figure out why they weren't taking to the program as they had in the 1970s. Their research showed, first, that viewers found the murderers too likable. They wanted their villains cold, calculating, unremorseful and unsympathetic. They wanted them to bully Columbo.

Surveys also revealed that the plots confused first-time *Columbo* viewers. New audiences weren't even sure who the villain was until Columbo began hounding them. Simmons' heavy focus on the murderer, combined with the inverted mystery format, seemed to be causing the public to view the show through the bad guy's eyes.

"There was much more concentration on the antagonist, and less focus on the clues, the classic cat and mouse," Bill Link deduced. "This season, we're restoring all that."

For Link, that meant the mystery should no longer be an afterthought. For Falk, that meant the clues needed to be more plentiful and more impressive. Falk now considered it a mistake that he had turned over all story development to Simmons, the easy scapegoat. For the first time, Falk vowed to regularly sit in on story meetings. He kept Gillis on as story consultant, but added two others—Bill Woodfield and Bill Driskill. The men would advise on crafting the stories, but mostly Falk wanted them to think up new clues. Falk constantly urged them to make the clues bigger, especially for the finale, his pop. Link went along, but didn't think every episode had to end with an out-of-nowhere stunner—

especially considering how hard it was to dream up the devilishly clever clues. "Peter, they're not all going to be terrific," Link would caution.

"Naw," Falk would respond, "it's gotta be a great pop! Gotta be good! I know you can do it!"

Through the summer, Falk alone held the title of executive producer. But as time neared to begin production on actual shows, he realized there were parts of the job he was not well suited to. He thought of Everett Chambers, even though their last stint together ended poorly. Falk asked Patrick McGoohan, whom he had continued to use as a sounding board, to gauge Chambers' level of interest. For the last two years, Chambers had been in Canada consulting for the series *Rin Tin Tin: K-9 Cop*. "Everett," McGoohan pleaded, "you've got to come back and help. Peter needs you." "I can't," Chambers replied, figuring Falk couldn't need him that badly if he wouldn't even make the call himself. "I'm in Ontario." A week later, Falk called. "I want you to come back." Chambers was amenable. "Let the studio make me an offer." Whether the decision was Bill Link's or someone else's, the studio made Chambers an insultingly low offer. He stayed in Canada.

Link preferred Jon Epstein, who had worked under Simmons on *The Trials of O'Brien* and under Levinson and Link on *Tenafly*, *Partners in Crime*, and *Scene of the Crime*. Epstein had also served as executive producer on dozens of other TV movies, mini-series and series, including the final seasons of *McMillan & Wife*. He was capable, likable and easy to work with—and famous throughout Hollywood for his annual A-List New Year's Eve party. His style and personality stood in stark contrast to Richard Alan Simmons'.

"Jon was not a writer. Jon was a producer," David Simmons noted. "Jon made things happen effortlessly, but he wasn't somebody who was going to be sitting in the editing room at 3 a.m. He was more of a smooth production person and I'm sure his marching orders were: keep Peter happy, but try not to kill yourself."

Falk was amenable to hiring Epstein as executive producer, but demanded on choosing the new line producer himself. He mentioned his need to former *Hill Street Blues* executive Bob Singer, a regular golfing buddy. Singer suggested his *Hill Street* line producer, Penny Adams. Up to this point, *Columbo's* production crew had always been older, industry-hardened males. The three who were just let go (Richard Alan Simmons, Stanley Kallis, and Philip Saltzman) were all in their 60s. Even Epstein was 61. Penny Adams was an energetic blonde in her 30s.

Falk interviewed Adams over dinner at the ages-old Italian eatery Cupa Loggia, making it clear exactly what he was looking for. Adams recalled, "When the show came back, they made Peter co-executive producer. Peter was not too happy because he had been maneuvered out of the way—as Hollywood producers very often do with actors. Peter didn't feel that his interests were being appropriately

INTO THE 1990s the primary influences on *Columbo* included Jon Epstein *(left)*, executive producer of Seasons 9 and 10, and frequent director Vincent McEveety *(right)*. *[Credit: Vincent McEveety Jr.]*

represented. His understanding for coming back for another season was Peter would hire his own line producer who wasn't, as he would call it, 'Universal's puppet,' someone he could rely on to give him information and keep him in the loop.

"It was a very personal kind of interview, because he already had my resume. In typical Peter fashion, it was marked up, with notes everywhere. He clearly knew my career. He asked questions about my career. But it was honestly a getting-to-know-you dinner. And towards the end of it, he indicated he was interested in having me on the show. He again laid it out for me what he needed; he didn't want a yes person, but he wanted someone who was looking out for his best interest as well as the show's. I said, 'Peter, they should be the same thing.' And he said, 'Yes, but they very often are not.'"

Adams asked whom else she had to interview with. Falk said no one; the decision was fully his. Adams said she was in, with the caveat that Falk not marginalize her, either by going around her when they had a disagreement or by belittling her in front of the cast or crew. "What do you think that professionally would do to my credibility?" she explained. "So whatever problems you have, I'm a big girl, I'm tough enough, I have three brothers, I can handle it. But I will not be mistreated in public." "That's easy," Falk said, smiling broadly. He put out his hand to seal the deal.

Adams recalled, "That was pretty much the end of dinner. And I had the job, so Epstein was basically stuck with me. But we actually turned out to be a very good team, Jon and I. I adored him. We both had Peter's best interest and the show's best interest at heart."

Columbo Cries Wolf

Story approval became fully Falk's domain. Jackson Gillis and Bill Link pitched him on *Double Vision*—the story of beautiful blonde twins; one is a sweet model, the other a malevolent schizophrenic who kills her sister and takes her place. Falk reflexively shied away from evil-women stories, but nonetheless let Gillis expand it into a full script three times over the next 18 months, each of which he'd reject.

For the new season, Falk did have one show completed, *Murder, a Self Portrait*. Simmons also had left another script, by Academy Award-nominated screenwriter Millard Kaufman, completed and ready to shoot. In *Last of the Redcoats*, TV journalist Norma Arnold arranges an on-air interview with the reclusive Nicholas Braden, "the last living member of the Redcoats, the legendary English trio that revolutionized the pop music of our times." They end up spending the night together, during which he discovers she has been secretly using a tape recorder in her purse during their conversations. He now refuses to do the interview. They argue and Norma kills him with a fireplace poker. After investigating, Columbo reveals Norma as the murderer as she interviews him on TV.

Falk shrugged. He liked only one of the projects in development, a Bill Woodfield script that pitted Columbo against a Hugh Hefner type. *Columbo Cries Wolf* featured one of the biggest twists the series had ever seen—magazine publisher Sean Brantley's partner, who wants to sell their business, goes missing. Columbo knows Brantley is guilty, and tears up his nymph mansion looking for the body. Then, three-quarters of the way into the episode, the victim resurfaces; her disappearance had been a publicity stunt to drive up the value of the magazine. Brantley then really does kill her and, in a setup reminiscent of *Blueprint for Murder*, stashes the body in a construction area that's already been searched. But Columbo remembers that the victim's pager was never recovered. So he dials her number—and the beeping leads him to her body.

Bill Link got the final clue from a journalist. "Somebody who was interviewing me for a mystery magazine told me, 'I have a great idea for an ending clue.' Usually, it's going to be awful. He tells me this clue—it's fabulous. So I said, 'We'll pay you $500 for that.' And we sent him a check."

To direct, Epstein tapped Daryl Duke, who had branched off from Universal fare like *Banacek* and Levinson and Link's *The Psychiatrist*, to bolder works like Falk's TV movie *Griffin and Phoenix* and the mini-series *The Thorn Birds*. "Daryl Duke was a very smart, fascinating, really nice guy to work with, but a guy who looked very weathered; he could have been about 90. But he was very hip," Adams said. "Daryl's idea was it's all well and good to make classic *Columbo*, to give the audience the show they've always loved, but that show is 10 years old and things have changed. And although your average viewer won't say, 'Hey, my tastes have changed,' they certainly would understand that after watching shows like *Hill Street*, that this was not *Barnaby Jones* time. By this time, people were taping feature films on VHS and watching them in their living rooms. A lot of changes had gone on in television, like *Miami Vice*, which I also worked on, with its (modern) style and art direction. People's minds were changed by watching good films. So Daryl, Jon and I had quite a few conversations about hipping it up a little bit without loudly deviating from *Columbo*, a chance to make it more late '80s. It so happens that that script was about *Playboy*. That helped in taking a little of the stodginess out of the work. We were out to make a kind of a hipper, more stylish version of classic *Columbo*. That was deliberate."

Falk was supportive, said Adams, "as long as Columbo was Columbo. Peter was pretty hip, too. He was no fool. He liked the sexiness of that show. He liked the idea that we would be attracting an audience that would find *Columbo* relevant. I mean every now and then he'd say, '*What*? We're doing *what*?' But, as I recall, he did not buck us at any time. Again, it might have been different if it wasn't already a show with girls in bikinis and that sort of thing, which was right up Peter's alley. So if we had started with one of the other shows, it might have been more confusing."

Agenda for Murder

For the next episodes, Falk began calling in favors from old friends. First, he contacted Patrick McGoohan, whose autocratic style would never have meshed with Richard Alan Simmons'. Falk had a great part in mind—*Agenda for Murder*'s Oscar Finch, a powerful defense attorney who kills to protect a Congressman friend he's positioning for higher office.

Falk was referred to the script by Bill Driskill, who had picked it up from his neighbor, fellow screenwriter Jeffrey Bloom. "I met Peter at Universal," Bloom recalled. "He was… very Columbo. A charming man with no affectations, a comfortable office, and walls peppered with evocative pencil or ink sketches of all sorts of people, famous and not. His own sketches. He was a talented artist. He was also eccentric. He was funny, and sly, and easy to like. When he smoked a cigar, ashes would fall onto his shirt and burn little holes that he never appeared to notice."

While others would help reshape the script, all of Bloom's instructions came from Falk. "No one knew Lt. Columbo like Peter did," Bloom said. "And as I came to find out, no one had anything to say about the show, except Peter. He was in complete control. It was the most purely creative television experience I ever had. No network executive could interfere in the creative process; no executive from Universal television. Writing a script for *Columbo* was entirely between Peter and a writer. Our meetings were at lunch in his office. We'd eat corned beef sandwiches and chat. Come up with ideas. Solve problems. It was joy."

Falk even provided the pop. The summer before, he had clipped an article about forensic dentists from the *Los Angeles Times*, which cited a story in *Police Chief* magazine about cases in which criminals were identified by the bitemarks they left behind in chewing gum or other food. Finch was to be a habitual nibbler, who is ultimately found out after he leaves telltale teeth marks in a piece of cheese at the murder scene.

Yet Falk claimed he was the only one who believed in the script. He recalled, "All of the staff writers said, 'Let's pass on this. Don't make it. It's boring. Nobody's interested in politics. It doesn't have an acceptable ending and this murderer is the dumbest murderer we've ever had on *Columbo*.' I felt that they were overreacting, despite some of their objections being valid."

So he sent the script to McGoohan. "This has something," McGoohan agreed. "I'll do this. We'll have to fix it a little bit...."

Falk expected no less. The two men discussed the structure of the script. McGoohan rearranged the scenes that took place once the investigation had begun, so that they were in a more dramatic order and occurred that same morning. He deleted a courtroom scene meant to show how skilled and brilliant his character was—if the dialogue for the rest of the script was written sharply enough, the audience would be able to recognize his skill and brilliance on their own.

"He kept all the good scenes and added new ones," said Falk. He considered McGoohan's greatest contribution to be his rewrite of the script's final confrontation, set in the midst of a celebration inside a packed hotel ballroom. "Unlike a lot of *Columbos*, the momentum of the story actually accelerated; it kept building until the final moment," Falk said. "We don't often have that."

However, McGoohan, the tyrannical director, endeared himself to no one else.

With the exception of Falk, he ignored the wishes and directions of the entire crew, from the location scouts to the producers, typically doing so in the most condescending ways imaginable.

"Patrick was a royal pain in the ass, from start to finish," Adams said. "He was a guy who had had a substantial career and wasn't going to be told what to do, from Jon Epstein as well as myself. I think that he did his best acting when he was busy trying to convince us that he was on our side, that what we were saying was a great idea, and that he subscribed to it completely. I guess he thought that we didn't understand that he was bullshitting us, or didn't care—one or the other. He was a man with a tremendous ego, very self-centered, and he was just going to do it the way he wanted to do it, regardless. He treated Jon with that same level of contempt, but he always talked to me as if I were 14 years old and a little timid. It was not my favorite hour-and-a-half of television."

Separate from McGoohan's rudeness, Epstein and Adams were concerned about the fallout from having a director run roughshod over the production. The two producers plotted how they would express their worries to Falk—which of them would play good cop, which would play bad cop—knowing that Falk adored McGoohan and his work. Epstein even had Bill Link approach Falk about keeping McGoohan contained.

Adams suspected the ploys worked, because as the shooting went on, McGoohan got ruder and ruder to her. "I really must have been annoying the hell out of him because he was not getting his way all the time," she said.

Although Robert Seaman had photographed all of the ABC *Columbos*, McGoohan wanted to bring in his own director of photography, and made life miserable for Seaman. Halfway through shooting, McGoohan replaced him with Jack Priestley, who had shot the actor's first *Columbo, By Dawn's Early Light*.

Priestley did provide some relief, because he knew how to handle McGoohan. "Jack was a hilarious guy, very talented, but with a real smart-aleck New York attitude," Adams said. "Jack sometimes took the air out of Patrick. Jack in his own irreverent way helped contain some of Patrick's big-for-his-britches-ness, his 'I'm British and the rest of you are stupid' kind of thing."

Although his performance was spectacular, McGoohan had once again burned bridges with the *Columbo* team.

Rest in Peace, Mrs. Columbo

Continuing to hit up old friends, Falk called to his office Peter S. Fischer, who had co-created *Murder, She Wrote* with Levinson and Link, and was executive producing its sixth season. Falk said, "You've got to help me. I need a show." As luck would have it, Fischer did have an idea for a *Columbo*, but wasn't sure Falk would go for it. Fischer recalled, "I described the opening scene to him with the funeral, and it's raining, and everybody's grim. 'It's called *Rest in Peace, Mrs. Columbo*, so it's obvious what happened, that his wife died,' I said, 'and it goes from there.' And he said, 'I love this idea. I love this.'"

In actuality, Mrs. Columbo isn't dead—Columbo is putting on a charade to trap his prey. Fischer wanted the entire episode shot in a film-noir style, with first-person narration, dark shadows, sultry music, a vengeance-seeking femme fatale murderer, and a hardboiled detective, minus the goofiness that had been creeping into recent episodes. Falk asked him to start work on the script immediately.

But after the *Old Fashioned Murder* debacle, Fischer wasn't so sure. "Peter," he said, "I'm not gonna sit there and work on a script and then have you rewrite the whole damn thing. I'm working on *Murder, She Wrote*, and I just haven't got the time."

Falk understood. "I'm gonna make you a deal. You write the story, I'm gonna give you notes, and that's it. Okay? The script the way you wrote it. I give you my word." Fischer hesitantly agreed, and found Falk to be true to his promise. Falk allowed Fischer to come in for a one-shot as executive producer and bring along some of his *Murder, She Wrote* crew, including supervising producer Robert F. O'Neill, director Vincent McEveety, and composer Richard Markowitz.

Fischer said, "When I finally got the script done, (Peter) shot it just about the way it was written. And I found that really solidified my opinion of him. He was a very direct guy and when he said something, he meant it. He didn't screw around with it. He just said the words that were on the page, and that was it."

The *Columbo* team was confident the series, at least creatively, was back on track. The wheel as a whole, unfortunately, was broken beyond repair. ABC had moved the *Mystery Movie* to Saturday nights, historically the worst night of the week for primetime ratings. That was the night audiences preferred to go out, rent videos, or watch the latest releases on cable TV. The few people who did stay in to watch network TV were typically tuned to NBC and its formidable sitcoms *The Golden Girls* and *Empty Nest*.

ABC was contemplating pulling the plug on the *Mystery Movie* before a single Epstein/Adams episode had even aired. Simmons' leftover *Murder, a Self Portrait* suffered the worst ratings of any *Columbo* made to that point. The other series fared even worse—particularly *Christine Cromwell*. In early January, days after dismal returns came in for the third of five *Kojaks*, ABC stopped production on *Christine Cromwell* after four episodes and voiced its pessimism about the other three series continuing.

Falk, who had just begun filming *Rest in Peace, Mrs. Columbo*, shrugged. Six two-hour shows in one season was much too much. He held an option for the next season—for three pictures.

Uneasy Lies the Crown

Still searching for the old magic, Falk returned to his stockpile of mothballed scripts to see if there were any gems he had bypassed. Steven Bochco's name jumped off the page. *Uneasy Lies the Crown* concerned a high-profile dentist who murders his cheating wife's lover by implanting fatal levels of digitalis in a new crown. During Season 4, Falk had pulled the show during pre-production because he didn't see a dentist as a worthy adversary for Columbo. After his option lapsed, Bochco—by then story editor for *McMillan & Wife*—took the script back and rewrote it for *McMillan*, produced by Jon Epstein.

Now Falk hoped it could be re-rewritten for *Columbo*. He sent Bochco's original script to Joseph Stefano, the screenwriter best known for *The Outer Limits* and Hitchcock's *Psycho*, with instructions to make murderer Wesley Corman a more typical *Columbo* villain. Stefano turned Corman into Max Bergman, "Dentist to the Stars"; his wife into Kitty, a "powerhouse Hollywood agent"; and his victim into Jimmy De Paul, a young movie heartthrob. Stefano packed the script with inside jokes about moviemaking.

The result was noticeably weaker than Bochco's. So story editor Bill Woodfield kept the culprit as a celebrity dentist, but threw away all of Stefano's other additions and reinstated almost everything that had been cut, including Corman's name, his father-in-law/business partner, and his poker-game alibi. Woodfield also turned Corman's poker buddies into celebrities, and transformed the wife from an aggressive professional into a shell-shocked, suddenly dependent spouse, similar to Mrs. Alex Benedict in Bochco's *Étude in Black*.

To add pep, Epstein hired Alan J. Levi—best known for action shows—to direct. "A director can bring certain attitudes to a show, but the characters and the workings of the show are already established," Levi said. "Now, *Columbo* is not an easy show. Peter was a perfectionist. We got along like brothers. I loved the little guy, but he was a curmudgeon. Many times I would print Take Three for me and Take 27 for him, because he 'didn't quite feel it.' And then I would take him into the screening room and show him the two prints and say, 'Now which one is your print and which one is mine?' And he'd (say, hemming and hawing), 'Well, I just felt different….'"

Murder in Malibu

Buoyed by the positive reaction to *Columbo Cries Wolf*, Falk thought it would be safe to draw on slightly racier material, and green-lit the gigolo story that Jackson Gillis had written two years earlier. Originally called *The Juggler*, the script had playboy Wayne Jennings murdering his wealthy, romance novelist fiancée when he thinks she's on to his philandering ways. Fearing he might be seen leaving her house, Jennings quickly juggles his plans. He decides to hang around another half-hour, then shoots the corpse with a different gun, calculating that if he's caught, ballistics will show that the body was already dead when he shot it.

Unfortunately, the script contained a number of preposterous situations. Jennings is so irresistible that every single one of the 11 women he interacts with becomes weak-kneed at his presence. That includes the victim's sister, played by Falk's *Cookie* co-star Brenda Vaccaro, who had shown nothing but disdain for him up until that point. Shortly after discovering Jennings shot her sister, she suddenly swoons and crumples into his arms.

That Gillis' scenario came across more as unsettling than sexy probably wasn't helped by Epstein's choice of director, Walter Grauman. The 68-year-old veteran had been helming action and mystery shows since the 1950s, including 49 installments of *Barnaby Jones* and 53 *Murder, She Wrotes*.

According to Adams, "Walter Grauman probably directed the first show they ever did at Universal. He was a nice man, but he had very much '70s television tastes, so he was a real old-timer. He came from: the direction is 'walk in a room, light a cigarette, pick up a drink, say your line.' All that shoe-leather ahead of getting to the point. It's something that *Hill Street Blues* just canned. Not all of that harumphing all the time. Walter was that classic '70s television type of guy."

Grauman did feel handcuffed working for the first time with Falk. "I had my own concept of how and what to shoot," he said. "And all of a sudden I found that Peter had his own concept, and it was nothing like my concept. So there would be constant—not arguing—but I would say, 'But, Peter, I wanted you to do so and so,' and he said, 'No, I want to do this.' 'So would you explain to me why?' And then he'd sort of explain it, and then there's not much I could do about it because it was his show."

This time around, Falk's improvisations made a bad situation worse. Gillis' weak final pop had Columbo announcing that the victim must have been dressed by a man, because her underwear was put on backwards. Falk was so determined to set up the big clue earlier in the story that he insisted on two early sequences—one at the victim's lingerie drawer and another looking at the evidence bags—in which Columbo spends an inordinate amount of time examining the woman's underpants.

Worse, in the final scene at a dress shop, the Sergeant asks Columbo to explain the significance of the backwards garments. According to the script, they were to turn to a scantily clad mannequin, and Columbo would briefly point out why the label should have been on the opposite side. While demonstrating, he'd suddenly realize all of the other shoppers were watching him. As Gillis wrote, "After a long horrified beat, Columbo jerks back his hands as though the mannequin were on fire and exit Columbo, *molto agitato*."

With the cameras rolling, Falk delivered the explanation in his own words, dragging it out so that he ended up repeating the word "panties" six times in a span of 45 seconds. Combined with his hasty-rather-than-horrified retreat, Columbo really did look like a pervert.

That said, the cast and crew had a blast filming the last show of the season. "It was a great location on the beach, and that always makes a difference," Adams said. "The weather was spectacular. It was fun. I always thought the show was a little more standard, but what worked for it was Brenda (Vaccaro). She's a pistol, so much fun to watch. That woman has so much energy. That lightens it a lot. And you get to do a show with Malibu as your backdrop."

ABC rightly read that this episode had an unusual, almost soap-opera vibe. So the network pulled it out of its normal Saturday night *Mystery Movie* slot and moved it to the following Tuesday evening, retitled *Murder in Malibu*. It ranked twentieth for the week, by far *Columbo's* best showing in a decade and bettering its Saturday replacement, a rerun of James Bond's *Octopussy*, by 50 percent.

Unsurprisingly, the *ABC Mystery Movie* was formally canceled for good. The network did pick up Falk's option for more *Columbos*, but they would be fewer and air on their own, as standalone specials.

Season 9 – 1989-1990

Murder, a Self Portrait
Filming Started: May 1989
Stars: Peter Falk, Patrick Bauchau, Fionnula Flanagan, Shera Danese
Director: James Frawley
Executive Producer: Richard Alan Simmons
Producer: Stanley Kallis
Co-Executive Producer: Peter Falk
Supervising Executive Producer: William Link
Teleplay: Robert Sherman
Air Date: Nov. 25, 1989
Nielsen Ranking: #59 (10.0 points, 18 share)

Columbo Cries Wolf
Filmed: Oct. 19 – Nov. 22, 1989
Guest Stars: Ian Buchanan, Rebecca Staab
Director: Daryl Duke
Executive Producer: Jon Epstein
Producer: Penny Adams
Co-Executive Producer: Peter Falk
Supervising Executive Producer: William Link
Teleplay: William Read Woodfield
Air Date: Jan. 20, 1990
Ranking: #45 (13.1 points, 23 share)

Agenda for Murder
Filmed: December 1989
Guest Stars: Patrick McGoohan, Denis Arndt, Louis Zorich
Director: Patrick McGoohan
Executive Producer: Jon Epstein
Producer: Penny Adams
Co-Executive Producer: Peter Falk
Supervising Executive Producer: William Link
Teleplay: Jeffrey Bloom (& Patrick McGoohan uncredited)
Air Date: Feb. 10, 1990
Ranking: #59 (10.5 points, 18 share)

Rest in Peace, Mrs. Columbo
Filming Started: Jan. 8, 1990
Guest Stars: Helen Shaver, Ian McShane
Director: Vincent McEveety
Executive Producer: Peter S. Fischer
Supervising Producer: Robert F. O'Neill
Co-Executive Producer: Peter Falk
Supervising Executive Producer: William Link
Teleplay: Peter S. Fischer
Air Date: March 31, 1990
Ranking: #46 (12.0 points, 22 share)

Uneasy Lies the Crown
Filmed: February 1990
Guest Stars: James Read, Jo Anderson
Director: Alan J. Levi
Executive Producer: Jon Epstein
Producer: Penny Adams
Co-Executive Producer: Peter Falk
Supervising Executive Producer: William Link
Teleplay: Steven Bochco
Air Date: April 28, 1990
Ranking: #38 (12.2 points, 23 share)

Murder in Malibu
Working Title: *The Juggler*
Filmed: March 19 – April 16, 1990
Guest Stars: Andrew Stevens, Brenda Vaccaro
Director: Walter Grauman
Executive Producer: Jon Epstein
Producer: Penny Adams
Co-Executive Producer: Peter Falk
Supervising Executive Producer: William Link
Teleplay: Jackson Gillis
Air Date: May 14, 1990
Ranking: #20 (14.0 points, 23 share)

18
New Respect

ABC had had enough of the *Mystery Movie*, but did want to continue *Columbo*, Falk permitting. The actor had already said he would be willing to return, but for no more than three specials. He also wanted to be rescued from the dregs of Saturday night, ideally returning back home to Sundays. On a handshake, ABC's Bob Iger agreed to run the first show on a Sunday, but warned that the network would reevaluate for subsequent shows, once *Monday Night Football* ended for the season.

Jon Epstein signed to return as executive producer, but Penny Adams left to work again with Bob Singer. Epstein requested Alan J. Levi succeed her as supervising producer. Most of the old story guard—Bill Link, Jackson Gillis, Bill Driskill—were not retained. That left only story editor Bill Woodfield to assist Falk and Epstein with the scripts. They were able to find three they liked.

Caution: Murder Can Be Hazardous to Your Health

The first was suggested by April Raynell, Falk's executive assistant since 1981. Raynell knew her boss was obsessed with ingenious clues and desperate for scripts. She mentioned Falk's needs to fellow studio executive assistant Judy Lamppu. She in turn contacted another friend, Patricia Ford, a former policewoman, to see if they could come up with a good *Columbo* script. Raynell promised to pitch their ideas to Falk, if she also got credit on the finished product. Their first idea, in which the victim was an illegal immigrant from Mexico, was rebuffed by Falk. He said that both the murderer and the victim needed to have a "higher profile." So Ford came up with a different tack—inspired by the TV series *America's Most Wanted*. The Fox show featured reenactments of crimes committed by fugitives from justice, and asked the audience for tips that could lead to their capture. In Ford's scenario, the show's dashing host kills a writer who threatens to expose his past as a porn star. If Falk wanted clues, Ford and Lamppu would flood their script with them.

Raynell added her name to the cover page, using the pseudonym Shelby Rose to fool Falk, and presented the first draft to her boss. Falk wasn't interested in reading it. So Raynell began boasting of all the unbelievable clues inside—but she refused to tell him what they were, unless he promised to read the script. He finally broke down, and Raynell described one of the clues: the victim could not have torn a certain news story from his printer because his fingerprints were on only one side of the paper. Falk was intrigued and started reading. He enjoyed it, but had several changes for Raynell to take back to her friends.

Once Falk optioned the script, Ford and Lamppu were invited to the story meetings. "I had never been to a story meeting before," Ford confessed. "I didn't know what they were like. And it was sort of a closed community. I understand those people have worked together for a long time. I don't think the story editor was too happy with us. He kept challenging me about being a police officer and saying he knew newspaper people who were always at the police station, and 'Do you know this one?' and 'Do you know that one?' No, I didn't. I worked undercover and I didn't have a lot of contact with newspaper reporters.

"There was some hostility to us as 'broads who didn't know anything.' The one who really liked us was producer Jon Epstein. He really showed respect to us, in the story meetings especially, because it could get a little heated sometimes when someone said they didn't care for this or they didn't care for that."

Falk had two specific scenes he wanted added. First, he said, it would be amusing to have Columbo visit an awards show and react to the booty-shaking dancers. (He was mistaken.) Second, Falk requested a sex scene for the X-rated movie from the murderer's past. Ford wrote the pornographic scene, though next to none of it was used. "I think they just wanted to see if we could write it," Lamppu said. "He also said we had too many clues. He wanted us to take some out—but we never did."

The first-time writers would revise their script based on recommendations from the story meetings, then give their new script to Raynell to turn in. Raynell tried her best to help with the writing, but her suggestions were so unusable, Ford and Lamppu ended up trying to avoid her. Twice after Ford and Lamppu gave her their latest draft, Raynell inserted a scene of her own before turning it in. Both times, the story crew singled out her additions as inappropriate. The first time, Ford tried to cover her tracks by saying she thought she'd deleted the scene on her computer, but forgot to hit Save. After the second time, Ford knew that she would have to submit future revisions directly to Falk.

"We were terrified April was going to sabotage the whole thing for us," Lamppu said.

That said, Raynell did make one major contribution that made it into the episode: the pop. A dog lover like Falk, she suggested the victim's golden retriever leave a telltale scratch on the murderer's car door, tying him to the crime scene.

Shortly after production began on *Caution: Murder Can Be Hazardous to Your Health*, Epstein's leukemia, which had temporarily sidelined his career 14 years earlier, relapsed. He was forced to take a leave of absence to receive chemotherapy.

Days later, Falk attended the Emmy Awards for the prior season, his first nomination in 12 years. Not only did Falk win, so did Patrick McGoohan for his guest appearance in *Agenda for Murder*. This time around, the victories were particularly gratifying. Falk later noted that his show had been back on the air for two seasons and still he was regularly being asked, "Why don't you bring back *Columbo*?" He blamed the show's low profile and poor ratings on being relegated to Saturday nights. The morning after the Emmys, his face was splashed across newspapers across the country, proclaiming that *Columbo* was back. Falk credited McGoohan as the one who returned his show to the public consciousness.

Columbo Goes to College

The script for the second show was supplied by Jeffrey Bloom, who had impressed Falk with his work on *Agenda for Murder*. "I collaborated on the story for *Columbo Goes to College* with Fred Keller, who I'd met years earlier," Bloom said. "Fred was well-read and had a good feeling for mysteries. We used the 'Leopold and Loeb' idea of arrogance gone wild for a springboard."

In their scenario, two spoiled college kids with domineering, perfectionist fathers are facing expulsion after their professor discovers they cheated on a test. The boys plot to murder him by remote control while they're sitting in class, listening to guest lecturer Lt. Columbo. During the lesson, the professor ducks out to the parking structure. Nearby they've parked their truck, equipped with a miniature camera and a gun behind its behind its grill. When the boys see him reach his car, they fire the gun by clicking their car remote. Bloom got the idea for the method of triggering the gun when he used his own remote to unlock his car and heard the sharp snap of the lock popping up.

Bloom had a field day devising clever dialogue for the boys, as they feigned helping the doddering detective with his investigation by leading him to all the wrong suspects. Falk was delighted. "These two kids are the youngest suspects Columbo has ever dealt with," Falk observed. "Usually he'd be dealing with their fathers. There's a big difference between going head to head in a cat-and-mouse game with the head of General Motors and with two kids in college. These kids pull their act on me, sort of a 'good cop, bad cop' routine, and then when I leave them alone, they hoot, they laugh. They have a great time imitating me. They can't wait for me to come back. Columbo's relationship with them is unlike any relationship he's ever had with any other suspects."

Bloom also wrote a juicy role for one boy's demanding father, a hot-tempered, high-powered lawyer. The casting could not have been better: three-time prior villain Robert Culp.

"Peter appreciated the way I wrote dialogue and attitude and plot that was distinctly *Columbo*, but he pushed me, energetically, to come up with new and unexpected final reveals," Bloom recalled. "At his urging, I rewrote the endings of my episodes several times before he was satisfied."

The final pop was nearly identical to the ending of *A Friend in Deed*, in which Columbo helped prime suspect Commissioner Halperin incriminate himself. In that episode, Columbo let Halperin glance at a file he's reviewing, trusting he'll note the street address of an ex-con he is trying to frame. Sure enough, Halperin hides evidence in the apartment—only the address didn't belong to the patsy. It's one that was just rented by Columbo. In *Columbo Goes to College*, Columbo makes sure the boys overhear his learning of an ex-con's car make and license plate number, which the boys stash the murder weapon in, only to later learn the car belongs to Mrs. Columbo.

Bloom had originally closed with a somewhat sympathetic confession by the boys—"You'd never understand," one said, with his buddy adding, "It was self-defense, Lieutenant. It was survival of the fittest. It's how we were raised. It's what we've been taught.... We never really had a choice."

Instead, Bloom improved the close by having the boys sneering and defiant until the end, vowing that their fathers would get them off. "Don't count us out, Lieutenant," one snarls, as he's dragged off by police. "Because my father doesn't like to see me fail."

The day filming wrapped, Falk was refreshed, almost jubilant. He was still working 14- to 16-hour days, but he was enjoying it. He knew that once again they had a winner on their hands. The producers and ABC agreed. While watching the dailies, they decided to fast-track *Columbo Goes to College* and schedule it as the season opener, five weeks away.

During a break in the action, all 50-odd members of the crew gathered, with a beaming Falk in front, to film a quick shout of "Happy Holidays" for viewers at home. Falk told a reporter that he was relieved to have cut back from six episodes a year to three, and he thought the scripts were steadily improving. In fact, if he could find another good one, he might consider shooting a fourth show before starting work on a movie in the spring. He had already committed to another three shows the following season. For the first time in 10 seasons of playing Columbo, Falk had the one thing he most coveted: time.

Three weeks later, on November 24, 1990, Jon Epstein died, at age 62. Levi recalled, "Me and Peter and everyone in the office, especially Peter's assistant, everybody was grossly affected. Jon was an extraordinary human being. Not only did he have a professional background and success, he was the sweetest guy on earth. We used to go to his New Year's parties, and he knew everybody and everybody knew him. The whole community was really downtrodden by that."

The crew dedicated the latest episode to Epstein's memory, and kept his name on the credits as executive producer for the remainder of the season. Sure enough, the ratings for *Columbo Goes to College*, back on Sunday, were the best the show had earned since its return.

Columbo and the Murder of a Rock Star

Work then began in earnest on *Columbo and the Murder of a Rock Star*. The script by Bill Woodfield featured a high-powered attorney who murders his cheating mistress—a pop singer. The story particularly appealed to Shera Danese, who wanted to be a singer before she had any aspirations of acting. She informed her husband that she'd like to play the part of the rock star victim. Falk said no, knowing the show opened with the character rolling around in bed, undressed, with a handsome young man. The killer's accomplice would be a safer role. Meanwhile, Alan Levi, who wanted to direct as well as produce, was hatching a plan to include his own wife, actress Sondra Currie.

While discussing casting with Falk, Levi said, "Peter, I've got a question to ask you. The policeman, your right-arm policeman during this show, do you have any ideas about it?"

"No, not yet."

"I've got an idea," Levi proposed. "What if it's a woman, a policewoman? It'd be an interesting relationship between the two of you."

Over the years, Falk had turned down other producers' periodic attempts to give him a female partner. The closest they came was in *Suitable for Framing*, which featured a brief scene of a short-skirted policewoman who could be timed running from the crime scene in heels. "Uh… I don't know," Falk replied hesitantly. "What do you have in mind?"

Levi asked, "What about Sondra?"

Falk looked at him blankly and replied, "Nah, that doesn't work for me."

Levi nodded, and they continued down the cast list. Suddenly, Falk said, "Hey, wait, I've got an idea. For the murderer's girlfriend, what about Shera?"

Levi looked up at him and said, "Nah, that doesn't work for me." After a beat, Levi broke off. "I'll see you later. I gotta go up to the office."

Falk persisted, "Won't you call her?"

Levi shook his head and walked out, closing the door behind him. Suddenly, he "pulled a Columbo"—reopening the door and sticking his head back in. "One more thing, Peter. If I call Shera and she accepts the part, I will trade you. I will accept Shera if you will accept Sondra as the policewoman, if Shera says she'll do it."

"You got a deal."

The wives were delighted to have the four of them working together. When Levi informed his star of the good news, Falk was unsure of what he'd gotten himself into. "Oh, boy. Okay, good luck to us," he smiled.

Universal was even more nervous. As soon as Levi submitted the cast list, he got a call from The Black Tower: "What are you trying to do down there? You've got Peter's wife on the show *and* your wife on the show? You're committing harikiri."

The next day, Falk had another suggestion for Levi: "I've got a great idea for the lead—Dabney Coleman."

Levi was apprehensive. Among other directors, Coleman had the reputation of being extremely difficult to work with. But Levi knew that Coleman's mastery of self-obsessed dismissiveness would make him a perfect *Columbo* villain. Just as importantly, Coleman was one of Falk's closest friends. Falk asked Levi to at least speak to him. Levi went to Coleman's house and the two had an enjoyable meeting.

Levi remembered, "Dabney has worked with a lot of directors who say, 'This is what I want.' And he says, 'I got this.' And they say, 'No, no, no, just hit your mark and say your lines, and that's good enough for me.' So I knew that Dabney just liked to be listened to. And if he has an idea, you listen to it, say, 'That's a great idea,' and try it. Then the next time if you say, 'No, for me, it would be better if…,' it'll be fine. So we hired him, and I got a second call from The Tower: 'And now you hire Dabney Coleman, with both wives? Well, the onus is on you, pal. You gotta run a tight ship.' It was a delight, an absolute delight. There were a couple of times (Dabney) had some good ideas, and I said, 'Let's do that.' And he became a little bunny rabbit in the corner. He was terrific. Everybody had a good time."

The filming proceeded swimmingly until it came time to shoot the extended final confrontation between Columbo and his prey in the lobby of the lawyer's mansion.

"We shot the first half of the scene and, at the end of the day, Peter and Shera got into a screaming fight and Shera walked off," Levi said. "She went home, and that was it for the day. But it was tense. The next day Shera did not show up for the second half of the scene. She said basically, 'Peter, FU.' She went shopping. We sent the police out to find her. And finally at 2:30 in the afternoon they found her shopping in Beverly Hills. So she never showed up."

The crew had to do a quick rewrite on the set, so they could finish the scene without Danese and give her lines to the other characters. "I had to move the second half of the scene outside and pretend that she was still inside," Levi said. "Shera's a very strong woman, and when she gets angry, you don't get near her. And she and Peter went at it like you would not believe. It turned out to be kind of a giggle between all of us, but it wasn't at the time."

Danese did record the singing for the rock star victim. Falk then became even more closely involved in post-production, despite his limited expertise in sound mixing. "He didn't have full understanding of the post process," co-producer Todd London said. "During the last day of the sound mix, he was unhappy with one of the music cues. He asked me if the orchestra was standing by."

Whether because of their waning quality or being relegated to a weekday timeslot, the season's last two specials slipped in the ratings. Falk, though, was enjoying himself again and had just purchased two blockbuster stories that were sure to shake up the *Columbo* universe.

Season 10 – 1990-1991

Columbo Goes to College
Filmed: Oct. 8 – Nov. 5, 1990
Stars: Peter Falk, Steven Caffrey, Gary Hershberger, Robert Culp
Director: E.W. Swackhamer
Supervising Producer: Alan J. Levi
Executive Producer: Jon Epstein
Co-Executive Producer: Peter Falk
Teleplay: Jeffrey Bloom
Story: Jeffrey Bloom & Frederick King Keller
Air Date: Dec. 9, 1990
Ranking: #21 (14.9 points, 24 share)

Caution: Murder Can Be Hazardous to Your Health
Working Titles: *Smokescreen, Cigarettes Can Kill You*
Filmed: Aug. 28 – Sept. 27, 1990
Guest Stars: George Hamilton, Peter Haskell
Director: Daryl Duke
Supervising Producer: Alan J. Levi
Executive Producer: Jon Epstein
Co-Executive Producer: Peter Falk
Teleplay: "Sonia Wolf "(Judy Lamppu), Patricia Ford & April Raynell
Air Date: Feb. 20, 1991
Ranking: #42 (11.8 points, 18 share)

Columbo and the Murder of a Rock Star
Filmed: Jan. 3 – 30, 1991
Guest Stars: Dabney Coleman, Shera Danese, Sondra Currie, Little Richard
Director: Alan J. Levi
Supervising Producer: Alan J. Levi
Executive Producer: Jon Epstein
Co-Executive Producer: Peter Falk
Teleplay: William Read Woodfield
Air Date: April 29, 1991
Ranking: #32 (12.6 points, 19 share)

19
Absolute Power

By the spring of 1991, Falk was overseeing literally every facet of the show. Dwindling film offers meant fewer distractions. According to Todd London, who was entering his fourth and final season on *Columbo*, "With each year that I worked on the show, there were fewer producers, and Peter Falk took on a larger role. He began to oversee the scripts, casting, editing, inserts. He would come to the mixes, direct ADR (automated dialog replacement) with the other actors. I think it made it easier to get what he wanted. The last episode I worked on we were a leaner producing machine. Just four of us."

Indeed, the title of executive producer was Falk's alone if he so chose. Alan Levi preferred to direct and left the series when Universal insisted he concentrate more on producing. Falk promoted unit production manager Chris Seiter to be the new line producer. The son of acclaimed film director William Seiter (*Sons of the Desert*) and silent film actress Marian Nixon, Seiter was known for his calm in the face of chaos. Falk also retained Bill Woodfield as story consultant for one final show.

ABC invited Falk to produce as many as eight new specials over the next two seasons. Realistically, Falk knew he would struggle coming up with half that number of usable scripts. He needed help. He hired Patrick McGoohan, promising to help him fund and produce a proposed feature-film version of *The Prisoner*. In the meantime, McGoohan agreed to co-executive produce the next two *Columbos*, and direct the first. But during pre-production, illness forced McGoohan to step away. The first show continued under *Murder, She Wrote* director Vincent McEveety, whom Peter Fischer had brought in for *Rest in Peace, Mrs. Columbo* and who would become Falk's most frequent director.

McEveety, according to his son Vincent McEveety Jr., "was always prepared, and was very good with actors. He was quick if you let him be quick, so when he got on a show he was able to deliver it. And he was a good guy, with very little guile. He absolutely loved Peter." Teamed with McEveety and the efficient Chris Seiter, who "kept things buzzing like a machine," Falk had senior leaders who could keep the show moving forward, while still indulging him. They accepted his pace. "Peter would do 50 takes if you let him," explained McEveety Jr. "He loved to play. 'I'd like to try one thing a little different....' That show was his baby."

Death Hits the Jackpot

The season's first show originated with a pitch by *Agenda for Murder*'s Jeffrey Bloom. "The California lottery was fairly new—maybe half-a-dozen years old—when the idea came to me for *Death Hits the Jackpot*," Bloom recalled. In his script, a Beverly Hills jeweler kills his gullible nephew to get his hands on a winning lottery ticket. "I mentioned to Peter that I rarely wrote a script with a specific actor in mind, but I'd been a lifelong fan of Rip Torn, and hoped that he would consider him for the lead. Peter did, and Rip got the part. I was very happy."

Rather than shoot the jewelry store scenes on the backlot, the production rented a storefront on Wilshire Boulevard and dressed it up as a high-end jeweler. Late one night, a thief threw a brick through the store's display window and stole an estimated $15,000 worth of fake merchandise, including a faux emerald-and-diamond necklace and a phony sapphire-and-diamond necklace with matching bracelet. Falk was amused by the incident and credited his highly convincing set decorators.

For the pop, Falk wanted the killer ID'ed not by his own fingerprints, but by a monkey's. So Bloom had to shoehorn a photogenic primate into his script. Bloom made his victim a photographer looking after a pet monkey that liked to grab at shiny objects—including a pendant the killer wore on the night of the murder. The unusual clue had originally been proposed by Bill Link at a story meeting two years earlier. The other writers told Link that monkeys didn't leave fingerprints. So in the middle of the story meeting, Link called the head of the crime lab at Parker Center in Los Angeles, whom he would occasionally run scenarios by to see if they were plausible. He asked him if monkeys left fingerprints. "That's the weirdest question I've been asked in 10 years," the expert replied. "I don't know offhand, but I'll ask our resident geniuses here in the lab. I'll get back to you in 10 minutes." Ten minutes later, the phone rang to confirm:

"Not only do monkeys leave fingerprints, they leave more indelible fingerprints than humans." Link was jubilant and worked the clue into Gillis' evil twin story, *Double Vision*. Right before that murder, the victim—a fashion model—was to pose for an eccentric photographer whose pet monkey would leave a telltale fingerprint on her necklace. But while Falk rejected *Double Vision*, he thought Link's pop was fair game.

Link recalled, "Years later, I'm watching a *Columbo* I had nothing to do with. We were at the Regency Hotel in New York City on a Sunday night, and I see a monkey introduced in a party scene, and I say, 'The SOB! He stole that clue out of the show he wouldn't do, and now he's stuck it in here!' Years later at a tribute, he says to me, 'Yeah, that was a great Jackson Gillis clue!' And I said, 'Peter! That wasn't Jackson Gillis! Don't you remember? I came up with that clue!'"

No Time to Die

One evening, Falk was dining with a friend who was an expert in the mystery field. Falk asked him who was the best mystery writer out there. His guest replied, "Ed McBain," the pseudonym that screenwriter Evan Hunter (*Blackboard Jungle*, *The Birds*) used for his 87th Precinct police novels. Falk had never read any of the books, although 30 years earlier he had appeared in an episode of a short-lived 87th Precinct TV series. Falk didn't have to hear any more. He promptly went out and bought the rights to two McBain books—*Jigsaw* (1970) and *So Long as You Both Shall Live* (1976).

Falk soon discovered that the 87th Precinct novels had little in common with *Columbo*, apart from detectives doggedly searching for clues to solve a crime. This wasn't a droll, good-humored, unassuming sleuth matching wits with his well-heeled prey. This was basically *Hill Street Blues*—a procedural featuring a team of hardened policemen on the gritty, violent streets of a big city.

Falk was not dissuaded, and in fact was applauded by McGoohan. Like Richard Alan Simmons, McGoohan had long encouraged Falk to think beyond the format, to realize that the most enduring component of *Columbo* was Columbo himself, Columbo the character. With that in mind, Falk brought in Robert van Scoyk to somehow transform *So Long as You Both Shall Live* into a *Columbo*. In the plot, one of the detectives has his bride kidnapped from their honeymoon suite by a crazed, scalpel-wielding stalker. The psycho plans to marry her in a private ceremony, consummate the wedding, and then kill himself and her, recreating how his mother was slain by his father. The entire squad room must work together and race against the clock to locate and rescue the bride before it's too late.

ON THE WEDDING scene set of *No Time to Die (left to right)*: post-production supervisor Stephen Swofford, tuxedoed star Peter Falk, and co-producer Todd London. *[Credit: Stephen Swofford]*

Van Scoyk converted one of the detectives into Lt. Columbo, minus almost everything that made him Columbo except the name and the raincoat. He considered making the Lieutenant the groom's father, but that would invite a host of story problems, including the necessity of having Mrs. Columbo appear at the wedding. Instead, Columbo became the groom's uncle, and he relies on an entire team to crack the case. There was no murder, no sly humor, no clever deductions, and no cat-and-mouse banter with the bad guy—in fact, Columbo doesn't even meet the bad guy until after the weirdo has been gunned down. The villain isn't a brilliant, wealthy, well-known professional; he's a downtrodden lowlife who lives in a shack off a dark alley. Van Scoyk's script was creepy and unsettling; Falk loved it.

Shortly before filming began, McGoohan again backed out of executive producing duties, citing problems "in the old health department." As he recuperated at home, he continued polishing future *Columbo* scripts for Falk.

For *So Long as You Both Shall Live*, Falk asked Alan Levi to step in as director and co-executive producer. Levi read the script, and immediately recognized how immense a departure it was for the franchise—a challenge he was excited to tackle. Levi went to Falk's office and said, "This is terrific. But if we're going to do a show like this, I suggest we *really* do it and not screw around with it. Let's not try and put it into a '*Columbo* capsule.' If we're going to make a different show, let's make a different show. Because if you make one that's slightly different, you're going to get roasted. This is a series of movies of the week in which you can really take a different tack on it. You've done hundreds that all had the same format. If we cast the right people in this, it can be something really special."

Falk agreed to not go halfway. He left the script as a relatively faithful adaptation of the novel, and allowed Levi to film it as a dark, suspenseful thriller. Falk's only significant change came on the last day of filming when he demanded that the final scene—a shootout in the psycho's all-white hideout—be relighted. The change caused a two-hour delay, but Levi was grateful to have kept the

---

Season 11 – 1991-1992

Death Hits the Jackpot
Filmed: July 1991
Stars: Peter Falk, Rip Torn, Gary Kroeger, Jamie Rose
Director: Vincent McEveety
Executive Producer: Peter Falk
Producer: Christopher Seiter
Teleplay: Jeffrey Bloom
Air Date: Dec. 15, 1991
Ranking: #25 (14.2 points, 22 share)

No Time to Die
Filmed: Nov. – Dec. 1991
Stars: Peter Falk, Joanna Going, Thomas Calabro, Daniel McDonald
Director: Alan J. Levi
Executive Producer: Peter Falk
Producer: Christopher Seiter
Co-Executive Producer: Alan J. Levi
Teleplay: Robert van Scoyk
Based on the Book: *So Long as You Both Shall Live* by "Ed McBain" (Evan Hunter)
Air Date: March 15, 1992
Ranking: #12 (16.5 points, 27 share)

production otherwise moving.

ABC moved the episode, retitled *No Time to Die*, back to a Sunday night, March 15, 1992. Falk crossed his fingers. He warned the press that he was trying something different. "We're not going to make a habit of it, but it was an interesting change of pace," Falk admitted. "The way he solves it has more to do with his obsession with details, with his compulsive thoroughness than with any inspired thoughts."

He also noted that his performance as Columbo is different than before. "He's under a little bit more stress," Falk said. "He's emotionally involved. He can't operate quite the same way because time is everything, so he has to get to it. His pulse is beating more."

Critics were stunned and generally panned the special. As *Columbo* expert Mark Dawidziak wrote in the *Cleveland Plain Dealer*, "Slow and excruciatingly deliberate, *No Time to Die* comes off as another cop story with a woman-in-jeopardy angle. We don't want Columbo to act like every other policeman on TV. If you must change the formula, don't change the character."

Falk admitted he was breaking the format, and half-apologized, explaining that it was the best script available. "I had to make a choice between what was on hand and the script that we chose to shoot," he said. "I was happier with the one we shot than I would have been with the alternatives we had. I just can't stand the ones that don't have a pop at the end, which are the hardest to come up with. We didn't have a good pop in any of the scripts I saw, and I thought they were all soft in the middle, so we decided to go with that one."

Nonetheless, the ratings were huge—generating the biggest audience *Columbo* would achieve outside of the 1970s. In fact, with the specials trending upward, ABC had been airing an old *Columbo* every Thursday since the beginning of the year. For the first time, *Columbo* was a weekly primetime series, albeit one comprised entirely of reruns. And once the network ran out of *Columbo* repeats, it aired the *Mrs. Columbo* pilot, followed the next week by *Prescription: Murder* and then *Ransom for a Dead Man*.

A Bird in the Hand…

Because Falk and his streamlined crew were so heavily involved in post-production on *No Time to Die*, work on the next *Columbo* did not begin until the spring of 1992. And because the last show was such a jarring, radical departure, Falk was determined to return to familiar ground for the next one. He had two treatments submitted by Jackson Gillis, who had written them more than two years earlier, when he was polishing *Murder in Malibu*. The first treatment, *Stunt Girl*, featured an abusively loud millionaire who, faced with mounting indictments, decides to flee the country. His wife Bonnie Sue and his financial advisor would stay behind to maintain the illusion that he was still in town. They would join him later, after they had methodically cashed out all of his securities. But as the millionaire flies off in his private plane, he notices a stowaway—Bonnie Sue, who shoots him and parachutes to safety before the plane crashes into a Mexican hillside. The financial advisor, evidently panicking, also disappears and becomes the prime suspect—until Columbo discovers his body, which Bonnie Sue buried near his beach house.

In Gillis' second treatment, *M.O. of a Golden Goose*, luxury-hotel-magnate-turned-pro-basketball-team owner Stanley McGee discovers his sponging nephew Harold has been selling inside information about the team to gamblers in Las Vegas. With McGee's former connections to the city, he knows that if word got out about his shady nephew, he'd lose his team. Harold, fearful he'll be cut off, wires McGee's car with a pipe bomb and writes a few anonymous threatening letters, to make the hit look like the work of professionals. But before using his car, McGee goes jogging and is killed by a hit-and-run driver. Harold meanwhile has been sleeping with McGee's wife, Dolores, and learns she has evidence that would point to him as the killer. He panics and kills her... only to later learn that it was Dolores who ran down Stanley, so she could be with Harold. As Gillis closed, "Harold has killed the goose who only wanted to lay him a golden egg!"

Falk wanted Gillis to proceed with the second story, but borrowing elements from the first. Stanley McGee became Big Fred, the owner of a pro *football* team, making it more practical for the team's strapping, 6-foot-tall (not 7-foot-tall) athletes to begin flirting with Dolores once she takes over the team. Dolores would undergo a *Lady in Waiting*-style transformation, as she begins to enjoy her newfound power and attention from strong young men. Her old squeeze, Harold, also becomes dispensable, and she kills him when he starts getting suspicious about her role in the hit-and-run.

The producers had hoped to use footage from an actual National Football League game, but filming started in July—months before the beginning of the NFL season. "So I called the NFL and asked if they had any stock footage," recalled associate producer Jack Horger. "'Oh, yeah, we've got some stock footage—at $5 a foot.' With the amount of football footage that was in this script, $5 a foot was way beyond our budget. Okay, so I'm screwed. We were not going to get one frame of NFL footage. So I called the Canadian Football League, which was playing football at the time. I got a television crew up in Edmonton that put two cameras on the ground, one camera in the stands, and one on the rim of the stadium. They photographed the whole game, the Edmonton Eskimos vs. the Saskatchewan Roughriders. Now Canada has a 110-yard football field, we have 100, so their center stripe is the 55-yard line. The crew carefully placed a bench on the sidelines in between the camera lens and the 55-yard marker. We had footage to make anything happen—touchdowns, tackles, fumbles. They even sent us a complete Roughriders uniform, so the Wardrobe Department could make one in the size of our actor."

Retitled *A Bird in the Hand...*, the show marked a clear return to the established *Columbo* formula, freshened up by several twists along the way, including an Act II Switcheroo: Columbo's original suspect, Harold, suddenly popping up dead. Falk even brought back composer Dick DeBenedictis after a 16-year absence to provide the haunting, pulsating score the show had been sorely lacking.

What didn't get used was the jaunty music DeBenedictis composed to play over the main titles, as Harold heads home after losing big in Las Vegas. In an early cut of the film, prior to DeBenedictis submitting his score, the assistant editor had used Tony Bennett singing "Rags to Riches" for the opening, just as a placeholder. When Falk sat down to view the final print, with all-original music, he was disappointed. "Where's 'Rags to Riches?'" he asked. "I love that song!"

"We don't own it," Horger explained.

"Well, buy it."

"Do you have any idea how much the rights to that song are going to cost? We don't have that it the budget."

Falk frowned. "But I *really* like that song. It just was so perfect."

As usual, Falk got his way, and the production found a way to license "Rags to Riches."

1992-1993 Season

A Bird in the Hand...
Working Titles: *M.O. of a Golden Goose, Point After Death*
Filming Started: July 28, 1992
Stars: Peter Falk, Tyne Daly, Greg Evigan, Steve Forrest
Director: Vincent McEveety
Executive Producer: Peter Falk
Producer: Christopher Seiter
Teleplay: Jackson Gillis
Air Date: Nov. 22, 1992
Ranking: #36 (12.2 points, 19 share)

Butterfly in Shades of Grey

By now, ABC had figured out that Falk would work at Falk's pace. Their contracts were becoming more open-ended, asking for up to three specials per year, but assuming that they would end up with one or, at most, two.

Falk planned to shoot the next two pictures back-to-back the following spring. In the first, *Butterfly in Shades of Grey*, William Shatner would play Fielding Chase, a bombastic radio host weirdly obsessed with his pretty young producer, whom he had adopted when she was a child. Chase shoots a journalist who attempts to free her from his control. Speeding from the scene, Chase frantically calls 911 from his car phone, pretending he's just left his home in the Malibu mountains—in an area that Columbo discovers does not get mobile reception.

Falk got the idea for the episode from Peter S. Fischer. "That was an interesting story because I just started with the idea that the phones wouldn't work in the mountains," Fischer recalled. "That was going to be the clue that got the killer at the end. Peter called me and I said, 'Here's the story, here's what I think will work,' and I told him the idea of going out in the middle of the mountains, but he couldn't get the phone to work in the mountains. I gave Peter the five-minute drill, and he said, 'Sounds good to me,' so I went off and wrote it."

Fischer gave it an unusual title for a *Columbo*—*Butterfly in Shades of Grey*—to describe the restrained daughter who yearns to break free. "She was very shy," Fischer explained. "She was unprepossessing and kind of socially inept, but she was a butterfly deep down, at heart, but she didn't let anybody know about it. It made sense to me. It's funny, because that was the first thing. I didn't have to search for a title, it just came to me immediately."

Shatner's character was clearly inspired by Rush Limbaugh. Shatner, though, didn't pattern his performance after the radio host. He tried to channel *Firing Line*'s William F. Buckley Jr. "I tried to do his voice and his arrogance of personality," Shatner revealed.

It's All in the Game

Falk then turned to the script he first began writing more than 20 years earlier. The project grew out of his badgering Levinson and Link to improve the scripts during Season 1, and their challenge to him that, if he thought it was so easy, he should try writing one himself. Falk thought back to an investigator he had met, who had become conflicted about a case because he was growing fond of his primary suspect. "I started by remembering a guy that I knew—not too well, but well enough that he would tell me things about his life," Falk said. After starting the actual writing, he quickly discovered how difficult it was to create and sustain the cat-and-mouse dance and top it with a jaw-dropping pop.

When ABC announced plans to revive the series in 1988, Falk dusted off and updated his screenplay, but his fellow executive producers convinced him it just wasn't ready. Now there were no other executive producers. He spent months further revising it, until at long last it seemed good enough to commit to film. In *It's All in the Game*, a beautiful middle-aged woman and her adult daughter conspire to kill a slick charmer who has been romancing both of them. To get Columbo off the scent, the mother flirts with the detective. He must trap her even as the two seemingly start to fall for each other.

Whether deliberately or subconsciously, elements of prior episodes started sneaking into Falk's writing: the mother who kills for her wronged daughter from *Try and Catch Me*, the parent who agrees to sign a confession to protect a child from *Mind Over Mayhem*, letting a sympathetic guilty party go free as in *Forgotten Lady*, establishing a later time of death by keeping the corpse warm with an electric blanket from *Suitable for Framing*, the killer insisting on a new tie for Columbo from *Requiem for a Falling Star*, and so on.

Falk's script was conventional as a mystery, and pedestrian as a drama—every five minutes there's a near-identical scene of mother phoning daughter to relay basically the same conversation. Yet the romance angle was wholly unique.

The project was so dear to Falk that he wanted someone perfect for the antagonist. During his search, he was contacted by Academy Award-winner Faye Dunaway, who was looking for tips on playing a forensic psychiatrist on a proposed series for NBC. Dunaway remembered, "I called Peter because *Columbo* is a cottage industry and nobody does it better than Peter and his people, so I said, 'How do you do a franchise character and make it work?' I began to have a dialogue with Peter, and I adore his work and himself as a person. And he sent me the script. He had written it and put it away until he found somebody he thought could play it. It had been in a drawer for years. So then I read it. I just thought it was so enchanting."

Dunaway would be sensational in the role—playing brilliantly off Falk, winning an Emmy, and being nominated for a Golden Globe for her performance—but it didn't come easy. She fully lived up to her reputation as difficult. After two decades as the terrorizer of production executives, Falk, as executive producer, was having the tables turned on him.

One friend shared that, away from work, Falk would complain Dunaway was driving him crazy. "The first week she went through two hairdressers and three makeup people," one buddy recounted. "She was a pain in the ass."

Universal executive Charlie Engel remembered one day getting an urgent call from the studio saying, "Peter's very upset. You'd better come out." Such calls,

Engel said, "were not rare. I went out to the set and said, 'What's up, Peter?' And he said, 'Faye won't come out of her dressing room.' I went to the dressing room with him, and he said, 'Go ahead, get her out.' And I said, 'Peter, you're the executive producer of this show. That's your title. You're in charge.' He knocked, and then I knocked and said to Faye, 'Please come out, we're ready to go.' She came out, but it was kind of funny because it was the pot calling the kettle black. Everybody said, 'Oh, Faye Dunaway's going to hate you, Charlie. Because you get her out of her dressing room when *she* is ready.' And I said, 'Well, I certainly didn't mean any disrespect, but it's a television show, not an Academy Award motion picture, and we have things that we have to do to shoot the episode.'"

Falk spent three solid months overseeing post-production on his pet project. He finally signed off on its release to ABC at 3 a.m. on a Sunday—hours before catching a flight to the East Coast to begin work on the film *Roommates*.

Undercover

By the time Falk returned to *Columbo*, he had only one story he trusted—his second *87th Precinct* story, *Jigsaw*. In McBain's book, the precinct's lone black officer, Detective Brown, must go undercover to obtain pieces of a photograph held by an odd assortment of hoodlums and bigots. When reassembled, the picture fragments show the location of loot stashed years before by bank robbers.

Falk liked the treasure-hunt story, but knew many of its details and overtones had to be changed. The novel was purposefully offensive—filled with racism, coarse language, and plenty of blood. Falk also wanted to give Columbo a bigger, more familiar role than in *No Time to Die*, where—apart from an opening-scene mention of his wife—our hero showed no humor, slyness, feigned befuddlement, or any other established personality traits. Equally problematic, *No Time to Die* had been an ensemble story in which different detectives alternated in taking the lead.

Falk also wanted a lighter touch. To adapt *Jigsaw* for *Columbo*, he hired Gerry Day, a 71-year-old female who was as adept at writing Disney fare as she was mysteries and westerns. First, she removed all traces of racism. Then she made Columbo the central character who goes undercover, taking on three different disguises and personas. Officer Brown was demoted to his partner. That meant giving Columbo lots of uncharacteristic tough-guy dialogue and action scenes—our hero brandishes a gun, smashes a door into a guy's head, is punched out, and gets knocked unconscious. Day also inserted numerous moments of comedy and hints that this fellow in the raincoat really is Columbo, including at the end when he says he's leaving to go play with his dog.

IN *UNDERCOVER*, Shera Danese played a suspect who didn't fall for Lt. Columbo's disguises. *[Credit: Gene Trindl/ABC]*

The book's ending was completely unusable. In *Jigsaw*, the detectives scheme to crack the killer's alibi-providing girlfriend by having the black detective break into the woman's apartment late at night and threaten to rape her unless she tells the truth. Falk pushed for a theatrical pop—albeit a silly one: the killer's fingerprint is found on a coin in a parking meter outside one victim's home.

One holdover from the book was the sliced-up photo revealing where the treasure was submerged, off of "Old River Road." Falk wanted to use the same photograph that was printed in *Jigsaw*. It sounded like a great idea to everyone—except for the Locations manager. "Where the hell are we supposed to find that?" he carped. He delegated the search for a matching location to co-producer Jack Horger.

"The job got booted down to me, to go out and find this Old River Road," Horger said. "I thought, 'Good luck with that.' So I took Lisa Tygett, my associate producer, and we drove all around Southern California. We ended up at the breakwater at Marina del Rey. There was a big parking lot and as we walked out onto the breakwater, there it was—with a road along the top of it. So I took pictures and they loved it. But in the photo the River Road had a lot of imperfections in it, a lot of joints and cracks; the breakwater did not. When I saw the dailies, I had to chuckle to myself. They had painted all those cracks on the breakwater to match that stupid picture. Then, of course, they repainted it back when they were finished."

1993-1994 Season

It's All in the Game
Working Title: *Two Women and a Dead Man*
Filming Started: April 27, 1993
Stars: Peter Falk, Faye Dunaway, Claudia Christian
Director: Vincent McEveety
Executive Producer: Peter Falk
Producer: Christopher Seiter
Teleplay: Peter Falk
Air Date: Oct. 31, 1993
Ranking: #26 (13.4 points, 21 share)

Butterfly in Shades of Grey
Filmed: March 1993
Stars: Peter Falk, William Shatner, Molly Hagan
Director: Dennis Dugan
Executive Producer: Peter Falk
Producer: Christopher Seiter
Teleplay: Peter S. Fischer
Air Date: Jan. 10, 1994
Ranking: #16 (15 points, 23 share)

Undercover
Working Titles: *Jigsaw, Columbo Goes Undercover*
Filmed: Feb. – March 1994
Stars: Peter Falk, Ed Begley Jr., Burt Young, Shera Danese
Director: Vincent McEveety
Executive Producer: Peter Falk
Producers: Vincent McEveety & Christopher Seiter
Teleplay: Gerry Day
Based on the Book: *Jigsaw* by Ed McBain (Evan Hunter)
Air Date: May 2, 1994
Ranking: #11 (14.1 points, 22 share)

Falk cast his close friend, Ed Begley Jr., as the killer; his wife Shera as a prime suspect; and Tyne Daly, the flirty drunk murderer from *A Bird in the Hand...*, as a supporting player. Daly recalled that while making the earlier show, "we had a great time. So (Peter) asked me to do another, which was a day job where I played another blowsy. That was a very blowsy period. We worked for one day. There were two scenes. And at the end of it Peter kissed me on the cheek. And his longtime producer said (huffily), 'Columbo doesn't do that!'" But the kiss stayed in.

This time, instead of apologizing to interviewers, Falk gladly confessed that he had once again broken the format. The main problem was that, while Falk did display an occasional hint of the old, good-natured Lieutenant, he too easily and fully transformed himself into two-bit thugs. Viewers were left with the impression that *everything* about the Columbo personality we've loved for all these years may be nothing more than an act the detective puts on for his suspects.

Audiences were intrigued, making *Undercover* the week's eleventh most-watched program. ABC had been waiting for the ratings before renewing *Columbo*. They gave Falk their blessing to continue.

Strange Bedfellows

By the fall of 1994, Falk had signed to do up to three more *Columbos* for ABC. Within a month, he received a script from Peter Fischer. In *Strange Bedfellows*, Graham McVeigh, the co-owner of a thoroughbred ranch, bumps off his gambling-addict brother and tries to frame a mobster to whom his sibling owed money. Feigning self-defense, McVeigh then murders the gangster, which upsets Vincenzo Fortelli, boss of the local crime family. Lacking concrete proof, Columbo agrees to work with Fortelli to compel McVeigh to confess—before the Don takes matters into his own hands.

Falk, unfortunately, decided to take matters into his own hands, rewriting the script himself... to Fischer's dismay. "That was a long involved process," Fischer recalled. "Peter and the director, Vince McEveety, changed so many things in the story that it didn't make any sense. Peter messed that one up *a lot*. He lost focus, because he was an extreme stickler about the clues that were used in *Columbo*. They had to be the right kind. I thought I had it there, but apparently he got a bug up his ass and just couldn't see it, and he changed everything around."

Among the gaps in logic, in one scene, McVeigh all but throws Columbo out of his home ("No, Lieutenant. There is no 'just one more thing.' Goodbye."). In the very next scene, McVeigh readily agrees to meet Columbo for dinner.

Falk's most regrettable deletion, though, might have been a lengthy exchange between Columbo and Fortelli at the Don's mansion. The four pages of dialogue were immaterial to the plot, but would have delighted longtime fans with their inside jokes and callbacks to earlier episodes. Columbo wants to get right to the point—what can the mob boss tell him about the murders. But it's Fortelli who prevaricates and goes off-topic, beckoning for a cigar. Fortelli was to ask Columbo if he had always wanted to be a cop and how much he makes in a year.

Fortelli would then inquire, "How long you had that suit?"

"Oh, that goes back," Columbo smiles.

"A lot of years."

"A lot of years," Columbo repeats.

"What'd you pay for those shoes?" Fortelli asks.

"I uh…"

"Goes back a lot of years."

"A lot of years," Columbo again repeats.

Fortelli wonders if there are things that the detective and the missus would like to do but don't have the money for, like go on a cruise together.

"We took a cruise," Columbo offers.

Fortelli is surprised: "You could afford…"

"No," Columbo interrupts, "couldn't afford it. She won a cruise on a lottery ticket—everything paid."

Fortelli eventually discovers that Columbo's wife does a lot of work through her church, helping underprivileged children. He insists—against Columbo's protests—on writing a $30,000 check for her favorite charity. "You're a stubborn son of a bitch with a small-minded mentality and despite you, those kids are gonna get the 30,000, 'cause I do things right. Now, let's see if you learned anything," Fortelli says. He then turns to the waiter: "Pour him his soup—and bring me an aspirin—the guy's giving me a headache."

In a delicious stroke of casting, Falk convinced Rod Steiger to play the mob boss. Yet Falk baffled the entire production team with his choice for the murderer:

Strange Bedfellows

Filmed: Nov. – Dec. 1994
Stars: Peter Falk, George Wendt, Jeff Yagher
Director: Vincent McEveety
Executive Producer: Peter Falk
Producers: Vincent McEveety & Christopher Seiter
Teleplay: "Lawrence Vail" (Peter S. Fischer)
Air Date: May 8, 1995
Ranking: #17 (12.4 points, 19 share)

George Wendt, the everyman barfly Norm from *Cheers*. Fischer recalled, "When I heard they were going to hire George Wendt, I said, 'No! This has got to be a guy like Jack Cassidy, Robert Vaughn. It's a guy who's smart, intelligent, good looking, suave. George Wendt! What, are you kidding me?'

"The opening scene where he goes to buy a gun in disguise—I'm sorry, you can't disguise George Wendt. He sticks out like a thumb. He goes into the pawnshop to buy the pistol in a mustache, but it's George Wendt! Right away I knew it was going to be trouble when I heard that he was going to be the villain."

Fischer continued begging McEveety to push back against Falk: "Vince, please for God's sake, can you get through to him?"

"No," McEveety apologized, "he's got his mind made up."

In the end, Fischer realized there was nothing he could do. "So I said, 'Fine, I'll just take my name off it. You guys do what you want.' So they did." And as he did on *Old Fashioned Murder*, Fischer changed his credit to his pseudonym, Lawrence Vail.

Strange Bedfellows was originally slated to air on a Sunday, May 7, 1995. But once NBC announced it would be counterprogramming with the network television premiere of *Jurassic Park*, ABC wisely pushed *Columbo* back one day. (Over 68 million people tuned in to *Jurassic Park*.) Safely back on a Monday, *Strange Bedfellows* pulled in good ratings, despite horrible reviews.

Five months after the show aired, Falk was accused of ripping the story off from a bit actor who had hoped to become a writer. While appearing as a cop in *It's All in the Game*, Frank DiElsi heard from Chris Seiter that Falk was in need of scripts. So DiElsi wrote his own, called *Never Trust a Gambler*, and submitted it to Seiter. Six months later, DiElsi was hired to serve as a voice coach on *Strange Bedfellows*. But by the time production was finished, he realized that the film appeared to be based on his script. He sued Falk, Seiter, McEveety, ABC and Universal for copyright infringement. The case was eventually thrown out without ruling whether or not any of his work had been copied. DiElsi had never registered a copyright for his script.

A Trace of Murder

As he entered his late 60s, Peter Falk finally started to slow down. Slightly. He continued doing the occasional film and TV movie, but he was just as energetic as ever, though maybe a touch more forgetful. "He was a chain smoker," said Charlie Engel. "In his office, he would light a cigarette, put it in the ashtray, and while we were talking light another, while the first one's still in the ashtray. He would put his glasses up on his forehead when we were talking and not working

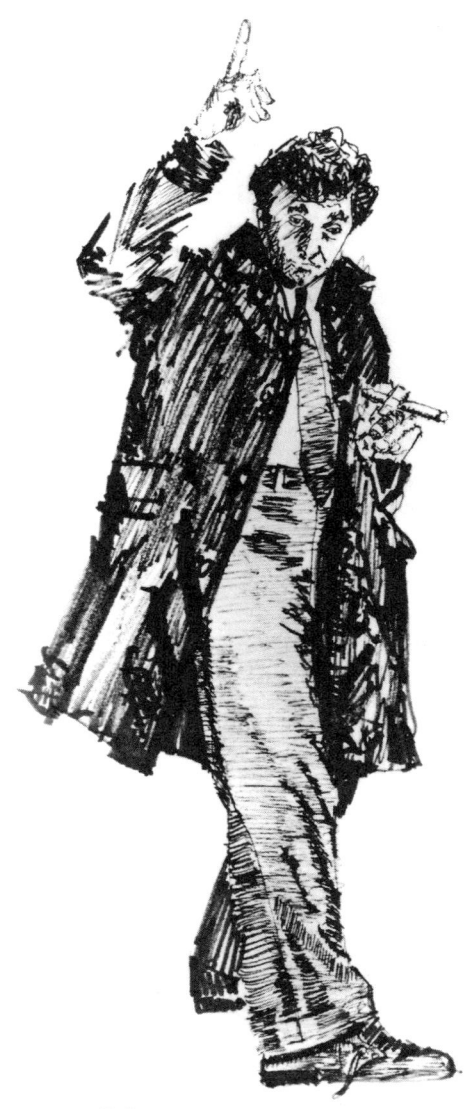

DURING THE ABC run, Falk featured this charcoal self-portrait on his office's notepads, along with the tagline "Just One More Thing...." *[Credit: Jack Horger]*

on a script, and then when it came time to go back to the script, he couldn't find his glasses. He would yell at his secretary, 'Where are my glasses?' Well, they of course were on his forehead."

The breaks between *Columbo* specials got longer. ABC was getting pickier about what it green-lit. Falk attributed the layoff to a lack of good scripts, although that problem was apparently not resolved by the time he was finally ready to suit up again more than two years later.

Bill Link had suggested one of his *Cosby Mysteries* writers, Charles Kipps, who had proposed incorporating more forensics and procedure into *Columbo* by making the murderer a CSI investigator. The murderer could then line up clues that point Columbo in the wrong direction—toward the husband of his mistress. The best thing about the script, at least for Falk's wife Shera, was its plum role of female conspirator. After 20 years of pleading, she finally got the opportunity to play the villain—as well as to wear 12 different fabulous outfits.

Falk had looked forward to playing Columbo in his old age, when the character's forgetfulness and other eccentricities might seem normal. Yet, his performance had the opposite effect. Columbo started to come across as borderline senile. In *A Trace of Murder*, he extraneously passes out bananas from a grocery bag and later apples from a gift basket. He issues an all-points bulletin for a missing cat ("That cat could be the only witness to this terrible crime! I want that cat!"). The other characters talk down to him and behind his back describe him as "goofy," "wacky," "crazy," and "dopey."

Worst of all, Falk thought the original ending—in which the lovers turn on each other—lacked finality, since no one is arrested. He inserted a laborious wrap-up, which dragged on for nearly six minutes explaining and re-explaining several clues. Whether the idea was to dumb down the show for new viewers, to pad out the running time, or to give more screen time to John Finnegan as Barney and director McEveety's son as Barney's busboy, it was completely unnecessary. Never before had an episode sputtered to a more tedious finish.

ABC promoted the program as *Columbo's* "25th Anniversary Special," even though *Murder by the Book* was 26 years earlier and *Prescription: Murder* nearly 30. It also programmed the show in unfamiliar territory on a Thursday night. Squaring off against the season finales of ratings powerhouses *Seinfeld* and *E.R.*, *A Trace of Murder* performed poorly and reiterated to Falk that if the show were to continue, he truly needed more help at the top.

A Trace of Murder

Filmed: Feb. – March 1997
Stars: Peter Falk, David Rache, Shera Danese, Barry Corbin
Director: Vincent McEveety
Executive Producer: Peter Falk
Producers: Vincent McEveety & Christopher Seiter
Teleplay: Charles Kipps
Air Date: May 15, 1997
Ranking: #41 (8.8 points, 14 share)

Ashes to Ashes

Playwright Jeffrey Hatcher had a number of successful stage productions under his belt, but—as a lifelong fan—he had always wanted to write a *Columbo*. Through mutual friend Dan Lauria, he was able to relay a script pitch to Falk: a Hollywood funeral director kills and then cremates a gossip reporter after she threatens to divulge that years ago he stole the diamond necklace off an actress' dead body. Hatcher shared, "When my father died, I spent time with the funeral director at the mortuary, and one day I asked, 'Any fun stories you can share with me?' I heard a few, about pacemakers, etc., and suddenly I had an idea for a *Columbo*. I know of no real famous Hollywood mortician to the stars, but there must be one. In New York, the funeral parlor to go to is the Frank E. Campbell Chapel. I went there and interviewed its manager. I got some very good inside information."

To Hatcher's amazement, Falk called him personally to tell him he liked the premise. "He brought me out to Los Angeles, we met at his office at Universal," Hatcher recalled. "We'd go to dinner, I'd go to his house. We worked in his studio, which was a converted garage. His process was to talk about the idea, flesh it out. Then he said (to) write the story—a 20-page treatment, which I was paid for. Then, when the treatment was solid, I was paid to write the teleplay."

Falk really liked that so much of the action took place in and around a Hollywood funeral home—a completely new setting for *Columbo*, and one that could inspire unique clues, such those associated with the process of preparing a body for burial or cremation. Falk was also tickled at Hatcher's suggestion that Dog find the first clue.

ABC gave the okay for two more episodes, the first to run in the fall of 1998, the second in the spring of 1999. But Falk needed more help. Chris Seiter was still available to produce, but for the first time in eight years, Falk could not hire co-producer/director Vincent McEveety. Vince McEveety Jr. said, "Dad had three accidents and then pneumonia. He had recently fallen on the set shooting (an episode of) *Promised Land*. The studios said, 'We can't have you if you can't complete a job. We have 10 guys standing behind you who can.' He was 68. He didn't want it to end—his mind was a steel trap—but his body was breaking down. He had worked constantly."

About the same time, Falk approached Christopher Plummer to play the funeral director, Eric Prince. Plummer was willing, but ABC balked at his asking price. So Falk went to his old friend Patrick McGoohan to see if his health would allow him to return. McGoohan agreed to help develop both of the next two shows, including starring in, directing and co-executive producing *Ashes to Ashes*.

Of course, part of any deal with McGoohan was also allowing him to rework the script. In particular, he zeroed in on making both Columbo and the murderer intelligent enough to, fairly early on, recognize what the other was up to. As originally written, Columbo was to return to the mortuary seeking a guided tour, pretending that he was interested in a prepaid funeral for himself and his wife. During an extended interview with attendant Gerald, Columbo was to muse, "Some of these caskets, they cost more than my car!" Gerald retorts, "Maybe we could bury you in your car." Gerald then begins taking Columbo on a tour, starting in the prep room, where Prince overhears the questioning and breaks in. McGoohan wanted to cut more quickly to the confrontation. He instead began the scene with Prince eavesdropping and made Prince, not Gerald, the one who answers Columbo's questions about cremation.

During Columbo's final interrogation of Prince, during the funeral for a famous hoofer, McGoohan had an old tap dancer perform alongside the casket. The performer taps out his routine in the background between the two men to accentuate the "dance" between them.

McGoohan could not restrain himself from adding bits of strained humor, such as supplying the lyrics for a series of corny songs at a morticians' convention ("For He's a Jolly Good Undertaker," "When a Body Meets a Body," "He'll Be Buried Six Feet Under When He Goes…").

Working together again, Falk and McGoohan had a wondrous time, and their scenes together crackled. Hatcher said, "Falk and McGoohan were very much in sync. You can see how much fun they had. They liked to throw each other fastballs, curveballs, lobs that held in the air for an odd moment to see what might happen. They didn't like to be bored. They kept each other on their toes."

During one confrontation, Columbo tells Prince that he knows he's guilty, he just doesn't have any proof—and then was to angrily storm off as Prince is delivering his final lines ("That's the tricky thing about burning questions. Once they're burned, they're just ashes."). During one take, Falk exited the scene a little early, so McGoohan was left to say his parting lines to an empty room. After a beat, McGoohan called out, "Have you gone?" The crew cracked up. They decided to leave the ad-lib in—although later McGoohan had to dub in the "Have you gone?" because the original track contained the crew's laughter and the assistant director calling "Cut."

Fittingly, the final scene in the show—which would become the final physical moments on screen of McGoohan's career—was the last sequence shot. Just before dusk on a drizzly Friday, the cast and crew arrived at the Lawry's California Center, a shuttered restaurant complex that doubled as the exterior of the funeral parlor. The two men squared off one final time, as Columbo revealed his proof.

Prince, with the police car waiting, asks Columbo, "Shall we go together?"

"That's up to you, sir," Columbo replies. "After all, it's your funeral."

According to Hatcher's script, Prince, instead of responding, was to walk alone to the police car, open the back door, and stand holding it as he looks back at Columbo. He pauses, then gets in and slams the door behind him—defiant until the end. McGoohan decided to instead end more collegially. He closes on the words "it's your funeral," as the men exchange sly smiles, under a lightly falling rain.

Reinvigorated by a strong script and each other to play off of, Falk and McGoohan seemed to step back in time. *Ashes to Ashes* was the liveliest *Columbo* in years, as if it had come from the classic days on NBC. ABC confidently scheduled the show on a Thursday night, going up against highly rated sitcoms and *E.R.* on NBC, *Diagnosis: Murder* on CBS, and the World Series on Fox. *Ashes to Ashes* fared a distant fourth.

Murder with Too Many Notes

During the production of *Ashes to Ashes*, Universal assigned two development directors, Nancy Meyer and Rob Levine, to help Falk find scripts. They would solicit and listen to pitches for new stories, hire writers, supervise their progress, and present the best options to Falk, Universal and ABC. Despite the reinforcements, the next script would find its way to Falk without them.

Jeffrey Cava, a young production assistant on Universal documentaries and a film-music superfan, had written a *Columbo* and dropped it off at Falk's office, where it lay, unread, for months. Cava ultimately convinced co-producer Jack Horger to give his writing a look. In Cava's story, *Murder with Too Many Notes*, flashy film composer Paradiso has been passing off the music of his young

---

Ashes to Ashes

Filmed: March 2 – 27, 1998
Stars: Peter Falk, Patrick McGoohan, Rue McClanahan
Director: Patrick McGoohan
Executive Producer: Peter Falk
Producer: Christopher Seiter
Co-Executive Producer: Patrick McGoohan
Teleplay: Jeffrey Hatcher
Air Date: Oct. 8, 1998
Ranking: #52 (7.4 points, 12 share)

apprentice as his own. When the assistant threatens to go public, Paradiso drugs him and places his body on a high-rise roof, above a freight elevator shaft. Paradiso then initiates the lift's slow ascent, so he has time to take the concert stage before the lift reaches the roof and pushes the body over the side of the building.

Horger loved it. It had excitement, clever clues, droll humor, inside secrets about scoring movies, and a classic *Columbo* feel. Its only problem was length. It ran over 130 pages and the current *Columbos* ran about 98 pages. A former editor, Horger helped Cava trim redundant lines and scenes to lop off 30 pages. Horger then "conned" Falk into reading it. Falk too liked it, and wanted to use it as the season's second show.

McGoohan agreed to direct. Falk wanted him to also play Paradiso, but—on the heels of *Ashes to Ashes*—McGoohan thought it too soon. Horger and Cava had hoped to cast Jeremy Irons as the murderer, but he was out of their price range. Nancy Meyer suggested stand-up comic Billy Connolly. "I had seen Billy Connolly in several things and could see him in the role of the flamboyant composer, so I brought him to Peter and Patrick's attention," she said. "I showed them *Mrs. Brown*, which was quite a dramatic role for Billy."

The casting meant changing the villain from the mysterious character Paradiso into a hard-drinking Scotsman, Findlay Crawford. That, alas, was just the beginning of McGoohan's changes. He spent the next three weeks completely bastardizing the script.

For "comic" effect, he inserted a nonsensical scene in which Columbo insists on giving the plastered Crawford a police escort home. Their cars, and the entire scene, crawl along, constantly stopping. The pointless sequence dragged on for nearly eight minutes. For a scene in which Columbo visits Crawford during a scoring session, McGoohan had the composer challenge the detective to a game of "Name That Tune," playing the unmistakable themes from *Psycho* and *Jaws*. Columbo is dumbfounded.

Cava's primary clue was based on how old-style industrial elevators, once common at movie studios, made an inaudible electrical connection as they passed each floor. He proposed that if the same electric circuit were simultaneously running the recording machines, the recorders would pick up a faint click every 20-some seconds, as the lift reached another level. He had Columbo visit with a music editor who is removing the clicks from a recording made on the night of the murder. The Lieutenant eventually traces the clicks to the backstage elevator and can prove it was activated well before the murderer took the stage. McGoohan omitted the entire clue and had the elevator instead make a loud rumble that startles the sound engineer. Strangely, the engineer lets the recording proceed and doesn't mention the interruption later.

Worse, McGoohan wanted to make the show more theatrical, particularly the ending. But in doing so, he omitted other clues that were supposed to incriminate Crawford. For the finale, McGoohan just had Columbo babble on about inconsequential circumstantial evidence until Crawford suddenly confesses.

Writer Cava was devastated when he saw what McGoohan had done to his script. Yet out of reverence, he dutifully held his tongue. Since Cava was already a staffer at Universal and in awe of McGoohan, he was given an open invitation to visit the set during the full duration of production. That gave him a front-row seat as the director systematically destroyed his script. McGoohan must have known it was difficult for the young writer to see his work changed so drastically. A few days into shooting, McGoohan turned to Cava and whispered, "Does it *hurt* yet, Jeff?"

Although he had not taken a writing credit since *The Prisoner*, more than 30 years earlier, McGoohan asked to be listed after Cava as co-screenwriter of *Murder with Too Many Notes*. Evidently the act was less to share the credit than to spread the blame.

As director, McGoohan ran a tight set. One morning, Connolly arrived intoxicated, and began forgetting lines and slurring the few he could recall. The director was livid. McGoohan was an equally heavy drinker, but would never allow it to affect his performance. The director called "Cut," and got in a shouting match with Connolly. The two retreated to their dressing rooms until the actor sobered up and was ready to return, with head clear and lines memorized.

Connolly's performance conducting music was reminiscent of John Cassavetes' imperfectly timed gesticulating in the previous conductor caper, *Étude in Black*. Coincidentally, they were the first and the last *Columbos* scored by Dick

---

Murder with Too Many Notes

Filming Started: Nov. 17, 1998
Stars: Peter Falk, Billy Connolly, Richard Riehle
Director: Patrick McGoohan
Executive Producer: Peter Falk
Producer: Christopher Seiter
Co-Executive Producer: Patrick McGoohan
Teleplay: Jeffrey Cava, Patrick McGoohan
Story: Jeffrey Cava
Air Date: March 12, 2001
Ranking: #24 (8.9 points, 14 share)

DeBenedictis, who regretted he was not allowed to do more to prep Cassavetes and Connolly. As DeBenedictis explained, "One of the problems with John and with Billy was that neither one of them knew how to conduct and I wanted to suggest to the director to not shoot them live because you can see they don't know what they are doing. John had the orchestra there and they were playing the Beethoven symphonies. In the case of Billy, it was underscore and he didn't know how to conduct. He did a very good job of faking it, and so did John. I wanted to coach them a little bit and I was told by the directors, 'Don't do that, let them do their own thing'; they wanted it to be more dramatically consistent than musically consistent, so I had to watch that and it was very frustrating."

So, too, was DeBenedictis dissatisfied with his score on *Murder with Too Many Notes*. "I was not pleased with what I did there," he said. "I was trying to make the film music he was doing sound different than the body of the score. Like in *Étude in Black* (where the score sounded distinct from the classical music the Maestro conducted), I wanted that there would be a differentiation between the two halves and I don't think I did a very good job. What I managed to do was dilute the effectiveness of the dramatic film score he was supposedly scoring. Instead of doing what I normally would have done, I was self-conscious of trying to make the difference between the music he was scoring and the music I was writing for the underscore. It kind of clouded my overall creativity, and I didn't come up with as a good a score as I wanted to."

Shooting wrapped in late December 1998, with plans for it to air in the spring. ABC thought differently. *Ashes to Ashes* had just brought in the lowest audience of any first-run *Columbo*. *Murder with Too Many Notes* was shelved indefinitely. Falk continued development work on other scripts, but with no indication that he'd even be permitted to don the raincoat again.

20
Columbo's Last Case

The longer the delay in airing *Murder with Too Many Notes*, the more it appeared that the show had met its demise. Team Columbo slowly began to disband. Some longtime members moved on to other projects; others opted for retirement. Falk filled his time with drawing in his backyard studio and taking supporting roles in minor films and lead roles in a few TV movies.

Like Falk, Nancy Meyer held out hope the franchise could continue. She hired screenwriters Mark Bruce Rosin and Barry Glasser. They pitched—and got her approval to write—*Hear No Evil*. "It's classic *Columbo*, pitting Columbo against a world of prestige and pretentiousness," Glasser explained. "The murderer is a glamorous, wildly successful author of historical romance novels like Barbara Cartland who then transitions to writing tell-all celebrity biographies. She is as big a celebrity as anyone she writes about. She meets a young deaf woman, who we find out is a journalist, who was snooping around her. She discovers that the journalist knows something about her that would destroy her. So she kills the journalist. The author's alibi is that at the time of the murder she was being interviewed on TV by Larry King. So Columbo goes to visit Larry King on set. It's a wonderful moment. Peter loved that."

In fact, Falk liked the entire script. ABC adored it, and was ready to go into production. But when talks turned to casting, Falk and ABC reached an impasse. Rosin recalled, "The reason it wasn't made was even though female stars were interested in playing the murderer, Peter wouldn't agree to them. He was intransigent in not agreeing with ABC. He had his own ideas. And after they waited patiently for a while to have him accept their ideas, they gave up. It was heartbreaking."

Finally, more than two years after *Murder with Too Many Notes* had been turned over to the network, ABC scheduled it to air on a nondescript Monday in March 2001. CBS and Fox were airing reruns, NBC a forgettable TV movie. Even then, expectations were low. Yet *Murder with Too Many Notes* earned solid ratings. ABC was impressed; if a lackluster entry fared so well, just imagine what they could get out of a livelier, demographically targeted program. ABC was committed to giving *Columbo* another chance, if they and Falk could agree on a marketable idea. They made clear they weren't interested in a *Murder, She Wrote* retread. It had to be something featuring young people in situations that would appeal to younger viewers.

Columbo Likes the Nightlife

In 2001, reality programming was the hottest thing in television, so Falk had his crew begin developing a story based on *Big Brother*. The murder would take place in a locked-down party house, which is under video surveillance 24/7 for the filming of a TV show. When Columbo arrives to investigate, he too becomes part of the show. Even though he had never viewed any reality TV, Falk liked the basic idea: "Columbo's wife is at home watching a reality show and now her husband appears on it!"

Yet Falk would not give the treatment his approval until the writers devised a strong pop. Meanwhile, ABC approached Falk about Columbo investigating in the world of "raves"—the then-trendy pop-up dance parties featuring techno music, strobe lights, and psychedelic drugs. "I'd never heard of raves," Falk later confessed. "When they told me about the rave world, I said, 'Oh, that's great. What is it?' I had no idea."

Falk was amenable to seeing a full story developed, so ABC immediately gave the go-ahead to up-and-coming writer Michael Alaimo. In *Columbo Likes the Nightlife*, a rave nightclub operator helps his girlfriend dispose of the body of her ex-husband by stashing it under one of the club's in-floor fish tanks. Columbo ultimately finds the corpse by noticing that one tank houses far fewer fish than the others. It was left to Alaimo to explain the surprise ending to Falk, aware of the actor's propensity to kill stories that have a pop that's flat.

As Alaimo recounted, "He holds his left arm across his chest and he supports his right arm on there, and he's got his right hand on his chin. It's that classic Columbo stance, and he stands there and he's quiet for like 30 seconds... and I'm just like dying, because if he doesn't like this, I don't know what I'm going to do. It was so tense and then, finally, he says, 'Oh, that's terrific!'"

The script was rushed into pre-production. Falk was able to lure co-producer

Jack Horger out of retirement, but the rest of his regular gang—producer Chris Seiter and their longtime editor, set decorator, art director, and production designer—were too old or too ill to participate. ABC took the opportunity to hire a younger, more progressive crew, headed by director Jeffrey Reiner.

Reiner intentionally avoided viewing earlier episodes, knowing ABC wanted something hipper, flashier and louder. "I treated it like I was making a movie," he said. "I came from independent movies. I had my style, so (despite) the fact that I was directing a *Columbo*, I didn't even think to go and look back. I watched it as a kid and loved the character, but it was a show about the nightlife. We even got The Crystal Method to do the music."

Just before filming began, Falk turned 75. Nonetheless, he embraced the modern story elements. He was less receptive to the modern storytelling techniques. Reiner recalled, "He was getting on in age, and we did have some battles in regards to stylistic things, like I made a joke, 'Why don't we just write CLUE in big letters on everything?' He wanted letters really big, so the audience knows. He was entering this other world, so it felt like why don't I just do what I do?"

To create a sleek, contemporary look, the set designers employed a great deal of glass surfaces—from the fish-tank floors to the victim's window-walled house and the glass coffee table he crashes on top of. For Columbo's visit to the glass house, the director of photography lit the scene from across the street and pulled the camera back to shoot in profile. Falk was confused. "Where's the light?" he asked.

"It's outside," Reiner said.

"Well, why isn't it inside?"

"Because that's the way you light in here," the director explained. "There's

---

Columbo Likes the Nightlife

Working Title: *Columbo Loves the Nightlife*
Filmed: Oct. – Nov. 2002
Stars: Peter Falk, Matthew Rhys, Jennifer Sky
Director: Jeffrey Reiner
Executive Producer: Peter Falk
Producer: John Whitman
Teleplay: Michael Alaimo
Air Date: Jan. 30, 2003
Ranking: #55 (6 points, 9 share)

enough ambient light."

Falk frowned. "Why's the camera over there?"

"For a profile."

Profile? "They're paying to see this," Falk retorted, pointing to his face.

"Peter, they're not *paying* to see you. It's on network television. It's free."

Falk remained as energetic and engaged as he had ever been, questioning everything and insisting on take after take until he got it just right. The least of Reiner's problems was that from the go Falk mistook him for Jeremy Kagan, who had directed *The Most Crucial Game* 30 years earlier and whose daughter appeared in *Columbo Likes the Nightlife* as a pink-boa'ed partier. "From the time we started working together, he never got my name right," Reiner said. "He called me 'Jeremy' from beginning to middle to end. And he could yell, so when he yelled, it was 'Jeremy!' He spent the whole movie calling me Jeremy. In the very first meeting, 'Jeremy, how are you gonna shoot the fishes?' It got to the point where, who cares? It didn't make a difference to me. At least it started with a J."

ABC loved what it saw—seemingly the perfect marriage of the classic Columbo character with a contemporary setting and style. The pace was markedly quicker than past shows. And to accommodate more commercials, ABC had the show trimmed to 88 minutes—a full nine minutes shorter than the two-hour episodes from the NBC days.

ABC scheduled *Columbo Likes the Nightlife* to air at their earliest opening, January 30, 2003, about a month after the picture came out of post-production. Unfortunately, the ratings were poor. The shows were now costing ABC about $4 million apiece—with nearly half going to Falk. Though discouraged, the network left open the possibility of continuing. Falk kept developing scripts. He had a circus story, among others. ABC preferred a show about lingerie models.

As time went on, Falk began to come to grips with his—and the Lieutenant's—mortality. He had always said that Columbo would never retire, since as Falk grew older he found the role easier and more natural to play. But now he sensed that the character was in danger of being retired for him. He desperately wanted to do just one more, to give the character a proper send-off. Falk took the best unproduced script he had—*Hear No Evil*—and personally rewrote it into the Lieutenant's final adventure, retitled *Columbo's Last Case*. ABC, however, was done with the show. Falk, Nancy Meyer, and Universal's Charlie Engel refused to give up. They tried selling the farewell special to the USA Network and others. No one was interested. Some industry watchers blamed Falk's age, that—now nearing 80—he was either insufficiently appealing to modern audiences or not

UNIVERSAL STUDIOS hosted an 80th birthday party for Peter Falk in September 2007. Here, he reunites with executive VP of programming Charlie Engel, who was beginning to realize that *Columbo* had come to the end of its run. *[Credit: Charlie Engel]*

up to the rigors of another go-round. Within six months, he would be diagnosed with the onset of dementia.

"*Columbo's Last Case* was a wonderful script, but his health was going and we never could get it shot," Engel said, with deep regret. "He had written it himself. It was going to be his last case. Unfortunately, we never got there."

Long before Falk passed, on June 23, 2011, at age 83, *Columbo* had been laid to rest. Who killed the character this time around? Certainly, a combination of factors contributed, starting with ABC's pullout.

"I think the show had just run its course," figured Horger. "We used to say, 'When are we gonna stop making these damn things?' and the joke was: 'It's just gonna Peter out.' That's basically what it did. I don't know if it was the network or his health or just that after 30 years maybe the public wanted something different. After a while, tastes change. Peter was getting older, the scripts were getting lamer, and ABC was getting filled up with other material."

For the most part, the autopsy report shows *Columbo* died of natural causes. The character was the creation of a bygone era, perfect for the tastes of the 1970s. Fifty years ago, pop culture was less violent, more refined, and more patient. The average viewer would sit back, undistracted, and enjoy witnessing the murder before their eyes and watching the resolution methodically play out in two hours of dialogue, with lots of pauses and a few detours. *Columbo*, at its best, remains as charming as ever. The rumpled detective may no longer be mainstream but, for those fortunate enough to remember—or discover—his genius, he will live forever.

Notebook
Sources & Scribblings

— Below represent only a fraction of the sources employed for this book, but do cite all major contributors including those from which a direct quote was taken. Quotes not referred to below were drawn from interviews conducted by the author, by Gergely Hubai (Dick DeBenedictis), or by Dene Kernohan (Jeffrey Hatcher, Charles Kipps, and Nancy Meyer).

I – Interview
Q – Quote
L&L – Levinson and Link
TAF – Television Academy Foundation
WGF – Writers Guild Foundation

For clarity's sake, this book refers to most episodes by their final name, even when discussing stages of production during which they were still operating under another name. These "working titles" are mentioned in the credits for each episode.

Chapter 2

(Page 13) L&L's background is drawn from countless sources, particularly *Stay Tuned: An Inside Look at the Making of Prime-Time Television* (Richard Levinson & William Link, 1981) and *I* Link (Rap Sheet 10-13-10)

Q Link on "I was told…": *I* Link (WGF)

(15) "Spats" Colombo: *Jewish Journal* 3-3-11

Early career, *Prescription: Murder* origins: *Allentown Morning Call* 6-23-72, 2-5-89; *Philadelphia Inquirer* 1-19-70; *I* Link (Rap Sheet 10-13-10)

(16) Stage cast vs. L&L, Gregory letter: *Agnes Moorehead on Radio, Stage and Television* (Axel Nissen, 2017)

Since Joseph Cotten's real-life wife was playing his mistress, before every performance she would slip her wedding ring to Cotten's on-stage wife, Agnes Moorehead.

(17) Play review: *Detroit Free Press* 3-20-62

(18) World Premieres, Jennings Lang: *Longview News-Journal* 5-29-66, *Press & Sun Bulletin* 6-4-66

Chapter 3

(20) Falk background: *NY Times* 6-25-11

(22) *Q* Falk on *Trials of O'Brien*: *Advocate-Messenger* 1-9-66

(23) *Q* Falk on running across script: *Sunday Gazette-Mail* 2-6-72

(25) L&L mesmerized by Falk: *The Columbo Phile: A Casebook* (Mark Dawidziak, 1989)

Chapter 4

(27) *Q* Link on "our best work": *I* WGF

Q Link on "we became producers": *I* Link (Rap Sheet 10-13-10)

(29) Falk swindled: *I* Hargrove. Hargrove and others credit Falk's pal-turned-investment-advisor, actor Wayne Rogers (*M*A*S*H*), for encouraging him to do *Columbo* to get his financial house back in order.

Sheinberg deal: *I* Hargrove

(30) *Ransom for a Dead Man* changes: Script 10-27 with revisions to 12-22-70, shooting schedule, call sheets, *I* Hargrove

"Notebook"

(31) *Q* Falk on brown: *Charlotte Observer* 12-31-72

Falk's contended that he used his personal raincoat on every show until the 1990s. However, the raincoat he wore in *Prescription: Murder* is clearly different from the one he wore starting with *Ransom for a Dead Man*, which has one fewer button, a loop on the left lapel, and no noticeable horizontal seam across the chest and back. The only question is—assuming Falk did at some point use his own coat—whether he used his own coat first or second. Second certainly is a possibility, since that's when he started using his own shoes. But to me first makes more sense, since what are the odds he had a raincoat in his closet that looked almost exactly like the one he used earlier?

Chapter 5

(33) Setting show: *I* Hargrove, *Mr. & Mrs. Hollywood: Edie & Lew Wasserman and Their Entertainment Empire* (Kathleen Sharp, 2003), *Stay Tuned*

(34) *Q* Levinson on sympathetic murderers: *LA Times* 2-15-75

(35-37) *Q*s Bochco on his start, fights, underwriting: *I* Bochco (TAF, 2002)

Battles with Falk: *Stay Tuned*

(38-39) Metty: *Steven Spielberg: A Biography* (Joseph McBride, 1997)

Did Link kill Levinson?: *I* Link (Rap Sheet 10-13-10)

Murder by the Book changes: Script 5-7 with revisions to 6-1-71

(41) *Dead Weight* casting: Memos 6-71

(41-42) Sick out, delays, Midget: *I* Chambers, production report 6-30-71, shooting schedule, *Stay Tuned*

Smight refuses to finish: *I* Chambers

(43) Albert curses out Falk: *I* Pleshette (TAF 2-9-06)

Overruns: Summary of costs

Q Link on first name: *I* Link (Rap Sheet 10-13-10)

(43-44) *Lady in Waiting* changes: Script 6-2 with revisions to 6-24-71

Suspension: *I* Chambers, production reports especially 7-13-71

Extra Dick Lance—given name: Richard Lanci—got his SAG card from doubling Peter Falk in *Lady in Waiting*, though it would not lead to many speaking roles, just billing as "First Patrolman" (who helps fish the commissioner's wife out of the pool) in Season 3's *A Friend in Deed*.

"Midget wants to direct": *Columbo Phile*

Numerous sources, including *The Columbo Phile*, give "Ted Leighton" partial story credit on *Lady in Waiting* and *Blueprint for Murder*. L&L occasionally employed the Leighton pseudonym—an amalgamation of their middle names—on projects they were not wholly pleased with. Dawidziak says the credits were taken from the syndication prints of the episodes in the mid-1980s, adding, "The credits as they appear in the book were checked and approved by Universal and William Link. Bill meticulously went through the manuscript line by line, submitting corrections, and he certainly was not shy about that." Yet Leighton's name does not appear on either episode on current prints. Another mystery!

(45) *Suitable for Framing* casting: Memos Gillis: *Journal Gazette* 5-21-88

(46) *Suitable for Framing* changes: Script 6-14-71

(47) *Q*s Falk on filming *Blueprint for Murder*: *Marion Star* 8-20-71

Blueprint for Murder became Falk's first and only director credit.

When the highway patrolman pulls over Elliott Markham and asks him for his license, the architect hands him a drivers license bearing a photo of Peter Falk—the same photo used on the "Frank Columbo" license. To his credit, the cop does try to hide the photo with his thumb.

An online debate has arisen over whether or not Columbo's true first name is "Frank." He definitely carried around a license signed "Frank Columbo." Yet none of the creative personnel had anything to do with it; they intentionally didn't give him a first name. My opinion: if we're arguing over prop licenses, you can insist Columbo's first name is Frank with the same certitude that Elliott Markham is really Peter Falk.

Blueprint costs: Summary of costs 8-13-71

(48) *Q* Falk on entrapment: *Chicago Tribune* 2-6-72

Give up smoking: *Columbo Phile*

Tramway: *Desert Sentinel* 9-9-71

Short Fuse changes: Script 8-17 with revisions to 8-31-71

(49) *Q* Falk on *Columbo* overload: *Democrat & Chronicle* 11-22-71

(49-50) Letters from *Columbo* viewers: Gross 11-17-71, Gritanza 10-30-71, Smith 2-15-71: Levinson collection, AFI

(51) *Q* Bochco on Emmys: *I* Bochco (TAF)

Chapter 6

(53) "Now I trust you": *Stay Tuned*

(55) *Q* Falk on "high degree of quality": *Daily News-Journal* 9-3-72

(56) *Stitch in Crime* changes: Script 5-22 with revisions to 6-19-72

(58) Replay video camera: *LA Times* 7-7-72

Cassavetes on orchestra: *I* Hargrove

Dog: *I* Chambers

Over the years, reports have erroneously claimed Dog was played by Henry, a basset hound rescued from a Burbank pound by trainer Ray Berwick and featured as a Season 6 regular in *Emergency!* Yet Henry made his *Emergency!* debut in 1976—years after the original Dog had passed—and the brown-and-white hound bears little resemblance to the black-and-white Dog II.

Étude in Black changes: Script 6-7 with revisions to 6-30-72

(59) *Greenhouse Jungle* changes: Script 6-20 with revisions to 7-11-72

The original script called for the victim to drive a Ferrari, but Universal had access to a bright yellow Jaguar that it preferred to send crashing down into the canyon. Film of the crash became stock footage, which Universal repurposed for later shows, including two episodes of *Barnaby Jones.*

(60) "What'd you pay for those shoes?": *Just One More Thing: Stories from My Life* (Peter Falk, 2007)

(61) Lakers: *Palm Beach Post* 8-11-72, *Kenosha News* 10-16-72

(62) *Requiem for a Falling Star* changes: Script 8-4 with revisions to 8-25-72

During the exchange between Columbo and the guard at the studio gate, Falk's copy of the *Requiem for a Falling Star* script appears to be sitting on the passenger seat of the Peugeot.

(63) *Étude in Black* to two hours: *I* Hargrove, Script additions 9-5-71

(64) *Double Shock* changes: Script 6-7-72

(65) *Q*s Butler: *I* Butler (TAF, 1-14-04)

(66) Raincoat in London: *LA Times* 11-6-72

Dagger of the Mind changes: Script 6-1 with revisions to 11-26-72

As scripted, Columbo was supposed to have his revelation about flicking a bead into the umbrella by watching a little old man in the park flicking breadcrumbs to the birds. When it came time to shoot the scene, Falk completely ignored the old man next to him on the park bench.

(68) *Most Dangerous Match* changes: Script 10-9 with revisions to 11-1-72

Q Cohen on giving idea: *Diabolique* 8-24-18

(69) *Q* Cohen on $100,000: *Montreal Gazette* 8-12-75

Chapter 7

(72) Paul Glass: *I* Hargrove, *Torn Music: Rejected Film Scores, a Selected History* (Gergely Hubai, 2012)

(73) Scoring *Columbo*: *I* DeBenedictis, *I* Hargrove

(74) *Q* Goldenberg: *Crime and Spy Jazz on Screen Since 1971* (Derrick Bang, 2020)

Chapter 8

(76) Benton's start: Correspondence 1-73

(78) *Lovely But Lethal* changes: Script 1-24 with revisions to 2-8-73

Ross hired and *Q*s: *I* Ross (TAF, 2-11-98)

(79) *Any Old Port in a Storm* locations: Shooting schedule

Any Old Port changes: Script 2-8 with revisions to 3-12-73

(80) Negotiations with Falk: *Dayton Daily News* 7-30-73, *Post-Star* 8-11-73, *Philadelphia Inquirer* 8-31-73

(81) *Candidate for Crime* changes: Script 2-7 with revisions to 10-22-73

L&L notes: Memo 2-8-73

(82) *Double Exposure* changes: Script 9-25 with revisions to 10-24-73

Q Culp: *Lafayette Daily Advertiser* 4-12-74

(85) *Shooting Script*: *I* Hargrove

To protect his integrity as movie critic for *Time*, Jay Cocks co-wrote *Shooting Script* under the pseudonym Joseph P. Gillis, the hack writer character in *Sunset Boulevard*.

(86) *Publish or Perish* backstory: *I* Hargrove, *I* Fischer

(87) Spillane Qs: *The Province* 1-22-74

(88) *Mind Over Mayhem* changes: Script 1-24-73

L&L notes: Memos 1-19, 1-26-73

Ross writes *Swan Song*: *I* Ross (TAF)

Swan Song victim Ida Lupino constantly scowls during her scenes. It wasn't completely an act. During her four days on the set, she was suffering from a cold and recuperating from broken ribs. (It was actually her third appearance since fracturing her ribs; she had just finished a *Streets of San Francisco* and a *Barnaby Jones*, in which she reinjured them.)

(90) Reshooting: *I* Hargrove, *Binghamton Press & Sun-Bulletin* 1-15-74

Scott Dilliard, the WICZ-TV cameraman who filmed Cash's concert in Binghamton, covered for Team *Columbo's* mess-up by telling reporters he "was filling in for an NBC crew that could not arrive on time."

(91) *Friend in Deed* changes: Script 1-3-74

(92) Q Levinson on "terrible": *Detroit Free Press* 3-21-74

Chapter 9

(95) How locations chosen: *TV Guide* 4-20-74, *LA Times* 8-17-76, *LA Times* 1-2-94

(96) *Lovely But Lethal* fat farm: *TV Guide* 4-20-74

Negative Reaction: *TV Guide* 10-26-74

(98) Q Baugh on "gaudy": *LA Times* 8-17-76

(99) Q Kline, *Étude* piano, *Double Shock* gym: *TV Guide* 4-20-74

Chapter 10

(103) *Exercise in Fatality* changes: Script 2-11 with revisions to 5-20-74

The actress playing the Tricon clerk messed up her first lines of dialogue, but delivered them so quickly, no one noticed and her flub was left in. She was supposed to tell Columbo to "fill out boxes A, B, C and D. E and F are for company *use* only." She accidentally said, "For company *policy* only."

(104) Projects waiting: Television Status Report 6-7-74

The seven completed scripts Hargrove and Kibbee left for Chambers included four he would film (*Negative Reaction, By Dawn's Early Light, Playback, Troubled Waters*) and three he would not (Bochco's *Uneasy Lies the Crown*, Brad Radnitz/David Rayfiel/Peter Fischer's *Sugar & Spice & Everything Nice*, and Ted Flicker's *Dead as a Duck*, the latter a rewrite of *Dead Swan*, a *McMillan & Wife* reject). The 12 story ideas were by Henry Garson/Lou Shaw (*Fade In to Murder*), Jim Menzies (*A Case of Immunity*), and Larry Cohen (*An Aptitude for Murder, An Aria for Murder, A+ for Murder, Death Is a Lonely Dance, Murder By a Thoroughbred, Murder Is a Star Vehicle, Murder Is the 8th Lively Art, Murder Is a Sport of Honor, Murder with a Feminine Touch*, and—with Sue Milburn—*No Tax on Murder*.)

(106) *Negative Reaction* drama: *TV Guide* 10-26-74

Casting: Memos

Among the actors on Chambers' short list to play ex-con Deschler was Bert Freed, the original Lt. Columbo from *Enough Rope*.

Falk drama: *Miami Herald* 6-22-74, *Des Moines Register* 7-21-74, *LA Times* 1-19-75

Q attorney on "working conditions": *Miami Herald* 6-22-74

(107) Q Sheinberg: *Des Moines Register* 6-28-74

By Dawn's Early Light casting: Memos

Asner: *I* Chambers

Academy search: Bob McCullough memo 5-28-74

(108) Football game: *Uniontown Evening Standard* 10-25-74

(109) Seignious' office: *Charlotte Observer* 8-17-74

McGoohan reworking script: *I* Chambers, "Patrick McGoohan & *Columbo*" (Peter

Falk, Barbara Pruett's McGoohan website)
Q Falk: Pruett
(110) McGoohan saluted: *Charlotte Observer* 10-25-74
Hiring Werner, drinking: *I* Chambers, *Honolulu Advertiser* 3-9-75
Some months after the filming of *Playback*, Everett Chambers received a call from director Stuart Rosenberg, who was considering casting Oskar Werner in his upcoming big-budget film *Voyage of the Damned*. Rosenberg had heard the rumors and wanted to know if "it worked out" with Werner on *Columbo*. Chambers held his tongue, implying a mild endorsement. Werner was given the part—the last movie role he would ever get.
(112) *Playback* changes: Script 5-16-74, *I* Hargrove
Gazzara moves from *Uneasy* to *Troubled*: Memo 9-20-74
(113) Vancouver trip: *Vancouver Sun* 9-24-74, *I* Chambers
Pacific Far East Line: Letter from LA Kimball 5-24-74
Master key: Letter from Captain JG Clark 8-8-74
Princess Cruise's requests: Memo from Max Hall, Letter from John Nyquist 8-7-74, Letter from Captain JG Clark 8-8-74
(115) Seasick: *I* Chambers, *San Francisco Examiner* 11-6-74
Troubled Waters changes: Script 4-30-74, *Lexington Leader* 7-27-75
(116) Q Falk on "you can make book": *Democrat & Chronicle* 9-13-74
(117) Blind man pop: *Columbo Phile*
Considered for *Any Old Port*: Benton notes
Q Hamilton: *Lancaster Sunday News* 2-9-75

Chapter 11
(120) Falk's favorites: *Columbus Telegram* 1-30-75
Qs Falk on "interesting," Fischer: *Detroit Free Press* 3-15-75
(120-121) Irving's crusade, Qs: *San Francisco Examiner* 3-19-75
(121-122) Day one meetings: Metzler diary 3-26-75

Case of Immunity casting: Diary 3-27, 3-31, 4-23-75
Learjet: Diary 3-28, 4-3-75
Storm: Diary 4-3-74, *Intelligencer Journal* 4-14-75
Need more extras: Diary 4-4-75
Survey: Diary 4-8-75
(124) *Now You See Him* changes: Script 1-29-75
Q Sloan: "Young Man with a Dream" (Michael Sloan, Michael-sloan-equalizer.com)
Orson Welles: Diary 4-11-75
(125) Fischer leaves: *I* Fischer, Diary 4-23-75
Falk tantrums: Diary 4-29, 4-30-75
(126-129) Meeting recapped: Diary, memo 5-1-75

Chapter 12
(130) Lally scene: Diary 5-2-75
Mankiewicz hired: Diary 5-12, 5-14-75, *My Life as a Mankiewicz: An Insider's Journey through Hollywood* (Tom Mankiewicz, 2012)
(131) Emmy joke: *My Life as a Mankiewicz*
(132) Jorge Rivero: Diary 5-23-75
Emilio Fernández: Diary 5-22, 5-23-75
(133) El teatro, backups: Diary 5-28-75
Falk fall: Diary 5-29-75
Car accident: Diary 6-2, 6-3-75, *I* Chambers
Bull footage: Diary 6-3-75
(134) Q Metzler on "at this late date": Diary 6-8-75
Marketplace: Diary 6-14-75
Matter of Honor costs: Summary of costs
(134-135) *Forgotten Lady* casting: Diary 6-3 to 6-30-75
Q Van Dyke on "second fiddle": Diary 6-30-75
(136) *Walkin' My Baby Back Home* rights: Diary 6-23-75
Broken ankle, Falk Q: *Buffalo News* 1-28-03
(137) McGoohan negotiations: Diary 7-1 to 7-11-75
"Blackmailer": Diary 7-11-75
Shooting overlap: Diary 7-24-75
Casting: *I* Chambers
Alicia Chambers did end up moving to New

York to pursue acting, but eventually became a high school drama instructor.
Location switch: Diary 7-21, 7-22-75
(137-139) McGoohan changes: Pruett
(139) McGoohan slow, drinking: Diary 8-18-75
Scheduling/looping fight: Diary 9-17, 9-23, 9-24-75
(140) *Now You See Him* long: Diary 6-14-75
Additional shooting *Now You See Him*: Diary 9-18, 12-29-75, *I* Chambers
McGoohan hired: Diary 12-10-75
(141) McGoohan on can't "lick the ending": Diary 12-11-75
Casting: Diary 12-16, 12-22-75
Bob Metzler could never get his *Columbo* script produced, but did convince the show to give his son Rick a role in *Last Salute to the Commodore* as Johnny the scuba diver.
(142) *Last Salute to the Commodore* changes: Script 11-14-75, *I* Chambers

Chapter 13
(145) *Q* Exec on "half of California," *Q* Falk: *LA Times* 5-17-76
(146) *Fade In* to Japan: Diary 7-8, 7-15-76
(148) *Q* Koenig: *I* Koenig (TAF, 1-14-13)
Fade In to Murder changes: Script 5-25 with revision to 7-12-76
During filming on the backlot, Falk shot scenes near the Jaws exhibit, as tourists rolled by on the Universal Studios tram tour. They, of course, were more excited to see Columbo than the prop Jaws, and would point and cheer. Falk had to call out, "You're supposed to look at the shark!"
Over budget: Diary 8-2-76
(149) Circus story rewrite, *Q* Metzler: Diary 7-21-76
Metzler on May: Diary beginning 6-30-76
Meeting postponed: Diary 8-6-76
(150) *Old Fashioned Murder* changes: *I* Chambers, *I* Fischer, Script 5-10-76
Q on "don't' shoot it": Diary 8-2-76
Location shooting, stylist: Diary 8-16-76
Set change: Diary 8-17-76
(151) *Q* Metzler on unauthorized rehearsal: Diary 8-31-76

Q Irving: Diary 9-9-76
(152) *Q*s Holm: *Chicago Tribune* 9-30-76
Metzler confronts Falk: Diary 9-7-76
Q Metzler on "destruction": Diary 8-12-76
Q Metzler on Day 30: Diary
(153) Falk to NY: Diary 9-24 to 10-1-76
Lesser of Two Evils: Script 7-23-76 with revisions to 8-24-76
"Tactical errors": Diary 10-4-76
Falk's "thank you": Diary 10-11-76
(154) Chambers termination: *I* Chambers, Diary 10-14-76
Falk was never wild about the notion of sending Columbo to Japan—he thought it too gimmicky—so the idea died with the departure of Chambers.

Chapter 14
(155-156) Producer search: Diary 10-14 to 11-29-76
Q Irving on self-respect: Diary 11-4-76
(156) Falk meets Simmons: Diary 12-28-76
Simmons meets Metzler: Diary 1-18-77
(157) Screens old shows: Diary 1-20-77
Simmons' ideas: Diary 2-1-77
(159) Morley: Diary 2-1, 2-23, 2-24-77
Q Metzler on Thompson: Diary 2-24-77
Try and Catch Me changes: Script 4-1, 4-5-77
(160) *3 Flats*: Diary 2-9-77
Q Falk on Columbo dead: *Dayton Daily News* 1-15-78
(161) *Make Me a Perfect Murder* changes: Script 8-1-77
Q Van Devere: *Palm Beach Post* 10-30-77
Lally quits: *I* Lally Jr. (columbo-site.freeuk.com)
(162) *Murder Under Glass* changes: Van Scoyk notes, script 8-19, 9-12-77
Q Demme: *I* Demme (DGA, Winter 2015)
(163-165) *How to Dial a Murder* changes: Script 2-18, 11-14 with revisions to 11-22-77
The judge who countermanded the dogs' death sentence was named Judge Metzler, almost certainly a nod to NBC's Bob Metzler, who left the show while *How to Dial a Murder* was in pre-production.

(165) *Conspirators* changes: Script 12-29-77 with revisions to 1-24-78

Q Revill: *News Herald* 12-2-15

Falk tantrum: *Courier-Journal* 2-8-78

(166) Q Falk on network: *Marshall News Messenger* 2-19-78

Chapter 15

(169) *Mrs. Columbo*: *American Film* June 1979, *I* Fischer

Q Danese: *Fort Lauderdale News* 11-16-78

(171) Q Falk on reviving *Columbo*: *Desert Sun* 8-13-79

Q Silverman: *Victoria Advocate* 7-15-79

Q Falk on raincoat: *Missoulian* 8-19-79

Q Falk on "I'm ready": *Akron Beacon Journal* 11-30-80

Jimmy Stewart: *Indianapolis Star* 10-14-79

Q Lafferty: *NY Daily News* 8-29-79

Q Falk on isn't dead: *Indianapolis News* 6-19-85

1981 revival plans: *Times Herald* 10-4-81

1984 revival plans: *Gazette* 12-29-84

1986 revival plans: *Courier-Post* 3-27-86

Chapter 16

(173) Spielberg may direct: *Salina Journal* 3-29-88

(174) Van Scoyk idea: Treatment 1-8-88

Q Link on Falk's script: *St. Cloud Times* 8-5-88

The Producers Building at Universal is now known as the John Ford Building. Falk's first-floor office was the first one on the right upon entering the center doors facing the commissary.

(176) Q Simmons on changes: *Northwest Herald* 2-4-89

Falk insisted that the raincoat he wore when the show was resurrected by ABC was the same one he'd worn through the 1970s, and that he did not retire it until 1992. *TV Guide*, however, reported in 1989 that the raincoat for ABC was an exact copy patterned after the original, aged by staining it with tea and repeatedly running it over with a car in the studio parking lot.

Q Falk on cigars: *TV Guide* 2-4-89

When Falk finally gave up cigarettes in the late 1990s, Columbo continued smoking, sort of. Falk tried to limit the cigar to one scene, and sometimes just held it, without bringing it to his mouth.

(177) Q Simmons on "that's not it": *I* D. Simmons

Murder, Smoke & Mirrors changes: Script 10-2 with revisions to 11-7-88

(178) *Columbo Goes to the Guillotine* changes: Script 7-16-93

Qs Singer: *I* Singer (TAF, 9-19-12)

(179) Q Martinelli: *I* Martinelli (TAF, 2-14-04)

(180) Tuba: *I* Ludwig

(181) Pressure on Simmons: *I* D. Simmons

Grand Deceptions changes: Script 10-31-88, 2-3-89

(182) Consider Moore: *Austin American-Statesman* 5-22-89

Consider Douglas, Weaver: *Post-Crescent* 5-31-89

(184) Q Danese: *Altoona Mirror* 11-3-89

Terminations: *I* Martinelli (TAF)

Chapter 17

(185) Audience survey, Qs Link: *Philadelphia Daily News* 10-26-89

(188) *Double Vision*: Notes 6-19-89, Scripts 12-8-89, 2-1-90, 11-8-90

Last of the Redcoats: Synopsis of 1989 script breakdown courtesy of Louise Hilton

(189) Q Link on beeper clue: *I* Link (TAF)

(190) Forensic dentists: *LA Times* 8-24-88

Agenda for Murder changes, Qs Falk: Pruett

(192) *Rest in Peace, Mrs. Columbo* changes: Scripts 11-9, 12-19-89

(193) *Uneasy Lies the Crown* Script 1-8 with revisions to 1-20-90, also undated Stefano version

(194) *Murder in Malibu* changes: Treatment 8-20-88, script 4-19-90

Q Grauman: *I* Grauman (TAF, 4-17-09)

Poetically, the Malibu home in which the murder takes place at is the same residence used as Charles Clay's estate in the similarly derided *Last Salute to the Commodore*.

Chapter 18

(198) *Caution* backstory: *I* Lamppu, *I* Mayo

Raynell became Falk's personal assistant in 1981 after he signed with Columbia Pictures. Carole Smith—who had been with him since 1968—went to work for John Cassavetes.

Caution became Mayo and Lamppu's one script credit. Jon Epstein had shown interest in them penning another *Columbo*, but they abandoned the idea once Epstein died, particularly after their relationship with Raynell became strained.

(200) Falk credits McGoohan: Pruett

(201) *Goes to College* changes: Script 8-28 with revisions to 10-3-90

Falk refreshed, Happy Holidays: *The Record* 11-25-90

(202) Danese casting: *LA Times* 4-27-91

Chapter 19

(207) Jewel robbery: *Cincinnati Enquirer* 7-25-91

Monkey: *Double Vision* script

Q Link: *I* Link (TAF)

Death Hits the Jackpot changes: Script 6-26 with revisions to 7-16-91

(208) Ed McBain: Dawidziak

(209) *No Time to Die* changes: Script 9-17, 10-1-91

(210) Re-light finale: *I* Levi

(211) Qs Falk: *St. Louis Post-Dispatch* 11-22-92

Q Dawidziak: *Cleveland Plain Dealer* 3-13-92

Stunt Girl: Treatment 1-29-90

(212) *Bird in the Hand* changes: Treatment 1-29-90, Scripts 8-15-90, 11-6-90, 6-7-91, 6-19-92 with revisions to 7-28-92

The special-effects expert who blew up the Rolls-Royce for the picture was able to make the car's hood fly exactly as high as and land precisely where the producers wanted. He also purchased the detonated vehicle and had it refurbished. The interior had already been removed due to fire regulations.

(213) "Rags to Riches": *I* Horger

(214) Q Shatner: *Cedar Rapids Gazette* 1-8-94

Q Falk on "I started by remembering a guy": *Wichita Eagle* 10-27-93

(215) *It's All in the Game* changes: Script 2-25-93

Q Dunaway: *Indiana Gazette* 7-15-92

(219) Q Daly: *I* Daly (TAF, 10-22-07)

Another change in *Undercover* from the book was increasing the treasure from $750,000 to $4 million.

The *Undercover* propman who supplied a phony newspaper needed a proofreader, misspelling "bizarre" in his headline "Two Die in Bizzarre Double Killing.")

Strange Bedfellows changes: Script 9-22, 11-9-94

While in the studio recording his play-by-play, racetrack announcer Trevor Denman was requested by one of the film's editors to slip in a mention of his uncle, a certain Mr. Kunkle. So one of the featured horses in the race became Uncle Kunkle.

(221) Lawsuit: DiElsi v. Falk, et. al., filed 1-23-96

(223) Hiring Kipps: *I* Kipps

(224) Plummer: *I* Hatcher

(225) *Ashes to Ashes* changes: Script revisions 3-3-90

"Have you gone?": *I* Hatcher

(228) "Does it hurt?": "Patrick McGoohan: An Appreciation" by Jeffrey Cava, 3-14-09 (columbo-site.freeuk.com)

Drunk Connolly: *The Scotsman* 3-26-18

Chapter 20

(231) Q Alaimo on pop: *The Californian* 1-15-03

(231-235) Unfilmed shows, demise of series: *I* Engel, *I* Glasser, *I* Horger, *I* Meyer, *I* Rosin, *NY Daily News* 3-27-07, *Pioneer Press* 5-6-07

Hear No Evil was the third project, following *Shooting Script* (1973) and *Last of the Redcoats* (1989), to involve a famous TV talk show host, feature a pivotal scene on their show, and be derailed by Falk as it entered pre-production.

Horger wasn't the lone holdover. He also brought along his longtime associate, Lisa Tygett, as post-production supervisor.

Index

— Italicized page number denotes photo

87th Precinct, 208, 216
A-Team, The, 82-83
Abroms, Ed, 32, 48-50, 69
Adam-12, 41, 43, 62, 82
Adams, Penny, 186-189, 191-192, 194-195, 198
Agenda for Murder, 189-191, 196, 200, 207
Ahern, Lloyd, 50
Alaimo, Michael, 231
Albert, Eddie, 41, 43, 49
Aley, Al, 129
Alfred Hitchcock Hour/Presents, 18, 42, 106
All in the Family, 69
Allen, Sian Barbara, 77
Altman, Robert, 145, 150, 152
Amy Prentiss, 107
Andrews, Anthony, 179
Antonowsky, Marvin, 137, 141
Any Old Port in a Storm, 75, 78-80, 89, 93, *102*, 117, 149, 157
Arkin, Alan, 172
Ashes to Ashes, 224-227, 229
Asner, Ed, 107
Astaire, Fred, 134-135
Averback, Hy, 44
Avery, Val, 40
B.L. Stryker, 173-182
Ball, Lucille, 62
Balsam, Martin, 106
Banacek, 53, 57, 116, 189
Baretta, 82, 132, 149, 168
Barnaby Jones, 63, 98, 189, 194
Barry, Gene, *24*, 26, 28-29, 45
Basehart, Richard, 107
Baugh, Michael, 98
Baxter, Anne, 62
Begley Jr., Ed, 219
Bennett, Tony, 213
Benton, Doug, 76-79, 81, 87, 92
Bercovici, Myrna, 76

Bergman, Ingmar, 145, 152
Berk, Howard, 107, 140-141, 146, 165
Berlin, Jeannie, 150-151, 153
Bikel, Theodore, 159
Bird in the Hand…, A, 211-213, 219
Bixby, Bill, 106
Blake, Robert, 149
Blinn, Bill, 155
Bloom, Jeffrey, 189-190, 200-201, 207
Blueprint for Murder, 46-50, 52, 103, 188
Bochco, Steven, 34-38, 43, 46-47, 50-51, 57-58, 68-69, 86-88, 112, 140-141, 193
Bogart, Humphrey, 62
Boone, Richard, 53
Brandt, Bob, 135
Bridges, Lloyd, 41
Brink's Job, The, 160
Buckley, William F., 214
Buono, Victor, 79
Burnett, Carol, 73
Burr, Raymond, 19
Butler, Robert, 65, 87
Butterfly in Shades of Grey, 214, 218
By Dawn's Early Light, 107-110, 120, 165, 191
Bye-Bye Sky High I.Q. Murder Case, The, *102*, 157-159, 160
Candidate for Crime, 75, 81-82, 93
Cannell, Stephen J., 82-83
Capone, Al, 58
Capote, Truman, 85-87
Carey, Timothy, 31, 40
Carlson, Richard, 15
Caron, Leslie, 135
Carson, Johnny, 85, 136
Cartland, Barbara, 230
Case of Immunity, A, 122-123, 126, 139
Cash, Johnny, 89-90, 92
Cassavetes, John, 10, 15, 27, *28*, 29, 31, 40, 42, 46, 57-58, 63-64, 74, 76-77, 106, 161-*163*, 181, 228-229
Cassidy, Jack, 40, 87, 112, 124, 126, 140, 221

Caution: Murder Can Be Hazardous to Your Health, 198-200, 205
Cava, Jeffrey, 226-228
Chambers, Everett, 40-43, 45, 104, 106-107, *108*, 109-117, 121-122, 125-126, 128-130, 132-137, 139-142, 145-146, 149-154, 156, 186
Charisse, Cyd, 135
Cheap Detective, The, 156, 160
Christie, Agatha, 34, 66, 157, 159
Christine Cromwell, 182, 192
Cobb, Lee J., 19
Cocks, Jay, 85
Cohen, Larry, 38, 68-69, 76, 78, 104, 129
Cohn, Harry, 21
Colasanto, Nick, 58
Coleman, Dabney, 203
Columbo (series), 9-12, 28-169, 171-235
Columbo and the Murder of a Rock Star, 202-205
Columbo Cries Wolf, 188-189, 194, 196
Columbo Goes to College, 200-202, 205
Columbo Goes to the Guillotine, 178-182
Columbo Likes the Nightlife, 231-233
Columbo's Last Case (see *Hear No Evil*)
Connolly, Billy, 227-229
Conrad, Robert, 103
Conspirators, The, 165-167
Cookie, 173, 194
Córdova, Pancho, 132
Cotten, Joseph, 15-17
Crosby, Bing, 19
Culp, Robert, 37, 40, 50, 60, 82, 86, 169, 201
Currie, Sondra, 202-203
Curtis, Tony, 106
Dagger of the Mind, 39, 66-67, 149
Dailey, Dan, 135
Daly, Tyne, 219
Danese, Shera, 148, 162-*163*, 189, 184, 202-204, *217*, 219, 223
Danger Man, 107, 136
Davis, Bette, 62, 157, 160
Davis, Luther, 159
Dawidziak, Mark, 9, 211
Day, Gerry, 216
Day, Robert, 141
De Palma, Brian, 85
Dead Weight, 40-43, 49, 51, 60, *96*
Deadly State of Mind, A, 116-117, 119, 162
Death Hits the Jackpot, 207-208, 210
Death Lends a Hand, 37-38, 40, 44, 47, 50-51, 74, 157
DeBenedictis, Dick, 58, 73-75, 77, 213, 228-229
DeBenning, Burr, *108*
Deighton, Len, 130
Demme, Jonathan, 162
Diagnosis: Murder, 116, 226
DiElsi, Frank, 221
Dishy, Bob, 59, 125-126, 153, 162-*163*, 169

Dodds, Edward K., 90-92, 104, 113, 121-122
Double Exposure, 48, 82-*84*-85
Double Shock, 64-65, 98, *100*-101
Double Vision, 188, 208
Douglas, Kirk, 182
Dr. Kildare, 18, 34, 76
Draper, Fred, 40-41, 77
Driskill, Bill, 112, 122-123, 126, 129-130, 132-134, 140, 145-146, 148, 150, 185, 189, 198
Dugan, Dennis, 141-142
Dugan, John T., 41, 60
Duke, Daryl, 189
Dunaway, Faye, 215-216
Duvall, Robert, 106
Elizondo, Hector, 122, 126-127
Ellery Queen (series), 98, 125-126, 130, 140
Ellis, LeRoy, 61
Engel, Charlie, 168, 174, 176, 215-216, 221, 233-234
Enough Rope, 15, 37
Epstein, Jon, 186-*187*-189, 191-194, 198-200, 202
Erhard, Werner, 162
Erickson, Keith, 61
Étude in Black, 57-58, 62-64, 66, 69, 73-74, 101, 193, 228-229
Exercise in Fatality, An, 103-104, 106, 118
Fade In to Murder, 99-*100*, 146-149, 155, 157-158
Falk (Mayo), Alyce, 20, 140
Falk, Peter, 9-12, 19-*22*-*24*-*28*-29, 31-32, 34-*50*, 53-*61*, 63-66, 68-69, 74-80, *84*-92, 96, 98, 103-*105*-107, 109-112, 115-123, 125-*138*-*147*-*163*, 165, 169, 171-*175*-*209*-*217*-227, 229-*234*
Fame Is the Name of the Game, 19
Family Holvak, The, 116, 139
Farentino, James, 53
Feibleman, Peter, 147, 149-151, 153-154, 156
Fernández, Emilio, 132-133
Fields, Bert, 44, 54, 140, 156
Finnegan, John, 41, 77, 223
Fischer, Bobby, 67-68
Fischer, Peter S., 86-87, 91, 103-104, 112, 116-117, 120-130, 146, 149, 152, 169, 191-192, 206, 214, 219, 221
Ford, Glenn, 106
Ford, Patricia (Mayo), 198-199
Forgotten Lady, 99, 134-137, 139, 143, 215
Franciosa, Anthony, 19, 28, 106
Frazen, Stan, 153
Freed, Bert, 15
Friend in Deed, A, 91, 94, 104, 201
Garner, James, 174
Gazzara, Ben, 27-*28*, 91, 112-113, 115, 122, 126-127, 162-*163*
Geller, Uri, 178
Gideon Oliver, 173, 182
Gillis, Jackson, 45, 48, 50, *54*, 57-58, 62, 64, 66, 68, 76-79, 112, 140-142, 173, 177-178, 185, 188, 194-195, 198, 208, 211-212

Girl from U.N.C.L.E., The, 76, 78
Glass, Paul, 72-73
Glasser, Barry, 230
Goldenberg, Billy, 32, 50, 72-74
Gordon, Ruth, 160
Gossett Jr., Lou, 173
Grand Deceptions, 181-183
Grant, Lee, 31-32, 34, 57
Grauman, Walter, 194
Greene, Lorne, 86
Greenhouse Jungle, The, 58-59, 70, 125
Gregory, Paul, 15-16
Griff, 86-87, 127
Griffin and Phoenix, 139, 189
Grossman, Ken, 96
Grusin, Dave, 74
Guardino, Harry, 40
Hairston, Happy, *61*
Hamilton, George, 117
Hargrove, Dean, 27, 29-33, 39, *54*-55, 57-58, 60-61, 63-66, 72-73, 76, 78, 80-83, 85-86, 88, 90-92, 104, 106, 112, 116, 123, 139
Harrison, Rex, 159
Hart, Harvey, *108*, 126, 128, 134, 155
Harvey, Laurence, 68
Hatcher, Jeffrey, 224-226
Hawaii Five-O, 112-113, 180
Hawks, Howard, 38
Hear No Evil, 230, 233-234
Hec Ramsey, 53, 62, 76, 92, 131
Hefner, Hugh, 188
Hendryx, Shirl, 55-57
Hill Street Blues, 57, 186, 189, 194, 208
Hirsch, Sylvia, 87
Holm, Celeste, 152
Hopkins, Anthony, 141
Horger, Jack, 212-213, 217, 226-227, 232, 234
How to Dial a Murder, 162-165, 167
Howard, Bob, 122, 153
Hudson, Rock, 29, 145
Hunt, Linda, 180
Hunter, Evan (Ed McBain), 208, 216
Husbands, 27-28
Iceman Cometh, The, 10, 21
Identity Crisis, 98, *100*, 136-*138*-139, 141, 144
Iger, Bob, 198
Irons, Jeremy, 227
Ironside, 76, 81, 129, 131
Irving, Richard, 19, 26-27, 31, 42, 55, 63, 91, 107, 111, 120-122, 125-126, 149, 151, 153-154, 156, 169
It's All in the Game, 214-215, 218, 221
Jericho, 18, 34
Jigsaw, 208, 216-217
Jourdan, Louis, 106, 135
Kagan, Jeremy, 61, 233
Kallis, Stanley, 176, 180, 184, 186

Kaufman, Millard, 188
Keller, Fred, 200
Kibbee, Roland, 80-82, 88-89, 91-92, 104, 116
Kiley, Richard, 124
King, Larry, 230
Kipps, Charles, 223
Kirby, Bruce, 77, 109
Kirby, Bruno, 109
Kjellin, Alf, 97
Klugman, Jack, 87, 145
Koenig, Walter, 148
Kojak, 116, 139, 155, 168, 182, 192
Kolb, Ken, 146, 151
Kowalski, Bernard, 111, 132
Kristofferson, Kris, 89
Kubrik, Stanley, 38
Lady in Waiting, 43-45, 50, 52, 95, 212
Lafferty, Perry, 171
Lally, Mike, 41, 130, 140, 161
Lally Jr., Mike, 161
Lamppu, Judy (Sonia Wolf), 198-200
Lance, Richard, 42, 44
Landau, Martin, 65
Lang, Jennings, 18
Lange, Hope, 31
Lanigan's Rabbi, 155
Lansbury, Angela, 135
Last of the Redcoats, 188
Last Salute to the Commodore, 140-145, 149, 166
Latham, Louise, *84*
Latimer, Jonathan, 58-59
Lauria, Dan, 224
Le Gallienne, Eva, 21
Leigh, Janet, 135-136
Lemmon, Jack, 22, 106
Leopold and Loeb, 16, 200
Lesser of Two Evils, The, 153-154, 156
Levi, Alan J., 193, 198, 202-204, 206, 209-210
Levine, Rob, 226
Levinson, Richard, 13-16, 18-19, 23-27, 29-30, 33-*35*-51, 53, 55, 57-58, 63-64, 66, 68-69, 72, 76, 81, 88, 92, 95, 117, 122-123, 125, 129, 156, 169, 173, 186, 189, 191, 214
Limbaugh, Rush, 214
Link, William, 13-16, 18-19, 23-27, 29-30, 33-*35*-50, 53, 55, 57-58, 63-64, 66, 68-69, 72, 76, 81, 83, 88, 92, 95, 122-123, 125, 129, 156, 169, 173-*175*-176, 185-186, 189, 191, 214
Lloyd, Norman, 43
London, Todd, 176, 204, 206, *209*
Lovely But Lethal, 77-79, 93, 96, *98*
Ludwig, Jerry, 180
Madigan, 53-54, 66, 76
Make Me a Perfect Murder, 161, 167
Man from U.N.C.L.E., The, 22, 78, 113
Mankiewicz, Tom, 130-131
Mannix, 18, 62

"Index" 247

Marion, Frances, 98, 100
Markowitz, Richard, 192
Martel, Arlene, 84-85
Martin, Ross, 45
Martinelli, John A., 176, 179-180
Mason, James, 159
Matter of Honor, A, 131-134, 139, 144
Matthau, Walter, 48
May, Elaine, 22, 28, 76, 80, 146-147, 149-151, 153-154, 156
McCloud, 29, 33, 49, 53-54, 73, 92, 107, 131-132, 145 155, 182
McCoy, 116, 139, 145
McDowall, Roddy, 48-49
McEveety, Vincent, 192, 206-207, 219, 221, 223-224
McEveety Jr., Vincent, 207, 223-224
McGavin, Darren, 106
McGoohan, Patrick, 107, 109-110, 120, 124, 136-*138*-139, 141-142, 156, 186, 189-191, 200, 206, 208-209, 224-228
McMillan & Wife/McMillan, 29, 49, 53, 57, 107, 131, 145, 155, 186, 193
McMillian, Jim, *61*
Medina, Patricia, 15,17
Mellé, Gil, 74-75
Meredith, Burgess, 149
Metty, Russell, 38-39
Metzler, Bob, 10, 121-135, 137, 139, 141, 146, 149-154, 156-157, 159-161
Meyer, Nancy, 226-227, 230, 233
Mikey and Nicky, 76, 80, 91, 103, 147
Miles, Vera, 77-78
Milland, Ray, 59, 72
Mind Over Mayhem, 87-88, 94, 125
Mission: Impossible, 34, 48, 65, 131, 178, 180-181
Mitchell, Thomas, 15-19
Monday Night Football, 181, 198
Montalbán, Ricardo, 132
Moore, Roger, 182
Moorehead, Agnes, 15, 17
Morita, Pat, 64
Morley, Robert, 157, 159
Most Crucial Game, The, 60-61-62, 70, 233
Most Dangerous Match, The, 67-69, 71, 88
Mrs. Columbo, 169-171, 211
Mulgrew, Kate, 169-*170*
Murder by Death, 140
Murder by the Book, 38-40, 44, 47, 49-51, 68, 72, 87, 102, 223
Murder in Malibu, 194-195, 197, 211
Murder Under Glass, 75, 162, 166, 174
Murder with Too Many Notes, 226-231
Murder, a Self Portrait, 184, 188, 192, 196
Murder, Inc., 68
Murder, She Wrote, 191-192, 194, 206, 231
Murder, Smoke and Shadows, 177, 183
Name of the Game, The, 26, 28-29, 31, 34, 39, 85, 90-91

Negative Reaction, 96, *99*, 104-106, 109, 118, 135
Nelson, Oliver, 73-74
Newman, Paul, 42
Nielsen, Leslie, 44, 137
Night Gallery, 39, 41, 64, 72, 77
Nixon, Marian, 206
No Time to Die, 208-*209*-211, 216
Now You See Him, 123-130, 140, 144
O'Connor, Donald, 135-136
O'Neal, Patrick, 45
O'Neill, Eugene, 21
O'Neill, Robert F., 34, 76, 78-79, 92, 192
Old Fashioned Murder, 149-153, 155, 157-158, 192, 221
Palance, Jack, 139
Paramor, Norrie, 74
Payne, John, 135-136
Pearlberg, Irving, 81
Penn, Arthur, 145
Penn, Leo, 179
Peppard, George, 53
Perry Mason, 45, 57, 59, 86, 116, 172-173, 181
Picasso, Pablo, 184
Pine, Les, 149
Pine, Tina, 149
Playback, 95, 110-112, 119
Pleasence, Donald, 79, 124, 169
Pleshette, Suzanne, 41-42
Plummer, Christopher, 106, 224
Post, Ted, 123, 132-134
Prescription: Murder (play), 15-17, 19
Prescription: Murder (TV), 19, 23-*24*-26, 29-30, 34, 37-38, 57, 74, 92, 162, 211, 223
Price of Tomatoes, The, 21, 156, 176
Price, Vincent, 77
Priestley, Jack, 191
Prisoner of Second Avenue, The, 32, 49, 53, 105-106, 184
Prisoner, The, 107, 137, 206, 228
Psychiatrist, The, 28-29, 39, 189
Psycho, 77, 193, 227
Publish or Perish, 86-87, 94
Quincy, M.E., 145-146, 155, 171
Radnitz, Brad, 131
Randi, James "The Amazing," 178
Ransom for a Dead Man, 29-34, 45, 54, 74, 136, 211
Rayfiel, David, 89
Raynell, April, 198-200
Redford, Robert, 132
Reiner, Jeffrey, 232-233
Requiem for a Falling Star, 47, 62, 71, 74, 78, 101, 215
Rest in Peace, Mrs. Columbo, 191-193, 197, 206
Revill, Clive, 165
Reynolds, Burt, 173
Richie Brockelman, Private Eye, 57, 142
Riley, Pat, 61

Rivero, Jorge, 132
Roar of the Crowd, 146, 149
Robards, Jason, 21
Robinson, Flynn, 61
Robison, Pat, 165
Rockford Files, The, 82-83, 142, 168
Rogers, Ginger, 134-135
Rogers, Wayne, 162
Rosin, Mark Bruce, 230
Ross, Stanley Ralph, 78, 89
Rowlands, Gena, 57, 110, 141
Ryan, Robert, 41
Sackheim, Bill, 155
Saint James, Susan, 146
Salkowitz, Sy, 181
Saltzman, Philip, 176, 184, 186
Sapinsley, Alvin, 146
Savalas, Telly, 54, 116, 182
Schell, Maximilian, 106
Schlosser, Herb, 153
Scorsese, Martin, 85-86
Scotti, Vito, 41
Seaman, Robert, 191
Seignious, George, 109
Seiter, Chris, 206-207, 221, 224, 232
Seiter, William, 206
Sex and the Married Detective, 180, 183
Shakespeare, William, 66, 146, 149
Sharif, Omar, 106
Shatner, William, 147-148, 214
Shaw, Lou, 146
Shaw, Robert, 79
Sheen, Martin, 78
Sheinberg, Sidney, 26, 29, 33, 39, 107
Shooting Script, 85-86
Short Fuse, 48-50, 52
Siegel, Don, 19
Silverman, Fred, 11, 168-169, 171
Simmons, Daniel, 179
Simmons, David, 165, 177, 184, 186
Simmons, Richard Alan, 21, 156, 162, 164-165, 169, 176-181, 184-186, 188-189, 192, 208
Simon, Neil, 32, 140, 156
Simpson, O.J., 141
Singer, Abby, 176, 178-179
Singer, Bob, 186, 198
Six Million Dollar Man, The, 98, 155
Sloan, Michael, 124
Smight, Jack, 42
Smith, Carole, 149, 153, 161
Smith, Jaclyn, 182
So Long as You Both Shall Live, 208-209
Spassky, Boris, 68
Specht, Robert, 76
Spielberg, Steven, 39-41, 46, 68, 72, 85, 173, 177
Spillane, Mickey, 87

Stack, Robert, 28
Stapleton, Jean, 169
Stapleton, Maureen, 169
Stefano, Joseph, 193
Steiger, Rod, 220
Stewart, Jimmy, 171
Stitch in Crime, A, 55-57, 62, 71
Strange Bedfellows, 219-221
Suitable for Framing, 45-46, 50, 52, *97*, 202, 215
Swan Song, 47, 89-92, 94
Swofford, Stephen, *209*
Szwarc, Jeannot, 77
Thompson, Gene, 159
Thomson, Fred, 98, 100
Tonight Show, The, 85, 136
Torn, Rip, 207
Trace of Murder, A, 221-223
Trials of O'Brien, The, 22, 25, 156, 162, 186
Troubled Waters, 112-115, 119-120, 131
Try and Catch Me, 159-161, 166, 215
Tygett, Lisa, 217
Undercover, 216-*217*-219
Uneasy Lies the Crown, 112, 193
Ustinov, Peter, 159
Vaccaro, Brenda, 169, 194-195
Van Devere, Trish, 161
Van Dyke, Dick, 106, 135
Van Patten, Joyce, 150
Van Scoyk, Robert, 162, 177, 208-209
Vaughn, Robert, 113, 115, 141-142, 221
Waddell, James, 108
Wagner, Robert, 45
Warden, Jack, 107
Ware, Peter V., 176
Wasserman, Lew, 38-39
Wayne, Carol, 169
Weaver, Dennis, 33, 131, 145
Webb, Jack, 62
Welles, Orson, 38, 124, 127
Wendt, George, 221
Werner, Oskar, 106, 110-111
Westheimer, Dr. Ruth, 180
Whitmore, Stanford, 29
Wickes, Mary, 46
Widmark, Richard, 53
Wierum, Howard, 17
Wild Wild West, The, 45, 103
Wilder, Billy, 11, 15
Williams, Hank, 89
Williams, Paul, 85
Wilson, Mark, 124
Woman Under the Influence, A, 57, 76
Wood, Natalie, 22
Woodfield, William Read, 178, 185, 188, 193, 198, 202, 206